Self-Help as Method of Conflict Resolution

Elie Pierre Eid

Self-Help as Method of Conflict Resolution

A Brazilian Perspective

Springer

Elie Pierre Eid
Instituto de Ensino e Pesquisa – INSPER
São Paulo, Brazil

ISBN 978-3-032-13904-7 ISBN 978-3-032-13905-4 (eBook)
https://doi.org/10.1007/978-3-032-13905-4

The original submitted manuscript has been translated into English. The translation was done using artificial intelligence. A subsequent revision was performed by the author(s) to further refine the work and to ensure that the translation is appropriate concerning content and scientific correctness. It may, however, read stylistically different from a conventional translation.

This Springer imprint is published by the registered company Springer Nature Switzerland AG
The registered company address is: Gewerbestrasse 11, 6330 Cham, Switzerland

For Marília.

Competing Interests The author has no competing interests to declare that are relevant to the content of this manuscript.

Contents

1 Introduction 1
1.1 Public and Private Spaces for Dispute Resolution 1
1.2 Relevance of the Topic 4
1.3 Scope of Approach and Methodology 7
1.4 Terminology and Concepts Employed 9
1.5 Structure 10
References 11

2 Self-Help as a Method of Dispute Resolution 15
2.1 Critical Analysis of the Prohibition of Self-Help 15
2.1.1 Grounds for Evolution 19
2.1.2 Analysis of the Brazilian Context 23
2.2 Criteria for the identification of self-help 27
2.2.1 Initiative of the Party 30
2.2.2 Unilateral Protection 39
2.2.3 Absence of a Third-Party Adjudicator 46
2.3 Self-Help Within the Framework of Dispute Resolution Mechanisms 48
2.3.1 Substance and Procedure in Self-Help 52
2.3.2 Self-Help and its Relationship with other Means of Dispute Resolution 55
References 57

3 Instrumental Function of Self-Help 65
3.1 Private and Public Conducts in Contractual and Non-Contractual Contexts 65
3.1.1 Self-Help and Imperium 69
3.1.2 Division of Powers Between the State and Private Parties for Unilateral Remedies 72

3.1.3 Impossibility of Subjection by Certain Forms of Unilateral Protection 75
3.2 Influence of Technology and the Automation of Legal Relationships 77
3.2.1 Algorithms and Automation 78
3.2.2 Internet of Things: Self-help and Digital Tangible Assets 80
3.2.3 Smart Contracts and Self-Enforcement 82
3.2.4 Cyberattacks and Self-Defence 84
References 86

4 Limits to Self-Help 91
4.1 Due Process of Law and Means of Dispute Resolution 93
4.2 Proportionality and Unilateral Enforcement 97
4.3 Criteria for the Control of Unilateral Protection 100
4.3.1 Material Criterion: Correlation Between the Type of Infringement or Threat and the Form of Unilateral Protection. 102
4.3.2 Formal Criterion: Procedural Guarantees as an Incentive for Self-Protection 104
4.3.3 Objective Criterion: Means Employed to Obtain Unilateral Protection 108
4.3.4 Subjective Criterion: Limitation on Personal Submission 112
4.3.5 Temporal Criterion: Timing of the Exercise of Unilateral Protection 116
4.4 Consequences of Non-Compliance With Control Criteria 117
References 118

5 Systematic Profile of Self-Help 123
5.1 Legal Framework of Self-Help 123
5.2 Sources of Self-Help 125
5.3 Individual and Collective Interests 127
5.4 Object of the Exercise of Power 129
5.5 Types of Unilateral Protection 130
5.5.1 Enforceability 131
5.5.2 Formative 133
5.5.3 Declaratory 135
5.6 Timing of the Exercise of Self-Protection 136
References 138

6 Conclusions 143

Abbreviations

ADCT	Act of Transitional Constitutional Provisions
ADI	Direct Action of Unconstitutionality
Art.	Article
BGB	German Civil Code
BGH	Federal Court of Justice (Germany)
BVerfG	Federal Constitutional Court (Germany)
CC	Brazilian Civil Code
CDC	Brazilian Consumer Protection CodeL
CF/88	Brazilian Federal Constitution of 1988
CLT	Brazilian Consolidation of Labor Laws
CP	Brazilian Penal Code
CPC	Brazilian Code of Civil Procedure
CTB	Brazilian Traffic Code
Inc.	Subsection
LGPD	Brazilian General Data Protection Law
LINDB	Law of Introduction to the Rules of Brazilian Law
OTAN	North Atlantic Treaty Organization (NATO)
RE	Extraordinary Appeal
REsp	Special Appeal
RO	Ordinary Appeal
STF	Federal Supreme Court
STJ	Superior Court of Justice
TJSP	São Paulo State Court of Justice
TST	Superior Labour Court
ZPO	German Code of Civil Procedure

Chapter 1
Introduction

1.1 Public and Private Spaces for Dispute Resolution

Aggression, violence, vigilante justice, private vengeance, and the arbitrary exercise of one's own rights — these are ways to describe self-help (Nieva Fenoll 2017, pp. 105–107), which is recognized as the earliest and most primitive method of resolving disputes by imposing the will of the stronger over the weaker (Vallimaresco 1926, pp. 14–15). Introductory studies in Procedural Law justify the rise of jurisdiction as a means of protecting an interest[1] through the initiative of its holder, opposing the law of retaliation and an asserted prohibition on self-help. Even if this perspective is accepted, a disconnect remains between the value placed on various self-compositive and third-party means of adjudication and the role of self-help in modern times, where there are both public and private forums for dispute resolution (Hensler 2014, pp. 45–51) , to prevent the physical enforcement of a claim (*nul ne peut se faire justice à soi-même*).

While this supposed omnipresence was defended, many events raised doubts about the adoption of state jurisdiction as the central focus of authority. Schünemann observed a paradox between this classical view, the consolidation of the Rule of Law, and the period that began with the era of codifications, during which there was considerable refinement of the limits on exercising self-help through the creation of new forms and the reinterpretation of past institutions to give them ethical and lawful authority parameters.[2] The reconstruction of two historical developments is essential to this modern origin. The principle of legality defined how the Public Administration conducted its actions. The delegation of its power to enforce its own acts and restrict private rights led to a unilateral approach, sometimes amplified by a margin of discretion.[3] This delegation of powers remains fundamental to its operations today,

[1] Under the Brazilian law, the term "interest" is adopted as the result intended with a legal position.

[2] Schünemann (1985), pp. 6–7.

[3] Fonseca (2012), pp. 47–48.

E. Pierre Eid, *Self-Help as Method of Conflict Resolution*,
https://doi.org/10.1007/978-3-032-13905-4_1

enabling it to act independently while assuming the legal responsibility of serving public purposes. In the private sphere, where the most significant concerns about the exercise of self-help arose, § 229 of the BGB highlighted the disconnect between the role assigned to the judiciary and the level of protection afforded to private individuals. This legal provision grants a general right of self-help, and, despite ongoing interpretative disagreements, part of its doctrinal approach involves contesting the argument of subsidiarity concerning the use of force by the State.[4]

The historical reassessment of self-help was also important for understanding its use. Scholars who studied this issue first identified the acceptance of unilateral protection by legal systems across different periods, with rules allowing both the exercise of subjection (physical or proprietary) and some freedom in unilateral action, even when authorities existed to protect individual interests. Secondly, they pointed out the mistake of opposing it to state justice, since there was a division of powers between the State and private entities and individuals.[5] Suppose the concept of a monopoly of jurisdiction can be questioned today. In that case,[6] one of its premises, related to the use of force, is challenged by the fact that the State has never held exclusive authority to enforce the protection of interests. This retrospective analysis suggests that public and private, self-compositive and third-party adjudication forums have always existed in history.[7] The main point, however, lies elsewhere. There was a discursive concern, partly with the alleged preservation of the individual, partly with the assertion of the state's (Bianca 2000, p. 131) authority in modern times, to define who would hold the power to determine legal protection. This seems to be an argument for a "non-historical rationalization": self-help emerged and developed alongside other forms of legal protection, and over the centuries, it was encouraged by the State itself, which reinforces the false nature of the justification given for the role of jurisdiction.

A closer look at self-help has uncovered a regulated aspect that can position parties as main actors within the complex framework of what has recently been studied as a method of dispute resolution.[8] Just as it has been recognized that jurisdiction is one of the functions of the State and could exist outside it, the effort should be to not only demonstrate the presence of self-help in our reality but also to establish clear boundaries for it, in order to define parameters for exercising unilateral protective powers.[9] Studying it today reveals its important practical potential as a response to the changing socio-economic landscape and the challenges of balancing self-determination, protecting one's interests, and adhering to legal restrictions.

The neglect of these characteristics results from factors such as (a) the still widespread inherent association between self-help and illegality; (b) the lack of clear understanding about what constitutes self-help; (c) the emphasis on incidental

[4] Beurskens (2017), p. 197.

[5] Luzzatto (1956), pp. 29–30 and Santamaria (1937), pp. 55–56.

[6] Picardi (2011), pp. 55–57.

[7] Colli et al. (2022), pp. 65–80.

[8] Montecchiari (2019), pp. 35–37.

[9] Klingbeil (2017), p. 40.

elements, which gives it a residual nature, such as personal aggression or urgency to act; (d) the absence of systematic analysis, which would define the scope of authorization and its appropriate use within a legal framework; and (e) the historical imbalance of power between private individuals and the State in the unilateral protection of personal interests. Therefore, the stigma attached to self-help, based on the idea that it disrupts public order and social peace, conflicts with its more refined forms of practice, many of which are detached from physical and personal confrontations.[10] These developments can be emphasized based on various factors: the relationship between formative rights, credit rights, and the exercise of power to protect infringed rights[11]; the appropriateness of specific contractual remedies for protection initiated by the contracting party[12]; the dispersal of guarantees whose enforcement depends on the creditor[13]; self-regulation[14]; the expansion of situations in which private enforcement is permitted[15]; changes brought about by technology and the self-executing nature of algorithms[16]; debates on the admissibility of atypical self-help powers and the freedom to contract in relation to them[17]; and the review of the limits of the self-executing powers of acts of Public Administration.[18]

Illustrating different realities, two examples can explain the current use and the advances mentioned. One is found in the first paragraph of article 1.210 of the Brazilian Civil Code, which authorizes the possessor to use force and take concrete action to maintain or restore possession in the event of disturbance, dispossession, or threat to possession. This is a well-known and longstanding case in which the right to act unilaterally is granted for the immediate protection in the face of a threat or violation of the right to possession. The other is drawn from a practice that has become increasingly common in recent times, namely the exclusion or blocking of profiles on digital platforms. After accepting the terms of use of a platform dedicated to electronic commerce and creating a virtual shop, the user begins to act in a manner contrary to the rules imposed in that environment. After several warnings, these behaviors persist, and as an initial sanction, the platform decides to restrict the use of certain functionalities, thereby limiting the commercial activity that can be conducted. As this fails to deter the undesirable actions, the user's profile is deleted as a final measure.

This brief scenario illustrates not only the broad scope of self-help — often misunderstood as limited or a residual concept — but also highlights the need to update our understanding of it as a means of unilateral protection of interests, rather than its usual exclusion from regular protection mechanisms. The present study aims to establish

[10] Griener et al. (2017), pp. 1120–1126.

[11] Lener (1985), p. 620.

[12] Salles (2019), pp. 70–86.

[13] Levada (2022), pp. 34–36.

[14] Renner (2021), p. 492.

[15] Purpura (2020), pp. 182–183.

[16] Bingwan (2018), pp. 111–138.

[17] Lepore (2019), pp. 33–38.

[18] Schirato (2011), p. 136.

criteria for identifying and applying unilateral protection under Brazilian law. First, the subject will be positioned within the context of dispute resolution mechanisms as a form of legal protection that can arise in situations ranging from the simplest and most subtle to the most forceful, with or without the use of force, and concerning objects beyond just the individual. Second, its application will depend on the limits set by the national legal system, an area that remains uncertain, especially due to the lack of doctrinal and jurisprudential solutions provided so far. This analysis considers the scope of authority granted to the State and individuals in accordance with the constitutional framework. Third, it aims to develop a systematic approach to this form of legal protection, similar to those established for other forms of protection.

1.2 Relevance of the Topic

"Given the pivotal role of self-help, it is surprising how little attention has been paid to defining its contours and providing theoretical justification."[19] The essential reconstruction of this subject faces several challenges: it is as ancient as it is overlooked, as broad as it is disorganized, as undefined as it is necessary, and as relevant as it is debated. Therefore, it is important to outline the thesis supported, according to the following question: can self-help be regarded as a legitimate means of dispute resolution? The answer involves three phases of analysis.

The first is the characterization of unilateral protection of infringed or threatened interests. The aim is to challenge dogmas such as the presumption that private self-help is exceptional and relies exclusively on explicit legal authorization; to differentiate between private and public self-help; to reject viewing substantive law solely as a tool, even though it provides means to protect various legal positions; and to emphasize the importance of judicial protection. The goal is to demonstrate how self-help is regularly employed and is essential for the functioning of legal relations, influenced by economic and social incentives. Therefore, a more careful approach should avoid rhetorical terms like resurrection, rebirth, or resurgence, given the numerous consistent instances of self-help since its origins law,[20] and which are part of a set of powers available to both private individuals and the State.

These dogmas originate from certain views within the doctrines of substantive and procedural law. For the former, institutions of Private Law and Public Law have acted as means to protect, enforce, or realize infringed or threatened interests, but in many cases, they were not identified or considered as forms of self-help. For the latter, the existence of jurisdiction and the right of action are viewed as solutions to self-help. Böhm's extensive survey demonstrated that much of modern procedural theory adopts the idea of replacing self-help and promoting social peace as the goal

[19] Sharkey (2010), p. 103.

[20] Cannata (2011), p. 379.

of judicial proceedings (*Prozeßzweck*).[21] Although this conception is still accepted, it can be questioned from various perspectives:

a. It is important to understand which type of self-help is referenced in these studies. In supporting the increase of jurisdiction, the State's monopoly on the use of force is assumed to override individuals.[22] The main idea of this proposal is private self-help, mainly because it views the system as "precarious and arbitrary, as it did not guarantee justice, but rather the victory of the strongest, most cunning, or most daring over the weakest or most timid."[23] At the same time, it was the State itself that exercised powers to unilaterally and coercively enforce its acts based on self-executing authority. This imbalance occurs because, on one hand, private self-help developed without regard for the principle of liberty, and on the other, public self-help was seen as an inherent feature of any administrative system act.
b. During the same period in which this antagonistic relationship between jurisdiction and self-help was established, several studies already pointed in another direction: (i) the use of force by the State as a measure of social security and trust did not eliminate self-help; on the contrary, it solidified it by recognizing the enforceability of rules by private individuals as well, where possible[24]; and (ii) fundamental rights of resistance, such as the right to oppose unlawful State demands, originate in the second half of the nineteenth century, a period that coincides with the development of the discourse of State supremacy through jurisdiction.[25]
c. The framework for depicting self-help considered physical force, aggression, and the personal domination of one individual over another. However, the evolutionary study of societies did not support the idea of a widespread state of barbarism that could be overcome by the emergence of the State,[26] nor did it reduce such acts to just brutality. Linking the subject to a primitive stage of human behavior can be reconsidered, both because the delegation of conflict resolution to a third party was gradual and never absolute, which suggests the ongoing autonomy of individuals for self-protection, and because the scope of conduct suitable for unilateral protection is complex. The idea that self-help exists outside the realm of law, in addition to making studying it pointless, equates it with personal violence. However, legislative developments have shown a different picture: the acceptance of one party's use of force against another has become rare and regulated, aiming to balance the preservation of human life with the allowance for unilateral action; today's acceptance of self-help results from a shift from person to property and legal positions, as a way of recognizing this legal authority protection.[27]

---

21 Böhm (2019), p. 300.

22 Saturno (1995), p. 244.

23 Cintra et al. (2015), p. 23.

24 Kelsen (1992), pp. 38–39.

25 Miranda (2020), p. 519.

26 Moraes (2022), pp. 314–318.

27 Cordero (2022), p. 213.

The second stage is to define the limits of self-help. The challenges involve the variety of legal relationships in which it may occur and the requirements for its regulation. On the one hand, there is support for the broad application of proportionality to evaluate both government and private conduct, without delving into the effectiveness of fundamental rights in each context or the specific rules that operate at the constitutional level to address potential excesses.[28] On the other hand, case law offers little assistance in this analysis, as it relies on grounds such as judicial reservation, good faith, excess of power, and abuse of rights,[29] without providing a precise specification of their relationship to unilateral protection. This climate of uncertainty highlights the inadequacy of the solutions presented so far and emphasizes the need to establish predictable criteria. These criteria, outlined across the material, objective, subjective, and temporal dimensions, consider the characteristics of due process of law under the Brazilian 1988 Federal Constitution, such as its scope and manner of application in various dispute resolution methods, and the alignment of fundamental rights with self-help, considering the personal and proprietary restrictions it entails.

To achieve this goal, it is crucial to identify the source of this protective power for both private individuals and the State. While it is challenging to list all reasons for the mistrust of private self-help, one significant factor is the neglect of individual autonomy. Díaz Alabart's observation supports this view: "the concept of self-help is, without doubt, a step forward in relation to the autonomy of the will of individuals who, based on freedom and dignity, have the right–insofar as they possess the capacity to understand and to will–to organize the personal aspects of their possible future protection."[30] From this point, the usual logic is turned around: private self-help is not necessarily governed by strict legal rules, nor are such actions typically considered crimes. Regarding public self-help, it is generally understood that self-initiated acts are justified by the importance of public interest or seen as an attribute lacking in private acts. These features lead Hamburger to refer to "extrajudicial adjudication,"[31] criticizing the historical imbalance between the State and individuals regarding the need to use the Judiciary to protect their interests directly. In this regard, studying the limits of self-help also requires reassessing the balance between public and private powers of unilateral protection within their constitutional framework.

The third stage is to define the profile of self-help in Brazilian law. By characterizing unilateral protection as a way to defend interests that are infringed or threatened, traditional doctrinal classifications such as defensive, repressive, aggressive, or reactive become more adaptable criticism.[32] Self-help should be examined within the context of dispute resolution mechanisms, which primarily aim to provide protection, satisfaction, or enforcement of a claimed legal right. In this context, there is no reason to ignore that unilateral protection adapts to the specificities of the conflict and may be constitutive, executive, declaratory, or precautionary. This adaptation

---

[28] Bauer (2023), p. 26.

[29] These are principles commonly invoked in Brazilian law.

[30] Díaz Alabart (2007), p. 23.

[31] Hamburger (2014), p. 129.

[32] Betti (1959), p. 529 and Schünemann (1985), p. 38.

helps determine who may obtain it, how it is obtained, what it applies to, and what outcomes it produces. This systematization emphasizes the instrumental nature of the concept and allows for its independent development understanding.[33]

As will be shown, conflict is a key element of self-help. This close link helps to distinguish the power of unilateral protection from other powers of the active subject, such as managerial, family, or regulatory powers. Therefore, viewing it as a means of unilateral dispute resolution is not just an option but a necessity for correct characterization. This leads to certain consequences. Unlike the approach suggested by Zamora y Castillo, subjective factors like selfishness, a sense of offense, or even a selection of illustrative examples to support this analysis are not particularly useful.[34] As a method of dispute resolution, self-help should be evaluated based on its appropriateness, its unilateral nature, and the different forms it takes. The important role of interested parties is often ignored, whether in their desire for and support of self-help because of its speed and efficiency, or because it acts as a tool of governance.[35] Just as other methods of dispute resolution have gone through phases of modernization, so too has self-help, but with a key difference: to understand its current uses, it is essential to overcome the obstacles of the past and recognize its ongoing role today well.

1.3 Scope of Approach and Methodology

The selected topic is interdisciplinary within the Field of Law. It is also explored in other fields, including Sociology, Anthropology, Philosophy, Economics, and History. To illustrate this broad scope, a brief mention of authors with very different influences, such as Kant,[36] Santos[37] and Bohannan[38] demonstrates the importance of self help in developing views on humanity, property, liberty, society, the use of force, and social issues control.

In the legal field, approaches can vary, such as examining the history of self-help and the evolution of human protection, its applications in a specific area of substantive law, applying the principles of Law and Economics, or conducting empirical research to evaluate how Brazilian courts oversee unilateral remedies. However, considering the issue at hand, this work concentrates on (a) self-help as a means of dispute resolution; (b) the delimitation of unilateral remedies as a form of protection for infringed or threatened interests; and (c) the systematization of this dispute resolution tool. To accomplish these goals, the analytical-functional method is used: analytical, because it seeks to establish concepts and present prescriptive elements for identification and

[33] Carimini (2018), p. 59.

[34] Zamora y Castillo (2000), pp. 47–48.

[35] Epstein (2005), pp. 15–18.

[36] Kant (2013).

[37] Santos (1977).

[38] Bohannan (1968).

classification; functional, because it aims to highlight the purpose and objectives, within the limits of the Brazilian legal system, of this protective power. Regarding these concerns, the scope (or mode) of the analysis is as follows:

a. This work aims to situate self-help within the framework of dispute resolution mechanisms. To achieve this, it is first necessary to define what self-help is and how to recognize it, and second, to explain why it should be considered a method of resolving disputes. Much of the scholarship on this topic has been developed by scholars of substantive law, offering valuable insights into specific cases such as the defense of non-performance, set-off, self-defense, guarantees, the expansion of the powers of the Public Administration, and others.[39] However, little of this has been analyzed from a procedural perspective, meaning with attention to the characteristics of protection, enforcement, or satisfaction of an interest by its holder. The justification for this being a topic for proceduralists is provided by Geri, who notes that self-help finds its "indefeasible logical foundation in the idea of protection, which represents a peculiar application (…) in relation to the prerequisites, the function, and, above all, the mechanism of operation."[40] In other words, if the expansion of the focus of Procedural Law aligns with the forms of legal protection offered outside the Judiciary,[41] there is no reason to neglect one of its forms, specifically unilateral remedies.
b. Many studies explore how self-help manifests in specific cases. This method reveals a rarely noticed contradiction: while it emphasizes the active subject's direct initiative, limiting it to certain situations reinforces the idea that self-help, especially in the private sphere, is rare or limited. This thesis takes a different approach. The framework for unilateral remedies should be established with its own criteria, allowing examples to serve as confirmation, which are also included in this work. The independence of this self-protection power yields outcomes similar to those of other legal remedies, such as adapting to various types of disputes.
c. Furthermore, these studies also offer detailed descriptions of the examined example, indicating that self-help is an incidental aspect or merely an antagonistic mechanism for resolving the observed dispute.[42] As will be shown, there is no conflict with state judicial third-party protection. In the words of D'Acunto, "contrary to popular belief, the dilemma of self-help does not concern the supposed opposition between state justice and 'private justice', but rather between state justice and its functions."[43]

---

[39] Von Tuhr (1888), Titze (1897), Landmann (1975), Popineau-Dehaullon (2008), Santamaria (1937), Mezzanotte (1995), Russo (2017), and Fonseca (2012).

[40] Geri (1971), p. 6.

[41] Yarshell (2020), p. 146.

[42] Feldman (2020), pp. 48–49; Lenzi (1996), pp. 114–116; Petrone (1997), pp. 109–111; Murino (2010), pp. 54–57; Carimini (2018), pp. 51–53; Belmonte (2023), pp. 231–233; Theodoro Júnior and Andrade (2023), pp. 97–99.

[43] D'Acuto (2020), pp. 15–16

d. Just as bilateral or multilateral remedies and third-party protections are categorized to organize their legal frameworks and boundaries systematically, unilateral remedies should also be approached in this way: (i) identifying the agents, meaning the parties with authority, both active and passive; (ii) understanding the sources of this authority, considering the legal and contractual rules that govern the scope and limitations of the acts performed; (iii) determining the interests to be protected, given the importance of safeguarding an individual's or a collective's legal rights; (iv) specifying the object of this unilateral remedy, which can involve the person, property, or legal positions; (v) identifying the forms of unilateral remedy based on the measure sought by the active party; and (vi) establishing the timing for exercising the unilateral remedy, taking into account the emergence or imminent occurrence of the conflict. The significance of these classifications can be justified by Saturno's perspective, which states that self-help does not contradict the essence of the Rule of Law, but "actually represents an element of its realization."[44]

1.4 Terminology and Concepts Employed

The proposed approach requires the prior definition of the concepts used. These serve to guide the reader and clarify the fundamental ideas they convey. All the following concepts are directly related to the substantiation of the thesis; some are relevant to various means of dispute resolution and therefore require specification.

1. Threat or injury: an unlawful act or fact, whether potential or consummated, that causes harm to a person.
2. Private self-help: unilateral protection of threatened or infringed interests, governed by the legal regime of Private Law.
3. Public self-help: unilateral protection of threatened or infringed interests, governed by the rules of Public Law. Public self-help, as an expression of self-executing authority in a specific dispute context, is different from self-help related to administrative acts, as the latter involves the power and duty of the Public Administration to review or cancel its own acts of initiative.
4. Conflict, controversy, or dispute: arises from the infringement or threat to a legally protected interest. This work uses the term "interest" because (i) self-help represents the exercise of a power to protect a legal position, which does not always derive from a credits or formative rights, but may also arise from a duty or an exception; (ii) a legally protected interest is one that is supported by the legal system and therefore deserves protection, regardless of its economic, social, religious, or other nature; (iii) the interest represents the concrete aspect of the latent state presented by the right, the exception, or the duty; it is through the interest that the entitlement and the need to satisfy that right, exception, or duty are justified.

[44] Saturno (1995), p. 249.

5. Third-party adjudication: legal protection provided by a third party, whose reference point is the parties involved in the dispute or the agent conventionally or legally designated to protect, realize, or satisfy an interest.
6. Protection, realization, or satisfaction of an interest: these are the possible outcomes of legal protection. To protect means to defend, safeguard, or assist an interest. To realize means to implement, put into practice, or carry out an interest. To satisfy means to fulfill, complete, or meet an interest. Each of these actions, in the context of self-help, must be situated within a dispute.
7. Methods of conflict resolution, controversies, or disputes are the pathways through which legal protection is obtained. These may be governed by legislation and thus institutionalized, or they may be based on agreements, with their structure determined by the parties involved.
8. Power of self-help: the legal concept defined by the specific right of self-protection or self-defense of individuals facing threats or violations of their interests.
9. Active party in self-help: the party that exercises the power of self-help.
10. Passive party in self-help: the party against whom the power of self-help is invoked.
11. Protection of rights, interests, or legal protection: the legal act of safeguarding, realizing, or fulfilling, regardless of whether a dispute exists. This protection can be unilateral, bilateral, multilateral, or provided by a third party.
12. Unilateral remedy: this is the remedy obtained solely through the conduct of the active party.
13. Bilateral or multilateral remedy: this is the remedy provided through the convergence of the wills of two or more parties involved in the dispute.

1.5 Structure

Once the thesis to be demonstrated and the method to be employed have been identified, the structure of the work aims to reduce the asymmetry present in the subject in Brazil. Critical review of the foundations and scope of self-help remains limited in the national literature and has only recently gained attention among scholars. It can be said that, even today, certain ideas persist, such as the existence of jurisdiction to prevent unilateral remedies, the overemphasis on the criminal aspect of such conduct, and a disconnect from the modern concept of division of responsibilities between the State and private individuals, which is reflected in the use of unilateral powers to resolve disputes. This situation differs from that of other countries, such as Germany, Italy, the United States, and England, where, for specific reasons, the subject has a long-standing tradition. Therefore, a work presented within the national context must be aware of the theoretical robustness found abroad, without ignoring the specific reality in which it is embedded.

Following this introductory chapter, Chapter 2 will outline the reasons for questioning the prohibition of self-help. Much of this stems from the approach taken by procedural doctrine regarding the role of jurisdiction and the model adopted for understanding various means of dispute resolution. Although this expansion considers different forms of legal protection, few advances have been made concerning unilateral remedies. These criticisms will lead to the development of criteria for identifying self-help (i.e., what it is), how it is exercised by the State and private individuals (i.e., how it manifests), and why it should be seen as a means of dispute resolution (i.e., its purpose).

Chapter 3 will examine the instrumental function of self-help. This function is defined by the presence of unilateral remedial powers within legal relationships that have distinct characteristics, which can be categorized as contractual and non-contractual relationships due to the differing limits of action in each case. The significance of this analysis also lies in the existence of such powers for the State, including in its foreign relations, and for private individuals. This analysis will also assess the impact of technology on these legal relationships, particularly in light of the growing use of self-help mechanisms based on algorithms and blockchain.

Chapter 4 will discuss the limitations of unilateral remedies. Here, it will be shown that the current requirements for such control are inadequate, particularly with the broad application of proportionality. To reach this conclusion, the work aims to demonstrate how due process adapts to various forms of legal protection and how the relationship between fundamental rights and self-help functions. Based on this, the work proposes criteria to assess the lawfulness of the conduct of active parties, which may be cumulative or not, depending on the type of protection involved.

Chapter 5 is dedicated to systematizing self-help within Brazilian law. Just as other legal remedies are classified, it is essential to define the profile of unilateral remedies based on the agents who invoke them, the types of protection they provide, their objectives, and the interests they aim to safeguard.

References

Bauer F (2023) Proportionality in private law: an analytical framework. In: Bauer F, Köhler B (eds) Proportionality in private law. Mohr Siebeck, Tübingen, pp 15–31

Belmonte E (2023) Compensazione e autotutela. Edizione Scientifiche Italiane, Napoli

Betti E (1959) Autotutela (dir. priv.). In: Enciclopedia del diritto, vol IV. Giuffrè, Milano, pp 529–537

Beurskens M (2017) Privatrechtliche Selbsthilfe, Rechte, Pflichten und Verantwortlichkeit bei digitalen Zugangsbeschränkungs- und Selbstdurchsetzungsbefugnissen. Mohr Siebeck, Tübingen

Bianca CM (2000) Autotutela (dir. priv.). In: Bianca C (ed) Enciclopedia del Diritto, vol IV (agg.). Milano, Giuffrè, pp 529–537

Bingwan X (2018) Adjudicating the regulatory penalties against non-professional taxis in China and the European Union. In: Krönke C et al (eds) Paradigms of internet regulation in the European Union and China. Nomos, Baden-Baden

Bohannan P (1968) Justice and judgment among the TIV. Routledge, London

Böhm P (2019) Prozessidee und Richtermacht. Österreich, Wien

Cannata CA (2011) Violenza fittizia e violenza reale nelle strutture primigenie del processo privato romano. In: Scritti scelti di Diritto Romano, vol I, a cura di Letizia Vacca, vol I, Giappichelli, Torino

Carimini F (2018) Sequestro convenzionale e autotutela. Edizione Scientifiche Italiane, Napoli
Cintra ACA et al (2015) Teoria geral do processo, 31th edn. Malheiros, São Paulo
Colli P et al (2022) History of conflict resolution in Europe – a project report. Rechtsgeschichte – Legal History, Rg. 30
Cordero F (2022) Le situazioni soggettive nel processo penale. Giappichelli, Torino
D'Acunto L (2020) Self-help in civil matters and state justice. Diritto Mercato Tecnologia
Díaz Alabart S (2007) La autotutela. In: Liber Amicorum Guido Alpa, private law beyond the national systems. British Institute of International and Comparative Law, London, pp 23
Epstein RA (2005) The theory and practice of self-help. J Law Econ Policy 1(1):1–31
Feldman R (2020) Der possessorische Besitzschutz und sein Verhältnis zum petitorischen Recht. Mohr Siebeck, Tübingen
Fonseca RG (2012) O fundamento da autotutela executiva da Administração Pública, contributo para a sua compreensão como problema jurídico-político. Almedina, Lisboa
Geri LB (1971) Profili sistematici dell'autotutela privata. Giuffrè, Milano
Griener J et al (2017) Self-help, reimagined. Indiana Law J 92:3
Hamburger P (2014) Is administrative law unlawful? The University of Chicago Press, Chicago
Hensler DH (2014) The private in public, the public in private, the blurring boundary between public and private resolution. In: Zekoll J et al (ed) Formalization and flexibilization in dispute resolution. Brill, Leiden
Kant I (2013) Metafísica dos costumes. Vozes, Petrópolis
Kelsen H (1992) Reine Rechtslehre, 2 Auflage edn. Österreichische Staatsdruckerei, Wien
Klingbeil S (2017) Die Not- und Selbsthilfe, eine dogmatische Rekonstruktion. Mohr Siebeck, Tübingen
Landmann V (1975) Notwehr, Notstand und Selbsthilfe im Privatrecht. Schulthess Polygraphischer, Zürich
Lener A (1985) Potere (dir. priv.). In: Enciclopedia del diritto, vol XXXIV. Giuffrè, Milano, pp 620
Lenzi R (1996) Condizione, autonomia privata e funzione di autotutela. L'adimpimento dedotto in condizione. Giuffrè, Milano
Lepore A (2019) Autotutela e autonomia negoziale. Edizione Scientifiche Italiane, Napoli
Levada FAM (2022) Garantias autoexecutáveis. Editora Revista dos Tribunais, São Paulo
Luzzatto G (1956) Von der Selbsthilfe zum römischen Prozeß. Zeitschrift Savigny Stiftung für Rechtsgeschichte 73, pp 30
Mezzanotte L (1995) Il diritto di ritenzione. Dall'autotutela alla pena privata. Edizione Scientifiche Italiane, Napoli
Miranda J (2020) Direitos fundamentais, 3rd edn. Almedina, Coimbra
Montecchiari T (2019) Ius singulare e autotutela privata, contributo allo studio di una categoria. ESI, Napoli
Moraes MZD (2022) Processo criminal transformativo, modelo criminal e sistema processual não violentos. D'Plácido, Belo Horizonte
Murino F (2010) L'autotutela nell'escussione della garanzia finanziaria pignoratizia. Giuffrè, Milano
Nieva Fenoll J (2017) Seis conceptos en busca de un objetivo, jurisdicción, acción, proceso, derechos, pena y delito. Polít Crim 12(23):103–123
Petrone M (1997) La compensazione tra autotutela e autonomia. Giuffrè, Milano
Picardi N (2011) La crisi del monopolio statuale della giurisdizione e la proliferazione delle Corti. Riv it sc giur 2:43–78
Popineau-Dehaullon C (2008) Catherine. Les remèdes de justice privée à l'inexécution du contrat. Étude comparative. LGDJ, Paris
Purpura A (2020) Autonomia privata, responsabilità e attuazione coattiva del credito. Giappichelli, Torino
Renner M (2021) Private ordering. In: Grundmann S, Micklitz H-W, Renner M (eds) New private law theory. Cambridge University Press, Cambridge, pp 484–494
Russo D (2017) Oltre il patto marciano. Edizione Scientifiche Italiane, Napoli
Salles RBDO (2019) Autotutela nas relações contratuais. Editora Processo, Rio de Janeiro

Santamaria MF (1937) La giustizia privata. Jovene, Napoli

Santos BS (1977) The law of the oppressed: the construction and reproduction of legality in Pasargada. Law Soc Rev 12(1):5–126

Saturno A (1995) L'autotutela privata. I modelli della ritenzione e dell'eccezione di inadempimento in comparazione col sistema tedesco. Edizione Scientifiche Italiane, Napoli

Schirato VR (2011) Repensando a pertinência dos atributos dos atos administrativos. In: Medauar O, Schirato VR (eds) Os caminhos do ato administrativo. Editora Revista dos Tribunais, São Paulo, pp 115–144

Schünemann W (1985) Selbsthilfe im Rechtssystem, eine dogmatische Studie am Beispiel der §§ 227, 229 ff. BGB. JCB Mohr (Paul) Siebeck, Tübingen

Sharkey CM (2010) Trespass torts and self-help for an electronic age. NYU Law Econ Res Paper 10:07

Jr Theodoro H, Andreade E (2023) Autotutela executiva, execução extrajudicial positivada. Forense, Rio de Janeiro

Titze H (1897) Die Notstandsrechte im deutschen bürgerlichen Gesctzbuche und ihre geschichtliche Entwickelung. Veit & Comp, Leipzig

Vallimaresco A (1926) La justice privée en droit moderne. Libraire de Jurisprudence Ancienne et Modern, Paris

Von Tuhr A (1888) Der Nothstand im Civilrecht. Carl Winters Universitätsbuchhandlung, Heidelberg

Yarshell FL (2020) Reafirmação e evolução da teoria geral do processo, projeções no ensino dessa disciplina no curso de graduação da Faculdade de Direito da Universidade de São Paulo. Revista Ius Dictio, janeiro-maio 00:143–146

Zamora y Castillo NA (2000) Proceso, autocomposición y autodefensa. Contribución al estudio de los fines del proceso, 3rd edn. UNAM, Mexico DF

Chapter 2
Self-Help as a Method of Dispute Resolution

This chapter explores the fundamentals of self-help in conflict resolution. While this section focuses on establishing core concepts and theories about the topic, the main challenges in systematically addressing it stem from these very aspects. The aim is not only to dispel the stigmas around self-help but also to define clear boundaries to prevent it from being mistaken for other forms of exerting power or exceeding what is permitted by the Brazilian legal system. Furthermore, its inclusion within the broader framework of self-empowerment strategies aims to highlight the complexity and fluidity with which disputes are resolved in both public and private settings. These aspects are often overlooked due to strict classification.

2.1 Critical Analysis of the Prohibition of Self-Help

The concept of self-help prohibition is viewed from four perspectives. First, the idea of the State as the sole controller of rights led to the belief that only the State is responsible for protecting them or that it alone has the legitimate authority to do so. In line with this social organization model, the actions of private individuals were criminalized, and excessive unilateral protection was considered illegal to reinforce the State's monopoly on the use of force.[1] Secondly, this supremacy sought to prevent the disturbance of peace and social coexistence by removing from individuals the power to pursue their claims without the intervention of an authority. Such interference contributed to civilizational progress, while at the same time overriding the self-determination of these individuals, on the presumption that any conflict should

[1] Zamora y Castillo (2000), p. 36.

E. Pierre Eid, *Self-Help as Method of Conflict Resolution*,
https://doi.org/10.1007/978-3-032-13905-4_2

be mediated.[2] Thirdly, the prohibition was designed to prevent acts of personal subjugation. The connection between subordination and the human being, or what is associated with vengeance, has endured over time and has, on one hand, contributed to expanding jurisdiction,[3] and, on the other hand, cast a marginalized view on self-help, which, both sociologically and legally, has underpinned much of the expansive argument for State-based dispute resolution.[4] Fourthly, it served as one of the justifications for the development of legal proceedings, framing them as a way to restrain acts of private defense. This organicist theory explained the supposed replacement of sanctions and punishments imposed by communities or non-state entities on individuals.[5] These justifications also influenced how self-help is viewed as a legally inadmissible means.[6] However, a counterintuitive conclusion might be drawn from certain key references to this widespread scenario.

Just as there was concern for individual protection, society has consistently recognized the existence of means involving the use of force. Assigning a residual, concurrent, or even primary role to self-help has been a consistent feature since ancient times, shaped by certain fundamental factors. Many acts aimed at protecting legal interests underwent a process of ritualization and normative integration, some of which were directed into the dichotomy between *negotia* and *iudicia.*[7] Without dismissing the debates about the origins of civil procedure, a consistent theoretical view suggests that some of these rituals reflected the acceptance of action by the interested party to serve their own interests on their own initiative, as was allowed, for example, during the period of the *legis actiones* and in the regulations of the Twelve Tables, or through the acceptance of moderate use of force under Justinian Code.[8] Some of these acts were linked to violence, while others were independent of any personal aggression; therefore, the identification of this range of conduct was also acknowledged by the legal order.[9] If the primary concern was the occurrence of violence, it was soon realised that such violence, in its authorised form, was merely one species of a broader genus and, over time, became residual.[10]Furthermore, the primacy of using force gradually shifted, being transferred to a public agent for its primary use. Despite the trend toward restricting direct action to protect an interest through the imposition of sanctions,[11] longstanding institutions such as self-defence, necessity, the right of retention, and the protection of possession and property, to name but a

[2] Schünemann (1985), pp. 2–3.

[3] Gil y Gil (1994), p. 19.

[4] Kneis (2005), p. 267.

[5] Luzzatto (1956), p. 30.

[6] Delgado Castro et al. (2017), p. 270.

[7] Kelly (1967), pp. 166–167.

[8] Luzzatto (1956), p. 59. Franchini (2012), p. 242.

[9] Cannata (2011), p. 379.

[10] Marino (2021), p. 40.

[11] Kelly (1967), p. 166.

few examples, remained resilient even during periods of greater restriction on private initiative.[12]

It would not be possible to admit that natural and intuitive human behavior could be eliminated simply by creating state structures that began to regulate and resolve conflicts. Self-help existed before the State, was incorporated by it, and continued to develop. If viewed as a form of protection for threatened or violated interests, social complexity made it impossible to fully replace the action of the interested party, or even, in such ancient times, to accept an overt state presence when, in reality, it was still precarious.[13] Even with efforts to control popular justice (*Volksjustiz*) by suppressing social organizations that aimed to impose physical and psychological consequences on those who violated its ethical and moral standards,[14] it cannot be said that self-help was eliminated or, ultimately, prohibited. Jhering identified the transition from a state of barbarism to a form of self-help supervised and regulated by law, describing as an "illusion" the notion that everything should be done by the State, thus distinguishing between the public system of law enforcement and the protection of private interests by the community.[15] Concluding that there was a prohibition did not stem from any outcome verified by the legal system, as restrictions were placed on individual activity to prevent the imposition of arbitrary will.

Later, Luzzatto observed this assimilation as the meeting point between the legal regulation of private autonomy and the historical pendulum of state presence as an intermediary in conflict resolution.[16] This line of thought can be summarized as follows: the State did not eliminate the possibility of unilateral initiative by rights holders, but instead defined the boundary between lawful and unlawful conduct for this purpose, since one of the manifestations of a right is the power to protect it.[17]

Over the centuries, there have been fluctuations in the relationship between power and personal subjection; however, a series of legal instruments has established the preservation of human life and confirmed the most desirable profile for self-help, within the limits of the legal system and with partial permission to use force. Within these boundaries, it is correct to observe that there was no monopoly on the use of force by the State, but rather a position of priority, coordinated with the actions of private individuals. Similarly, self-help was not limited to acts of aggression or opposed to public order and still included a range of protective actions that extended beyond physical acts. This is also explained by Kaser and Hackl, who pointed out the futility of treating it as a "war of all against all," given this limitation of unilateral power. This stage of domestication revealed the inaccuracy of identifying self-help as something outside the scope of law.

Its prohibition, coupled with the provision of State protection, is therefore a post hoc construction. More accurate views of these phenomena show that it was

---

[12] Franchini (2012), pp. 169–170.

[13] Haferkamp (2003), §§ 226–231, p. 1073.

[14] Marino (2021), p. 38.

[15] Jhering (1866), p. 116.

[16] Luzzatto (1956), pp. 40–41.

[17] Dedek (2018), pp. 98–100.

not possible to assume a state of legal uncertainty and abuses that needed to be addressed by an organized public structure. In this context, several points should be highlighted: a re-examination of the emergence of the institution, which suggests that regulation does not stem from disorder, but from the diversity of local rules that allowed for varying degrees of arbitrariness and personal sacrifice. This goes beyond the polarization between the State and the individual.

From an evolutionary perspective, it is also incorrect to claim that there was an effort to eliminate self-help.[18]In addition to its incorporation into the legal order as mentioned above, the supposed homogeneity of the advance of public over private spheres began to be questioned in the nineteenth century, when a reconstructive recovery took place, and the presence of numerous forms of self-help in the past was observed.[19] This was one of the significant contributions from German doctrine, and it soon became clear that "it is not possible to assert that any act of self-help is illegal or punishable" or "that the mere existence of the Judiciary entails a prohibition on self-help."[20]

Suppose the division of powers between the State and private individuals has changed. In that case, it is inaccurate to recognise a linear evolution from the State monopoly on force to the prohibition of self-help.[21] The range of acts for direct and unilateral protection has also made it impossible to equate self-help with violence or with a disordered understanding of society. Nevertheless, the narrative constructed up to the mid-twentieth century was highly successful, attributing not only an omnipresent connotation to jurisdiction, but also to the State itself.[22]

Only in more recent times have these ideas been contrasted due to the emergence of a comprehensive theory of self-help, which has expressed its full development[23]in both public and private applications.[24] This is due to specific characteristics, such as dissociating self-help from violence through the presence of more refined and legally authorised mechanisms; its inevitable presence for social coexistence and the dynamic economic reality; its function as a first measure of protection for a legal position; its perception as a non-bureaucratic means, as the intervention of a third-party adjudicator is unnecessary; the revision of public functions regarding acts of aggression and a broader scope for private action; and its suitability for resolving a range of disputes.[25] Thus, it cannot be said that self-help was limited to emerging from the shadows and occasionally gaining legal recognition. Its dissemination was influenced by legal, social, and economic factors that established it as a means of

---

[18] Kaiser (1983), pp. 56–57.

[19] Jhering (1866), pp. 117–18.

[20] Bensey (1835), p. 1.

[21] Titze (1897), p. 125.

[22] Marino (2021), p. 43.

[23] Haferkamp (2003), §§ 226–231, pp. 1073–1078.

[24] Lichtman (2004) p. 2.

[25] Stănescu (2015), pp. 18–19.

dispute resolution,[26] as well as challenging the widespread premise that jurisdiction and Procedural Law are its antithesis.

2.1.1 Grounds for Evolution

The theory of formative rights was essential in recognizing, within the scope of powers held by the right-holder, the possibility of unilateral exercise for the protection of interests.[27] Lacking an enforceable title and independent of any authority's intervention, it became clear that it was possible to substantially prevent or remedy a violation of a legal position through submission alone, without needing cooperation from the opposing party. Although the term "formative right" has gained significant acceptance,[28] the origin of *Gestaltungsrecht* suggests a more precise meaning. As a result of this configuration, it may lead to concrete manifestations in legal position. In some cases, this power is withheld, and its exercise requires a judicial decision,[29] as an alternative to what is termed the technique of self-help (*Selbsthilfetechnik*); in others, although freely exercised, it is not aimed at this purpose, as in the case of the right of option.

The identification of the category of formative rights of self-help (*Selbsthilfegestaltungsrechte*) led doctrine to classify them as original formative rights.[30] This sensitive dogmatic analysis not only led to the reclassification of numerous legal institutes[31] but also revealed something more profound: the presence of formative rights in various branches of law carried with it this unilateral power of protection.[32] The presence of self-help was more evident than previously imagined, as was the capacity of substantive law to provide solutions to infringements or threats to rights.

While formative rights were already present in various legal systems, a significant change occurred with the identification of the characteristics of the powers held by some of them.[33] The concrete, unilateral, and submissive action revealed a straightforward technique, which involves considerable economy of effort in protecting a legal position.

The lack of need for procedural activity drew attention to both the agility of operating effectively and the legal protections afforded by substantive law itself, independent of any third-party adjudication apparatus.[34] The origin of the modern concept of self-help is rooted in this foundation. Viewing it as an inherent means within

26 Delgado Castro et al. (2017), pp. 267–269.

27 Helmreich (1967), pp. 37–45.

28 Marino (2020), pp. 107–118.

29 Motto (2012), pp. 79–82.

30 Helmreich (1967), p. 39.

31 Betti (1959), pp. 529–530.

32 Bötticher (1964), pp. 2–3.

33 Feldman (2020), p. 8.

34 Petrone (1997), pp. 32–33.

the legal system, human behavior, and social relations—recognizing that individuals have limits but also the freedom to protect their interests—and emphasizing its speed, simplicity, and efficiency, free from third-party intervention, justified its gradual development and assimilation.[35]

This observation is not limited to the historically established cases that have since been reclassified. There was a movement toward expansion due to these attributes, while elements that previously characterized it—such as the use of violence, the urgency that would prevent authorities from intervening, or physical submission—proved to be incidental. Therefore, it is essential to classify these various characteristics into three categories to explain the development, based on how suitable self-help is to the conflict: (a) the origin of the power; (b) the regulation of the power; and (c) the object of the exercise of power.[36]

From the origin of self-help power, one must understand whether it comes from the State or the individual. To clarify this division, the difference between public self-help and private self-help is used, although, in terms of purpose and structure, both can serve the same function of protecting interests.[37] The distinction, however, is important because the paths each follows are different. While the State's power to exercise self-help is central to its activities—whether in reviewing its own actions, enforcing them independently, or restricting individuals' rights beyond certain normative limits—the suspicion of private self-help took longer to fade, due to the reasons explained in the previous section.

On the one hand, this is due to the debate over the legitimacy of violence, which, as seen, influenced restrictive conceptions of individual liberty. On the other hand, this suspicion largely stems from the notion of the state's supremacy over individuals, in the belief that the State would seek social peace by preventing each individual from protecting their own interests due to the restriction of the principle of liberty.[38]

It would not be possible to address this division without taking fundamental rights as a starting point. In this context, they perform a dual function. The first is to limit State power, serving as a barrier to violations of legal certainty, legality, liberty, property, and dignity. This observation aims to prevent the use of force from being understood as a state weapon against the individual, a form of authorization for the invasion of their personal or proprietary sphere in an exclusive and authoritarian manner. Fundamental rights are limits to the unconvincing thesis that, in the rule of law, public agents would have primacy in the use of force by virtue of alleged sovereignty, since the State must act in the interests of these individuals.[39]

Furthermore, it would be hard to argue that this monopoly constitutes a constitutional principle, as the restrictions placed on individuals also come from other fundamental rights. The level of private power allowed or restricted by the legislator influences how the State's use of force is balanced and applied. The law does not

[35] Alland (2001), p. 77.

[36] Eid (2024), pp. 259–263.

[37] Lampis (2019), pp. 120–121.

[38] Schauer (2015), pp. 124–128.

[39] Schimpfhauser (2009), pp. 70–71.

establish this supposed monopoly; it merely defines the scope of action for State agents. An example of this is the presence of private security companies operating alongside or in parallel with public security. The second role of fundamental rights is abstention, meaning they require the State not to interfere in private decisions, since individuals are intended to exercise these rights actively.

This margin of freedom is a key element of private self-help, symbolizing autonomy in protecting legal rights. The debate centers on the individual's right to defend their legal domain against violations or threats by others.[40] The discussion of legality in this context assumes a different character, as it is argued that such conduct is not possible without legal authorization, even though this principle applies broadly in private relations. This restriction is accompanied by another argument widely disseminated in procedural doctrine: the right of action is the right to call upon the State to resolve conflicts, on the premise that self-help would be prohibited. In other words, such an analysis equates the interpretation and application of the principle of legality for private individuals and for the State. Therefore, the challenge lies in defining the boundaries of private acts of self-defense without applying the assumptions of public self-help, based on the scope of grounds for excluding unlawfulness, as discussed in Chapter 4.

The regulation of power is closely connected to the discipline of self-help. The contrast between third-party regulation and self-regulation characterizes it; the former involves creating rules by a third party, usually the State, to manage the conduct and relationships of other entities or individuals, while the latter is defined by regulations established by the recipients themselves. This division has had a significant impact on self-help, considering its integration into both public and private spheres, and, above all, features such as globalization, the pursuit of legislative harmonization, and cross-border and digital relations.[41] Thus, its dissemination has been considered a strategic choice, mainly because it avoids the need for state judicial proceedings, which often lead to delays and disputes over jurisdiction, legitimacy, applicable law, and other issues, keeping in mind that "civilised self-help has the advantages of speed, efficiency, flexibility and cheapness upon which the smooth functioning of business life so much depends."[42]

Just as it is said that new rights now require judicial protection, new rights and reasons have also emerged, leading to the use of self-help in this context of multiple normativity. These regulatory choices, therefore, emphasize an opt-out approach that prioritizes general principles over specific jurisdictions, reversing the usual order: first, the power for unilateral protection is granted, and only afterward is its validity evaluated. In addition to the theoretical analysis of formative rights and the specific regulations of each country, some examples of self-regulation and third-party regulation can be highlighted, considering their contribution to the spread of the institute.

40 D'Acunto (2020), p. 3.

41 Stănescu (2015), pp. 22–23.

42 Goode (1988), p. 151.

The Uniform Commercial Code (UCC) of the United States adopts self-help as one of its guiding principles. Enacted in 1952, it was strongly influenced by the interests of economic groups in the banking sector and guided by the conception of property rights in that country. This is reflected in *sections* 9–609 and 9–610 of this statute.[43] The first provision allows the creditor, after default, to take possession of the asset given as security by the debtor without the need for judicial proceedings (*self-help repossession*), a situation limited by the *'without breach of peace'* clause, to render the asset unusable or to dispose of the security. The second sets out how this act of disposal should take place, which may occur through sale, lease, or other commercially reasonable means, including acquisition by the creditor themselves.

These provisions established a unitary model, subsequently adopted in Australia, New Zealand, Canadian provinces, and in some Central and Eastern European countries, including Hungary, Croatia, Poland, and Romania. For the same reasons, the structure defined by the UCC inspired soft law guidelines on security interests from various international organisations seeking normative harmonisation, such as the European Bank for Reconstruction and Development (EBRD), the United Nations Commission on International Trade Law (UNCITRAL), and the International Institute for the Unification of Private Law (UNIDROIT).[44]

The possibility of creating self-help scenarios has served as an incentive for self-regulation, granting, for example, the power to impose consequences for unlawful acts, and as a tool for governance. The subject is notably broad, especially considering the contractual freedom to establish rules of conduct for agents who agree to be bound by them.

The immediacy and coercive nature of self-help are relevant to the preservation of structures that operate in this manner, protecting a range of rights.[45] Using self-regulation by digital platforms as an example, self-help can take many forms and benefit a variety of participants. Consider cases where the platform prevents the sharing of a video that violates copyright, limits the work of drivers for breaking the terms of use of ride-hailing apps, or blocks profiles that spread false information, hate speech, or child pornography. The quick response of self-help is crucial for maintaining desired relationships in self-regulated environments and acts as a means of controlling and excluding undesirable content.[46]

Finally, the purpose of exercising power indicates what will be the target of the interested party's unilateral action. It has already been noted that self-help has evolved, no longer being solely a personal and aggressive form of protection. It can be recognized that part of its modern use stems from a shift from focusing on the person to concentrating on assets and legal situations.[47] The acceptance of efforts by an interested party to physically subjugate another has become a residual concept, as it has become necessary to balance the protection of human dignity with the allowance

[43] Mccall (1973), pp. 75–76.

[44] Stănescu and Gikay (2017), pp. 101–103.

[45] Bachman (2006), pp. 126–127.

[46] Goldman (2021), pp. 23–25.

[47] Alland (2001), pp. 75–76.

for unilateral action. Current forms lead to the restriction of rights, seizure, appropriation, or transfer of assets, as well as the prevention of abuses of legal positions through indirect coercion, among other consequences.[48]

From this observation, several consequences can be identified. One is the recognition that many rights allow for some degree of direct protection by their holder, even if their full realisation depends on a judicial decision. If a claim is not fully satisfied, a margin of freedom remains for actions aimed at obtaining some applicable protection by the interested party. For example, although a creditor cannot invade the debtor's assets to unilaterally and forcibly satisfy the debt, they may resort to coercive measures such as registering the debtor's name with a credit protection agency. Another consequence is the possibility of intermediaries who are not responsible for providing the protection sought by the holder, but act to facilitate or cooperate in its realisation. Examples range from the most straightforward to the most advanced, such as legitimate defense, where a property owner uses animals to deter an intruder, or the use of algorithms to optimize the detection and removal of fake profiles on social networks. Ultimately, self-help can offer various forms of protection to those who practice it. These changes have made it possible to apply classifications usually reserved for judicial protection. Therefore, depending on the criterion used – Chapter 4 is dedicated to this systematic profile – self-help may be executive, constitutive, declaratory, conservatory, among other modalities reflecting the variation above.[49]

2.1.2 Analysis of the Brazilian Context

After publicly and unexpectedly revealing a significant liability due to accounting fraud, a retail company surprised consumers and creditors by filing for judicial reorganization. Before this, the company had entered several contracts with one of its main creditors: one for providing credit to suppliers, another appointing the creditor as the custodian of its funds, and a third for offsetting and settling transactions. Insolvency was regarded as a contractual default, prompting the creditor to invoke two clauses: one allowing for the acceleration of all debts, and another permitting the creditor to offset all its credits against the amounts deposited with it. The second clause was designed to quickly address defaults by enabling the creditor to take the quantities deposited, redeem investments, and settle transactions early—measures that prevented losses amounting to billions.[50]

Following the adoption of a strike movement demanding a career and salary plan, profit-sharing, and changes to working hours, workers halted their activities to pressure the employer to meet these demands. To prevent the continuation of these claims, the company decided to initiate a collective labour dispute and challenge

[48] Beurskens (2017), pp. 16–21.

[49] Geri (1971), pp. 16–17.

[50] STJ, *Jurisdictional Conflict* No. 194,336, Justice Og Fernandes, 26/01/2023.

the action, alleging that the rights sought were excessive and that there was non-compliance with the legal requirements for a lawful strike. The court ruled that there was no illegality; however, not all the employees' claims were granted. Specifically, the court limited the claims to compensation for the days of the strike, restricted temporary job security to employees with open-ended contracts, and denied payment of profit-sharing.[51]

During an inspection of a residence, the electricity utility detected tampering with the meter. Notified of the debt arising from the correction of these modifications and allowed to contest the inspection, the consumer chose not to defend himself and refused to pay the debt, as well as failing to pay the most recent bill. Subsequently, the utility company proceeded to disconnect the service by cutting off the electricity supply, a move that was challenged in court but was ultimately unsuccessful.[52]

The driver was caught by electronic equipment travelling on a motorway at a speed 50% above the maximum permitted. This offence, classified as very serious under the Brazilian Traffic Code, carries penalties including a fine, immediate suspension of the right to drive, and seizure of the driving licence (Article 218, III). The challenge to the constitutionality of the seizure of the licence, on the grounds of violation of due process, was rejected on the basis that the unilateral measure by the Public Administration was intended to provisionally protect situations of high risk to road safety, postponing the right to adversarial proceedings and full defence to the administrative or judicial process. The administrative measure would therefore be a consequence of the self-executing and imperative nature of police powers.[53]

The example above illustrates how often courts face issues related to unilateral protection initiated by the interested party. While these are just a sample, they show the variety, importance, and commonality of self-help in everyday life and its different roles. Many other examples could be found throughout laws or established by custom. However, the goal here is not to list all of them; rather, it is more helpful to understand the development of the topic in our context to see why it has diverged from other dispute resolution methods.

Several reasons are prominent in this analysis, considering (a) the theories surrounding the right of action; (b) the criticism focused on the freedom inherent in private self-help, while public self-help has benefited from administrative action independent of strict judicial intervention; (c) a perspective still linked to personal submission as a result of self-help; (d) the acknowledgment that many dispute resolution methods would be more appropriate if based on the idea that consensus leads to better outcomes, a characteristic absent in self-help; and (e) finally, the tendency to directly apply elements of the Theory of Procedure to various dispute resolution methods without proper adaptation.

The separation between the right of action and substantive rights was one of the pillars for recognising the dichotomy between a claim directed against the State and

[51] TST, RO-1533-35.2012.5.15.0000, Specialised Section for Collective Disputes, Justice Mauricio Godinho Delgado, 21/02/2014.

[52] STJ, REsp No. 1,412,433/RS, Justice Herman Benjamin, First Section, judged on 25/4/2018.

[53] STF, ADI 3951, Reporting Justice Edson Fachin, Full Court, judged on 29/05/2020.

a claim arising from the violation of a right.[54] The former arises from the exercise of a public subjective right to resolve disputes. Here lies the primary feature that distinguishes the right of action as a counterpoint to self-help. Wach employed the term *Rechtsschutzanspruch* in reference to the protection offered by the State to resolve conflicts of interest. The core of his argument rested on the idea that "the regular exclusion of self-help from the domains of Private Law goes hand in hand with the guarantee of State assistance in legal protection, through proceedings, for threatened interests."[55] This distinction between the right violated or threatened and its protection evolved to the point where, at the heart of the right of action, there is the right to appropriate, timely, and effective judicial protection. It is noted that the right of action comprises a complex of legal positions and procedural techniques, such that this right could not fail to be fundamental, since "it arises from the very existence of rights and, thus, is the counterpart to the prohibition of self-help.".[56]

The emphasis on how and to what extent the State must provide judicial protection, based on the scope given to the right of action, presupposes certain considerations. First, the distinction between the interest that was violated, and its protection suggests that judicial protection takes precedence over an individual's freedom to pursue it. There is a relationship of superiority of the former over the latter, influenced by the common belief that self-help is either forbidden or discouraged. However, self-help should not be confused with illegality; basic teachings still affirm that jurisdiction exists to prevent individuals from taking the law into their own hands, positioning the State as the entity responsible for enforcing the law.[57]

Although a critique of this relationship with the concept of substantive right of action has been outlined, the school of thought associated with it did not consider the different configurations of self-help to challenge the discourse of procedural doctrine and acknowledge the coexistence of various forms of unilateral protection.[58]Secondly, the broad interpretation of Article 5, item XXXV of the Brazilian Federal Constitution of 1988, as access to legal protection through various means, does not necessarily align with the debate over which of these means provide access to justice and why, although this constitutional provision may serve as a starting point for reevaluating the dominance of judicial protection.[59] This was also insufficient for self-help to be included in this framework, as the interpretation of this article equated consensual means, such as arbitration, mediation, and conciliation, types included in policies aimed at expanding dispute resolution avenues.[60] In this context, the concept of access to justice encompasses protection by the interested parties themselves, provided that it is legitimate only if it results from a convergence of wills. There is an attempt to connect various dispute resolution methods to the

---

[54] Wendelstein (2021), p. 140.

[55] Wach (1885), p. 4.

[56] Marinoni (2020), p. 128.

[57] Dinamarco (2013), pp. 188–191.

[58] Couto e Silva (1997), pp. 177–179.

[59] Watanabe (2012), p. 88.

[60] Grinover (2018), p. 62.

idea of access to justice, without explaining how this relationship is established in terms of sufficiency, completeness, and scope; it is overlooked that these are some of the ways self-help and third-party adjudication manifest, and the complexity of such protection must certainly be examined to understand the current meaning of the constitutional principle mentioned.

The analysis of the preference for judicial protection over protection initiated by the interested party has a gap. The idea of a right of action versus self-help is based on the prohibition of private action, despite the significant and broad use of such action by the State.[61] The partial view mentioned earlier confirms that the restriction was not explicitly connected to unilateralism but rather to who would have the initiative. According to Maurer, self-executing powers give the Public Administration the authority to impose coercively what, for private individuals, would typically require an enforcement order obtained through judicial means.[62] Submission may occur, for example, in the exercise of police powers, which serve as a form of such conduct aimed at legal protection by restricting the rights of private individuals. These barriers can lead, for instance, to the imposition of fines, suspension of licenses, or closure of establishments, among other consequences.

The duty of the Public Administration to protect the interests entrusted to it becomes concrete through self-executing powers, meaning the act is carried out by the public entity itself without needing approval from a third party. Just as priority was recognized for protecting rights through the courts in private disputes, the State made an exception to this preference in its own favor. Therefore, the current system of judicial protection should be compared to direct protection by the party as a whole—whether the State or the individual—to reduce power imbalances and examine the possible forms of protection.

Viewing the right of action as opposed to private self-help is also connected to the longstanding fear of equating it with human subjugation. If, from a reconstructive perspective, it has been demonstrated that characterizing it as unlawful or limiting it to physical force is inappropriate, it is equally important to emphasize that the different ways of exercising it have moved it away from this outdated concept view.[63] Its presence, as demonstrated, indicates a range of legal protections that are far from human subjugation and may be related to consent.

Although it is exercised unilaterally, will remains a significant source of opportunities for its application, often in situations of self-regulation. Its use as a means of protection against contractual breaches, for example, would be a typical case where the parties wish to balance risks, to take swift action without harming future review of their conduct. As noted, excluding self-help from an integrated study of dispute resolution mechanisms on the assumption of a lack of consensus ignores all these developments.[64] The point previously emphasized is thus reiterated: a theory

---

[61] Medauar (2021), pp. 18–19.

[62] Maurer (2000), p. 241.

[63] Talamini and Cardoso (2022), pp. 196–199.

[64] D'Acunto (2020), p. 9.

of dispute resolution mechanisms must consider the different types of protection provided under the rule of law.

Finally, a barrier that persists in achieving this objective is the adoption of the Theory of Procedure as the starting point for analyzing any dispute resolution mechanism. Since it is commonly asserted that self-help is prohibited as a precondition for the right of action, and this is one of the pillars of that theory, it is not surprising that even today expressions such as "alternative means" or "jurisdictional equivalents" are used. Although a substantial critical framework exists regarding these notions, it is essential to highlight them because they continue to perpetuate a restrictive conception of unilateral protection by the interested party.

The right of action does not exist to prevent extrajudicial mechanisms for dispute resolution. It is not an exclusionary principle, but rather a principle whose relevant purpose is to promote the protection and satisfaction of rights through state judicial protection.[65] This does not mean that it is the only route, nor that it cannot coexist and interact with others. Furthermore, specific points deserve emphasis: it is not necessary to rely on the Theory of Procedure for principles such as adversarial proceedings, full defense, or due process of law to extend beyond state judicial proceedings, since the vertical and horizontal effectiveness of fundamental rights provides solutions for this scenario.[66] It is relevant for providing theoretical contributions to understanding any form of procedurality, but not for simply transposing concepts and classifications specific to state judicial systems' proceedings.[67] Procedurality, as a means of limiting state activity and guiding private conduct, will not always be present in all types of protection, as may be the case in self-defense, necessity, or a state of siege, which does not preclude subsequent review of the acts performed.[68] The forms of legal protection, typically examined from the perspective of judicial protection, also exist in other dispute resolution methods, showing their independence from the right of action.

2.2 Criteria for the identification of self-help

One of the main issues in studying self-help is defining it, whether because it relates to the complex area of legal powers or because its requirements are not always clearly outlined. Several factors can be identified as contributing to these challenges, as analyzed in legal scholarship. The lack of a comprehensive legal framework to define its scope results in a narrow view of private self-help, which is often examined only sporadically based on scattered legislative provisions. The apparent lack of a general rule authorizing private self-help, along with Article 345 of the Brazilian Penal Code, which supports restrictive views on its use, arguing that it is only allowed

[65] Comoglio (2000), pp. 262–263.

[66] Couto e Silva (2011), p. 93.

[67] Yarshell (2022), p. 419.

[68] Romano (2021), pp. 219–221.

in specific, highly varied cases. Another issue is the common adoption of a negative view of self-help, whose usefulness is highly doubtful, as it simply excludes judicial intervention in providing legal remedies.[69] Associating it solely with the absence of a judge or third party to resolve the dispute makes its meaning broader and less specific, in addition to the recurring confusion with other legal institutions.[70]

These issues are also connected to the fluid and dynamic nature of self-help, which can often go unnoticed by observers. On one hand, suspicion surrounding private self-help could prevent recognition beyond those cases explicitly allowed by law, as seen in typical situations or when considered an exercise of individual freedom. The legal scholars who acknowledge the absence of a general prohibition on self-help are the same ones who resist recognizing a broad private right of power.[71] The contradiction suggests that it would be unsustainable to deny this power while simultaneously questioning the state's monopoly on the use of force. Conversely, the State's unilateral exercise of protection has not yet achieved sufficient autonomy, despite its widespread acceptance. Self-executing authority, in summary, is a characteristic that arises from the lack of need for judicial authorization to implement an administrative act. Within this context, some of these measures may be aimed at unilateral protection.

Thus, it is necessary to determine when and how self-executing authority will possess this characteristic, and relying solely on this negative perspective is insufficient. Lastly, the separation between unilateral protection exercised by private individuals and by the State puts the same phenomenon on opposite sides, undermining a unified and structural conceptual and practical approach. Although the characterizations of private and public power may differ, direct legal protection by the interested party will be present in both cases.[72]

The search for a concept of self-help also faces certain obstacles. It is common for means of dispute resolution to lack normative definitions, requiring legal scholarship to undertake the task of defining them. Determining what constitutes self-help also stems from this issue.

It is possible to identify three groups that pursue this conceptualization. The first, mentioned earlier, is the negative one: some authors define self-help as protection without the need for judicial proceedings.[73] This idea has evolved into the concept of the absence of a third-party adjudicator, but without offering criteria to differentiate this power from others that are not aimed at legal protection. According to this view, the constellation (*Selbsthilfekonstellationen*),[74] the mosaic,[75] or the polyhedron.[76] Specific cases of unilateral protection would form a barrier to defining a concept applicable to all situations. The second is a positive concept, which stems from

[69] Vallemaresco (1926), pp. 14–15.

[70] Nerson (1969), p. 8.

[71] Dagnino (1983), p. 248.

[72] Lampis (2019), pp. 117–118.

[73] Addis (2021), pp. 47–48.

[74] Beurskens (2017), p. 197.

[75] D'Acunto (2020), p. 6.

[76] Tango (2014), p. 18.

protecting a legal position that allows independent and unilateral action by the injured party. Therefore, self-help is seen as direct protection by the interested party of legal positions that are at risk or have been violated. The third is a subjectivist concept, which links self-help to the selfishness and partiality of the agent, distinguishing it from other forms of exercising power, such as familial or managerial power.[77] This criterion, lacking any theoretical objectivity, could lead to problems that go beyond the confusion caused by these two personal elements. Self-help does not always come from an agent's selfish motivation; it might, for example, result from an unavoidable need of the circumstances forcing action, from mutual agreement, or from the legal system's focus on efficiency and speed. Furthermore, partiality does little to clarify the role of the interested party, as their involvement in resolving the conflict is inevitable in any case of self-settlement.

Since the positive concept of self-help is most closely defined, it is essential to consider an additional element. To pinpoint the legal protection exercised directly by the party whose interest has been harmed or threatened, one must examine the characteristics of the passive subject, that is, the individual against whom such protection is aimed. The effectiveness pursued through the conduct of the interested party takes on the form of proper protection with impositivity, meaning the obligation to submit to the protection sought.[78] This must be analyzed in context: subjection can exist in different categories of powers, is part of the broader spectrum of formative rights, and, contrary to what might be assumed, is not the same as the impossibility of reaction.[79] From the perspective considered here, such subjugation occurs when the active subject protects their interests independently of the will, cooperation, or acceptance of the passive subject. This scope includes both the powers of the State and those of private individuals, providing a unified approach to these actions. One meaning of the term "legal protection" is the safeguarding, realization, or satisfaction of harmed or threatened interests; therefore, we refer to judicial protection when provided through the courts, or, more broadly, to the protection of rights, given the existence of various means for such protection.[80]

Thus, self-help is a form of legal protection that can be obtained unilaterally by the party whose interest has been harmed or threatened. This definition comprises the following constitutive elements, discussed below: The initiative of the interested party, unilateral protection, and the absence of any need for a third party to provide it.

[77] Zamora and Castillo (2000), pp. 50–51.

[78] Schünemann (1985), pp. 28–29.

[79] Fornaciari (1999), pp. 22–23.

[80] Yarshell (2006), p. 25.

2.2.1 Initiative of the Party

The conceptual framework begins with the power of action held by the interested party. This distinction is crucial to prevent unilateral protection from being confused with the legal protection provided by third parties. The reasons for such initiatives may vary between the State and private individuals, but the common element is the act of safeguarding a legal position. At this point, it is important to revisit the debate on the difference between substantive claims and procedural claims to identify the various types of protection. Although this discussion has mainly focused on the substantive claim—which concerns the enforceability and characteristics of subjective rights—and the procedural claim, which involves asserting this enforceability in court, the broader consequences of a threat or violation should also be examined.

Firstly, the subjective situation is not limited to a position of enforceability against a legal duty but also includes the power to intervene in another's legal sphere, and is therefore opposed to subjection.[81] Thus, the interested party's initiative may occur to fulfill or protect, wholly or partly, a subjective right, as well as to exercise formative rights.[82] Secondly, when the Public Administration is responsible for defending specific interests, its protection can be exercised either in court or outside of court. In the latter case, third parties may be subjected either through the exercise of powers derived from the mandatory nature of administrative acts or through contractual relationships. Thirdly, the distinction between substantive and procedural claims reflects an even broader division, known as rights and obligations remedy.[83] This sequence should not be viewed solely as right and action, since there is a dimension between the right and the means of protecting it, which may involve self-compositive or third-party adjudication, thereby expanding the scope of. *ubi ius, ibi remedium.* The protection of a legal position can be achieved through various means, either provided by third parties or by the interested parties themselves, with or without the involvement of the State. This relationship allows for two approaches: the concept of protecting rights occupies an autonomous space[84] and deserves to be examined beyond the scope of judicial protection. Recognizing that one of these forms is unilateral, it becomes necessary to consider substantive law as a tool for safeguarding the substantive right itself.

From this broad view of the interested party's initiative shows that self-help is not limited to acts of aggression. Its forms will depend on (a) the nature of the conflict and the criteria of appropriateness to determine if and when it will be used, and (b) just as there are different types of judicial protection, there are also various ways to protect rights, which are reflected in self-help. In this context, a key question arises: does every violated or threatened interest permit, to some degree, unilateral protection directly by its holder? This will be examined in the following sections.

---

81 Amorim Filho (1960), pp. 9–10.

82 Pinto (2005), pp. 178–184.

83 Chizzini (2018), p. 37.

84 Noronha (2016), p. 93.

2.2.1.1 Self-Help by Individuals

Self-help exercised by individuals faces considerable skepticism. Its exceptional status is justified because individuals can only protect their interests unilaterally if explicitly authorized by law; judicial protection is regarded as the primary means to satisfy such interests; individual actions are limited since they are still connected to acts of force and violence; and it is assumed that private acts do not have the same enforceability as public ones acts.[85]

Much of the opposition to these arguments has already been discussed. Now, it is crucial to decide whether, in defending interests, such action is limited to a narrow view or if there is a wider scope for conduct that can, wholly or partially, offer some level of protection. This analysis hinges on two fundamental rights: the right to liberty, to examine whether private autonomy encounters such barriers when pursuing self-help, and the right to legality, to determine whether the requirement for legal authorization is mandatory under Brazilian law system.[86]

The an analysis of the principle of liberty must start with certain premises, such as defining its content, its relationship to other principles, its scope within the Federal Constitution, the ways it can be limited, and specifically whether it includes the autonomy to defend infringed or threatened interests. Regarding the principle of legality, the premise that individuals are allowed to do anything not explicitly prohibited by law must be weighed against the prevailing view that private self-help is exceptional.

The purpose of the principle of liberty is to protect an individual's right to self-determination and the formation of legal relationships. It involves defining, by law, choices, behaviors, life plans, and preferences, with the emphasis on the free development of personality. It is commonly divided into positive liberty – the ability to make and carry out such choices – and negative liberty – the absence of restrictions – though a more precise understanding of its legal structure requires further clarification. From the perspective of individual autonomy, liberty reflects dignity because it allows for making choices, which must be understood within their scope. Making these choices and engaging in these behaviors are based on expressions of freedom such as freedom of contract, movement, association, assembly, thought, expression, and religion. Therefore, freedom is not only a fundamental right but also a core principle of other fundamental rights (*Muttergrundrecht*), which obliges the State not only to abstain from interfering with its exercise but also to guarantee its realization actively.

The importance of liberty lies not only in the general freedom to act but also in the specific form of action, as Aarnio notes, whether to prevent overuse and trivialization of this principle or to ensure that fundamental rights are not overlooked. In other words, its analytical value is in identifying the type of liberty involved and, consequently, defining its limits within the rule of law, including the barriers that exist

---

[85] Werner (2000), pp. 9–10.

[86] Beltran (1996), pp. 28–29. Grinover (2018), p. 19. Yoshikawa (2008), pp. 24–25. Salles (2019), p. 46.

for each form of self-determination, since part of the legitimacy of legal position. The nature of the system depends on the margin of liberty granted.

This delimitation must account for the interaction between individuals. Any restriction on an area of liberty requires adequate justification rooted in another fundamental right. After all, an advanced concept of liberty involves not only social coexistence but also the protection of shared goals. The collectivist perspective on liberty explains, for example, why contractual autonomy or property must serve a societal purpose.[87] However, this way of thinking must be approached with caution: restrictions on liberties, justified by the claim of serving the "public interest" or "common good," cannot conceal the fact that limiting one fundamental right is often aimed at achieving another.

This warning extends the already criticized dominance of the public interest over private interest, which still influences a centrist perspective on the right to action, as previously discussed. Moreover, a perceived conflict between collective and individual interests implies that individuals may not be able to defend their own legal rights from threats or violations directly, or only in minimal situations. This is because the goal is to promote social stability or prevent a reversion to barbarism. Based on this standard approach, individual autonomy would be greatly limited in favor of collective interests, without explicitly referencing another fundamental right that takes precedence.[88] The restrictions on individual self-help are usually justified by an alleged need for judicial protection to prevail, as a means of safeguarding humanity and, ultimately, as an expression of solidarity. Therefore, although not without severe criticism.[89] The paradigm used to justify this limitation is the potential for violating public peace, as individuals in this dimension of freedom could inflict physical and psychological harm upon one another.

In analyzing the relationship between individual rights and collective interests, Alexy highlights the existence of a significant argumentative burden for limiting individual rights by collective interests, especially when state actions do not directly impinge on fundamental rights.[90] Regarding self-help, besides the issues already mentioned about its link to violence, post-war constitutional debates centered on limiting individual actions to enhance the state's protection of people.

It has even been stated that "the most forceful sanction for state indolence is private self-help",[91] on the premise that public officials should protect individuals from one another. The advancement of fundamental rights has significantly mitigated this extreme reduction of individual autonomy in safeguarding one's own interests: the reconciliation and balance between the Social State and private autonomy; the reassessment of the authoritarian profile underlying the argument that the State should prioritize controlling individual initiatives; the harmonization of liberty, democratic deliberation, and state control; the enhancement of self-management

[87] Martins-Costa (2005), p. 43.

[88] Silva (2013), pp. 743–744.

[89] Schmidt (1973), p. 16.

[90] Alexy (1995), pp. 257–258.

[91] Isensee (1983), p. 56.

and self-organization of society in fundamental matters; the shift in perspective from state surveillance and regulation of private individuals to the acceptance of sharing and cooperation in public and private activities; and, above all, the recognition that "dignity aims to guarantee the individual, in their irreducible intrinsic value, a sphere of freedom and protection that cannot be affected by collective interests."[92]

The traditional reasons used to reject private self-help have changed significantly and no longer match the reasons for limiting liberty. When unilateral protection does not involve acts of personal violence, the original concern no longer applies. When physical force is involved, law enforcers limit it through sanctions. Therefore, there is no justification for suppressing individual protection in favor of a public dispute resolution role, especially as this is increasingly viewed as just one of several ways to address harm or prevent threatening interests.[93] This conclusion also exposes the contradiction in the argument historically used to reject private self-help, especially since it is the State itself that sets limits on access to the Judiciary, creating room for conflicts that often remain unresolved.

Does the unilateral rejection of an unlawful act form part of individual autonomy? The specific freedom of self-help must be derived from the constitutional text, with the recognition that individuals can act, within the limits of the legal system, to safeguard their interests as an expression of self-determination. It would not be very sensible to accept the range of choices, projects, and conduct offered by the principle of liberty without the ability to defend them. Moreover, the rule of law is the foundation for defining this right to protect rights, as it ensures the principle of liberty as the core of exercising multiple fundamental rights, whose infringement is asserted against both individuals and the State. The contemporary nature of the principle of freedom assumes that individuals are also responsible for its effectiveness, with the capacity for organization, expression, and direction, whether individually or collectively.[94]

The counterpart to this greater autonomy is, furthermore, increased flexibility in state action, the expansion of public spaces for deliberation, coordination, and above all, consensus-building, with a reduction in authoritarian approaches. Thus, the right to self-help of injured or threatened interests has multiple constitutional references. In addition to the general aspect of liberty provided for in Article 5, caput, of Brazil's 1988 Federal Constitution, specific freedoms of self-help derive from the right to property (Article 5, *caput* and item XXII), due to its historical foundation around protection against risks or dangers; from the right to physical, moral, and psychological integrity (Article 1, III), to prevent or reject unlawful acts committed in various spheres of human activity; the right to security (Article 5, caput), one of its features being personal security in both private and public settings, against private individuals and the State; autonomy of will (Article 5, II), with private initiative in response to the dynamics of life events and the creative development of mechanisms to overcome unlawful acts; and the right to strike (Article 9), for the defense and assertion of infringed labor rights interests.

---

[92] Gutmann (2011), p. 38.

[93] Sinel (2017), p. 34.

[94] Augsberg (2021), p. 39.

Accepting private self-help as a form of individual freedom contrasts with the idea that its prohibition is predetermined.[95]

Firstly, the issue resides in a discursive dispute, a clash of perspectives about the extent of autonomy in defending one's own rights, rather than an analytical examination of the limits of fundamental rights. Examining a timeline from the nineteenth century to recent times reveals both supportive and opposing views on unilateral conduct for protecting, realizing, and fulfilling private rights. To cite examples from opposing sides, one might mention von Tuhr's view, for whom such prohibition gives way "to the legal interest in preserving and realizing one's own rights",[96] and Blomeyer's position, who asserts that "the need to seek judicial protection corresponds to the prohibition of enforcing private rights through self-help".[97]

Secondly, the prohibition assumes a conflict between the right to freedom and the right to action, which does not seem to exist. To argue that the right to action serves as State protection instead of private protection of interests, in addition to relying on the false idea that private individuals would be immobilized for this purpose, ignores the fact that the scopes of protection for these rights are wholly separate and distinct.[98] The right of action does not restrict individual freedom nor does it conflict with it; instead, one of its features is the coexistence of the State's judicial function with other forms of dispute resolution, including those rooted in other fundamental rights.[99]

Thirdly, this antagonism is based on an outdated perspective that concentrates power in the hands of the State, even though this hermetic view has been dismantled in numerous areas due to the inevitable division of public and private tasks in pursuit of common interests.[100]

Thus, the scope of this freedom of self-help is defined by legality. It is necessary to assess how it applies to private individuals to determine whether the premise that private self-help is permitted only if legally authorised is correct. Article 5, II of the Brazilian Federal Constitution of 1988 provides that "no one shall be obliged to do or refrain from doing anything except by virtue of law", from which it follows that any restriction on freedom, imposed by the State, must be based on a democratic decision resulting in the enactment of a norm by the Legislative Branch. The meaning of law as employed in the constitutional text is interpreted as a normative category resulting from the legislative process, enacted for general and impersonal application, or a subordinate act supported by it.[101] Therefore, in the absence of a norm prohibiting the actions of private individuals, freedom guarantees their exercise. As a principle, legality guides individuals, aims to establish equality among them, and serves as an

---

[95] Saturno (1995), pp. 260–261.

[96] Von Tuhr (1888), p. 43.

[97] Blomeyer (1982), p. 1.

[98] Silva (2014), p. 71.

[99] Cordeiro (2018), p. 446.

[100] Hensler (2014), pp. 45–46.

[101] Schoueri et al. (2021), p. 28.

instrument for the realisation of other fundamental rights.[102] Generally, it defines their conduct through the prescriptive function of legal norms.

Another question must be addressed. Does the law impose a general restriction on private self-help, meaning its use is only allowed when explicitly permitted by law? Although the Brazilian legal system does not have a specific rule of general authorization for private self-help, it cannot be concluded that the default is a broad prohibition. Acts of self-help by individuals, as private acts, are subject to the same limitations of free will as any other private act. The origin of such acts is the will of the agent, constrained by grounds for excluding unlawfulness, such as the proper exercise of a right, self-defense, and necessity. This does not prevent legislation from establishing specific circumstances where the power of self-help is granted—to clarify its use, promote private action, impose certain admissibility requirements, or even exclude such power.

Self-help, therefore, is any voluntary act inherent to exercising freedom. The right to protect, unilaterally and directly, injured or threatened interests is part of the powers derived from the autonomy of will, and excessive acts or omissions can lead to the agent's liability. Consequently, whether based on the constitutional principles of freedom and legality or on the authorizing margin at the infra-constitutional level, a review of Article 345 of the Brazilian Penal Code shows that it is not possible to infer an explicit prohibition of all forms of individual self-help 116, as will be addressed in section 3.1.

Consequently, the ban on private self-help appears to stem from a doctrinal assumption, repeated over time due to concerns about the state's role in resolving disputes, rather than from a broad legal prohibition. Therefore, the issue is not simply whether private self-help is allowed, but rather to what extent and based on which criteria it can be used exercised.

2.2.1.2 Approaches of the State

The implementation of the content of an administrative act without judicial authorisation is referred to as self-executing power. The subjection of third parties to an administrative act unilaterally enforced is classified as imperativeness. According to prevailing doctrine, this is the power of public administration to compel compliance with an obligation without the subject's consent or the intervention of the Judiciary.[103]

The term "self-help" is used in Brazilian Administrative Law to denote the power of the Public Administration to review, remedy, or invalidate, *ex officio*, its own administrative acts. This meaning is distinct from that examined thus far, which concerns the unilateral protection of interests violated or threatened by others. To ensure terminological consistency and facilitate understanding of the arguments advanced in this study, self-help is restricted to the administrative act of state self-help, also known as public self-help. Self-help in relation to the administrative act

---

[102] Leão (2023), p. 79.

[103] Cretella Júnior (1972), p. 48.

should be understood as the duty to review or invalidate, with the purpose of control by the party responsible for the defect or the reason for correction. Public self-help is an administrative action aimed at the unilateral protection of interests that have been violated or threatened, with the capacity to bind third parties. It is a specific aspect of action in the context of the self-executing power and imperativeness of administrative acts, particularly in response to unlawful acts by others.[104]

Public self-help may also arise in other contexts, such as consensual ones. The remediation of unlawful acts in contractual legal relationships may allow the contracting parties themselves to take the initiative. Thus, within this range of approaches associated with public self-help, the public entity may, for example, order the closure of a commercial establishment that breaches health regulations or withhold payments if a private party fails to fulfil an obligation stipulated in an administrative contract.[105]

Unlike private self-help, public self-help has always been regarded as a matter of course.[106] The idea of the State's monopoly on the use of force was not limited to enforcement actions from judicial authority; it also justified the mandatory nature of administrative acts. The absence of a need for judicial intervention was seen as crucial for the independence of the Public Administration, whether due to the separation of powers or the presumed legitimacy of its actions. Restrictions on liberty and property were closely tied to organizational power, stemming from police authority. These features are described as attributes of administrative acts when compared to private acts.

Self-executing power, imperativeness, and the presumption of legitimacy provide the means for the exercise of public self-help and have traditionally been viewed as projections of the state's supremacy over the individual. These theoretical foundations and the existence of a state apparatus to achieve such objectives have contributed to the establishment of a paradox: while public self-help has been conceived as an activity inherent to state functions, private self-help has been viewed as exceptional, due to this concentration of powers in the hands of the State.[107] Suppose the previous section demonstrated the fundamental right to self-help. In that case, it is now necessary to assess the above justifications to determine whether the asymmetry of powers between state agents and private individuals still holds.

Certain premises underlying the development of Administrative Law and the functions of the Public Administration deserve to be established.

The first concerns the well-known debate over the justification for prioritizing the public interest over individual interests, a relationship traditionally regarded as a principle of Public Law. This idea included the unilateral protection of interests, as it was believed that the exercise of authority, as an expression of power, placed the State in a position of superiority. The effects of this perspective shift have led to the understanding of the authoritative and imposing nature of Public Administration.

[104] Ragazzo (2006), pp. 12–13.

[105] Bomfim and Fidalgo (2008), p. 283.

[106] La Torre (2011), pp. 9–15.

[107] Hamburger (2014), p. 131.

The view that proportionality acts as the balance to protect those rights, and the idea that public and private interests are deeply interconnected through collective consideration, and that sacrificing an individual right must be justified by recognizing an equivalent right in return standing.[108]

The second aspect is the oversight of administrative action through procedural safeguards, which reinforce fundamental guarantees and reduce arbitrariness. Even when such action leads to public self-regulation, the principles of adversarial proceedings, full defence, and prior justification are generally ensured. Thus, a legal relationship is established with the administered parties to legitimise administrative actions.[109]

The third aspect is the focus on the principles of efficiency and good governance, from which the duties of government and the role of the State as a facilitator arise, to organize, promote, and cooperate in economic and social development. The sense of superiority gives way to a more horizontal approach through a variety of tools for information, participation, regulation, and engagement with the private sector individuals.[110]

The fourth aspect involves a typological review of administrative acts, which limits the imperativeness and self-executing authority to specific categories, subject to the principle of legality. By recognizing that not all administrative acts are imperative and self-executing, focus has been given to external oversight of administrative acts, especially where judicial authorization would be necessary for their enforcement.[111]

The fifth aspect is the spreading of consensus within Public Administration. From this perspective, there have been significant changes not only in the principles of Administrative Law but also in the practical approach of public entities, aligned with legislative frameworks that promote amicable settlements between the State and private parties. The effects on how administrative claims are resolved include a reduction in the imposition of penalties, an increase in voluntary compliance by individuals, and a preference for a relational model over one of subordination.[112]

All of this indicates specific changes in public self-regulation. Legality remains the primary means of limiting state power, ensuring submission only when there is a legal or contractual provision.[113] Even when imperativeness is authorized, consent may dictate the measure imposed, transforming administrative action into an agreement, as provided for in Article 26 of the LINDB[114] or Article 32 of Law No. 13,140/2015. Instead of implementing administrative acts, the State may promote private parties to organize themselves for autonomous and collaborative regulation. Fundamental rights also help limit the necessity of restrictions to instances where there is enough justification for restricting liberty or property.

---

[108] Moreira Neto (2008), pp. 104–105.

[109] Medauar (2018), p. 161.

[110] Schmidt-Aßmann (2006), pp. 172–177.

[111] Schirato (2011), p. 136.

[112] Almeida (2012), p. 297.

[113] Gordillo (2011), p. V-37.

[114] This law provides general rules applicable to the Brazilian legal system.

Therefore, before executing and imposing its own acts, Public Administration has the responsibility to assess which means would be less burdensome and more efficient, so that the chosen course of action is not to impose on private parties, but to cooperate with them.[115] Before the execution and imperativeness of administrative acts, there are measures to avoid subjection, such as warnings, notifications, or notices regarding the administrative intention, since otherwise, "it would amount to the pleasure of violence, to the arbitrary and unjustified use of force for its own sake, to a fait accompli, which is inadmissible in the rule of law."[116]

In the context of contractual legal relations, the self-regulation of Public Administration can be equated with the same cases allowed for private transactions, such as the right of retention, material acts based on the exception of non-performance, or the enforcement of contractual guarantees. This equivalence is further justified by the public entity's challenge to the scope and application of exorbitant clauses, as well as the scenario introduced by Law No. 14,133/2021, which aims to reduce the unilateral actions of the Brazilian Public Administration in administrative contracts.

The attributes of administrative acts must also be examined. The position of superiority over the acts of private parties has led to the understanding that there is an "execution privilege" in public administration.[117] Is it correct to say that enforceability and imperativeness are absent in individual acts? This can be answered as follows: while for the State, execution and imperativeness come from legal authorization, for private individuals, they are expressions of exercising freedom; performing individual legal acts simply means acting without interference from third parties. Usually, private individuals choose to educate their children, contract, fulfill obligations, defend themselves, and so on. The unilateral subjection of another in private acts also reflects the agent's freedom, whether that subjection is non-contractual, like in legitimate self-defense, or contractual, as in retention.

Furthermore, the idea that only administrative acts are presumed legitimate must be challenged. Many legal acts, including private acts, benefit from this presumption (Articles 113, 219, and 422 of the Brazilian Civil Code). Likewise, just as some Public Administration acts rely on another authority for their enforcement, many private acts also display this trait. The invalidation of private legal transactions cannot be done unilaterally by the interested party, as a judge must recognize the defect. Claims by the Public Treasury, recorded as outstanding debts, are subject to the tax enforcement process and their satisfaction, which may involve property seizure, pending judicial approval, and oversight. The differences between public and private self-help also deserve reconsideration, since consensual mechanisms can bring them closer together.

Therefore, the way the contrast between public and private self-help is framed should be reexamined. It is not about endorsing a privilege or the State's dominance

[115] Guerra and Palma (2018), p. 147.

[116] Sundfeld (2003), p. 83.

[117] Fonseca (2012), p. 27.

over the individual—especially given the many tools available to prevent subjugation—at the expense of the individual's right to self-help. The key point is to recognize that legal actions, whether public or private, can have self-executing power and authority—publicly through legality; privately through individual freedom—within the framework of unilateral legal protection for violated or threatened interests. Self-help that relies on legal authorization is public, as it follows the legality regime, which aims to control others in specific situations and ideally is preceded by consensual or voluntary means.

2.2.2 Unilateral Protection

The second identifying element is unilateral protection. Third-party and bilateral or multilateral protection are excluded. Additionally, there is a semantic issue to resolve: the terms "protection of rights," "protection of interests," or "legal protection" are used in this work to signify the same outcome as judicial protection. Nivarra demonstrates that discussing meanings is not purely formal, as it involves a broader issue of understanding what it means to give concrete effect to an interest and the various dimensions of this activity. The act of protection, therefore, is the act of safeguarding, realizing, or satisfying an interest in the face of some actual or potential opposition or impediment.[118] In this context, it is noted that self-help is described as "compulsory enforcement".[119] This observation highlights a generalization that overlooks the specificities of the legal position involved, whether they are being violated or threatened. The study of rights protection has long focused on judicial protection alone, without fostering the necessary dialogue and systematic approach to other forms of protection, both within and outside the judiciary, in both public and private spheres. Therefore, it is proposed that unilateral protection be adapted to meet the diverse needs of these legal situations.

Turning to the traditional justifications for judicial protection, several characteristics should be highlighted: a predominantly state-centered approach, continuing the historical perspective on the relationship between law and procedure; an emphasis on adaptability and procedural mechanisms to ensure effectiveness; the treatment of substantive rules as the practical realization of interests—particularly regarding the regulation of specific rights—and as a system for determining which interests are recognized; debates about the scope of the term "judicial protection," along with various ways of classifying it based on the particularities of substantive law; and the inclusion of evaluative elements such as pacification, fair settlement, elimination of litigiousness, and so forth. Although it has been a central theme in procedural scholarship, judicial protection has not been a central theme. Achieved harmony with

[118] Nivarra (2018), pp. 17–23.

[119] Bongiorno (1984), pp. 52–53. Lepore (2019), pp.131–132. Loterstein (2013), pp. 1, 372–1, 373. Hattenhauer (2011), p. 271. Duchstein (2015), p. 105. Klingbeil (2019), p. 185. Theodoro Jr. (2023), pp. 110–113.

other forms of rights protection. It is fair to say that, as a result, forms of protection provided independently of judicial intervention and embedded in the routine of legal relations have taken a long time to be studied, just as it is accurate to say that such study has focused on mechanisms with a degree of institutionalization, as evidenced by concepts like the justice system or multi-door justice.

This did not prevent the recognition of other types of protection, enforcement, or satisfaction, driven by a broad understanding of the effectiveness of legal measures in protecting individuals.[120] This development occurred for reasons such as the consolidation of the theory of remedies in response to public and private wrongs, including in countries with a civil law tradition; the creation of structures for the certification and mediation of such wrongs, and the autonomy of the parties involved in resolving them; the expansion of mechanisms for contractual and non-contractual redress directly by the injured party; the demystification of the idea that acts of enforcement could not be personal or could not be carried out outside the judiciary; the identification of techniques offered by substantive law for resolving disputes; and the adoption, by legislation in numerous countries, of instruments to overcome losses and financial crises without relying on government intervention authorities.[121] These incentives stemmed from criticism of the dominance of judicial protection, as well as from a structural change in the relationship between conflict and the corresponding protection.

For a long time, this duality was restricted to the model of law and procedure, which was secularly constructed around the triad of claim, action, and judicial protection. Gradually, it became clear that the last two elements were not necessary for the concrete enforcement of an interest, and criticism was also directed at the "right of action" doctrine,[122] particularly in relation to extrajudicial means of resolving disputes. Judicial protection came to be seen as one of several forms of protection of rights, sharing space with other methods of dispute resolution. In the rule of law, the protection of rights is achieved concurrently, taking into account the framework of fundamental rights that allows for various avenues of protection. This right to protection has multiple constitutional references, including the right to action, access to justice, the right to self-help, and autonomy of will. This also demonstrated that protection may occur at different levels and with varying degrees of intensity, depending on the limits for its exercise.[123]

Both of the scenarios have influenced self-help. While some studies have asserted that it "is (officially) prohibited in civilised human communities and generally leads to the 'imposition' of dispute resolution by the stronger party",[124] the exploration of the concept has made it possible to state that it is the "possibility of achieving, by

---

[120] Smorto (2015), p. 186.

[121] Samuel (2001), pp. 113–174. Stănescu (2015), pp. 4–12. Smith (2019), pp. 278–279. Popineau-Dehaullon (2008), pp. 382–386. Romano (1958), pp. 40–46. Follieri (2016), pp. 16–23. Majo (2001), pp. 142–152.

[122] Medicus (1974), p. 314.

[123] Chizzini (2018), pp. 7–9.

[124] Fairén Guillén (1992), p. 17.

extrajudicial means, a result, in whole or in part, analogous to that which would be obtained through legal proceedings."[125] This discrepancy highlights the previously mentioned lack of harmony and also uncovers theoretical developments based on criteria of systematization that differ from those of judicial protection. Self-help has been classified in various, though somewhat inconsistent, ways. This is because an instrumental perspective on unilateral protection, considering the specificities of disputes and the situations outlined by the legal system, is lacking. These issues create contradictions summarized by the universalism of classification, which stems from the particularism of legal hypotheses, and by the unusual nature of unilateral protection based on normative typification. From this context, for example, Betti's well-known criteria emerge, which state that self-help is active if force is used, and reactive if it occurs as a response to an injury.[126] And Schünemann's classification, which categorizes it as aggressive or defensive.[127] For these reasons, it is essential to examine how unilateral protection is established and the benefits it should provide.

2.2.2.1 Unilateral Protection as Safeguarding, Enforcement, or Satisfaction of a Violated or Threatened Right

There are challenges in characterizing unilateral protection. It is important to understand what it involves and to determine whether its forms differ from those of judicial protection. Certain elements help describe the protection of rights. Various definitions have been proposed to determine when a legal position warrants protection, such as the opposition of interests, legal crises, unjustified resistance, and resisted claims. Although each of these has specific features, they all share the core idea of the need for protection, which is built around the principles of judicial protection: the necessity of judicial intervention to enforce a particular interest, usually because it cannot be achieved by the right-holder alone; the political decision to assign the judiciary the task of resolving specific issues, even when no conflict arises from them; and the exclusive authority of the judiciary to resolve certain disputes.

Unilateral protection moves in the opposite direction, as it is the right-holder themselves who possess the powers to protect, enforce, or satisfy their infringed or threatened rights.[128] The need for protection is thus viewed differently: it is essential to assess which unilateral acts can effectively safeguard that interest. Identifying such acts within the scope of the powers held by the Public Administration or private autonomy is not always straightforward. This is a contentious point, although it is generally accepted that unilateral protection involves the "overcoming of the harmful event through conduct aimed at restoring or maintaining the balance of the situation that has been violated or threatened."[129] This definition must consider the actions

---

[125] Geri (1971), p. 3.

[126] Betti (1959), p. 529.

[127] Schünemann (1985), p. 38.

[128] Carvalhosa (2004), p. 128.

[129] Ricciardoni (2011), p. 16.

available to the interested party that can provide different levels of protection, satisfaction, or realization of the interest. Therefore, it is necessary to establish the guiding principles of such conduct: (a) identification of the harm or threat; (b) determination of who holds the infringed or threatened interest; (c) assessment of whether the interest allows for unilateral protection by its holder; (d) delimitation of the acts to be performed by this holder to remedy, in whole or in part, the harm or threat; and (e) exclusion of acts that do not serve this purpose or that depend on a third-party adjudicator.

Some examples clarify the presence of these elements[130]: termination of an employment contract, by unilateral act of the employer, due to just cause on the part of the employee; collective mobilisation of employees in a strike in response to violations of their labour rights; extrajudicial enforcement of a fiduciary guarantee in the event of default; an express termination clause triggered by breach of contract; unilateral material acts of transfer of possession, retention, and satisfaction in the enforcement of a pledge; various instances of retention due to contractual non-performance; enforcement by the creditor themselves of an obligation to perform that has not been fulfilled by the debtor; acts of possessory protection; blocking, exclusion, or restriction of fake profiles on social networks; control of freedom of expression in digital environments by the provider; blocking of videos on a digital platform for breach of intellectual property rules; confiscation of products and foodstuffs in violation of health and safety regulations; public security measures to suppress or prevent current or imminent danger; the use of force by the State in its international relations in response to unjust offences.

When self-help is viewed as a form of enforcement, it is typically considered just one type of rights protection.[131] The development of judicial protection theory clearly shows how protection, enforcement, or satisfaction are tailored to address violations of interests. The classifications of judicial protection also serve as classifications of rights protection, since they are based on specific needs presented.[132] The unilateral act of fulfilling a claim to performance serves as a form of executive self-help. However, as the examples above demonstrate, it is also appropriate to describe constitutive self-help when it is necessary to change a legal situation; declaratory self-help when a doubt involves a fact or the existence, non-existence, or nature of a legal relationship; preventive self-help to ward off a threat; precautionary self-help to safeguard or secure an interest; and individual or collective self-help depending on the number of interest holders. Therefore, whether the conduct of the active subject is a reaction, action, defense, aggression, repression, or any other form, it is essential to evaluate its purpose and results. Sinel notes that the list of potential behaviors is so extensive and varied (over-inclusivity) that the concept of self-help would become meaningless without a strict connection between the conduct and the

[130] These examples consider Brazilian law.

[131] Klingbeil (2019), p. 185. Raimo (2018), pp. 68–69, 2018. Follieri (2016), p. 97.

[132] Noronha (2016), p. 93.

result.[133] Therefore, the classification depends on the type of protection, not on the agent's actions.

The longstanding debate regarding the timing of exercising judicial protection is not only reflected in the division between condemnatory, declaratory, and constitutive protection, but also in the need for the claim to performance to be realized in the physical world. In the field of self-help, all of this is independent of any certification decision or enforcement order,[134] and produces inevitable consequences, such as the prevalence of unilateral protection over the prior determination of the existence of an infringed or violated interest; the definition of the offense or violation of the interest by the holder themselves; the absence of control background to the legitimacy of acts directed against the legal sphere of others; establishing when an act is suitable for the intended protection. The process for determining whether harm or threat has occurred, for carrying out acts of protection, satisfaction, or enforcement, and for achieving legal protection generally falls under the exclusive judgment of the active party, which introduces uncertainties regarding the lawfulness of self-help. Although these characteristics are regarded as efficient advantages,[135] they also present drawbacks in balancing their role as a unilateral power and a legitimate means of dispute resolution. Therefore, the above criteria help identify when the agent is operating within the scope of self-help. Still, the assessment of its lawfulness will depend on the requirements outlined in Chapter 4.

2.2.2.2 Utility and Levels of Unilateral Protection

As a result of unilateral action, questions arise regarding the scope of legal protection directly received by the active party. One area of interest in acting pertains to the level of protection provided by judicial relief, specifically determining when a claimed legal position has been resolved.[136] This correspondence simplifies the identification of the moment when the judge declares, constitutes, condemns, anticipates, safeguards, or satisfies. In the case of self-help, since it depends on the conduct of the active party, it is not always straightforward to determine whether such conduct has provided the intended protection, enforcement, or satisfaction. No matter how much the party acts, there is no guarantee of obtaining, in whole or in part, legal protection, either because their actions may be limited by the constraints imposed by the legal system or because they have proven ineffective in removing, preventing, or overcoming the harm or threat.[137]

Therefore, the usefulness is also evident in this analysis as it concerns the benefit derived from the agent's conduct for unilateral protection, which may vary in degree

---

133 Sinel (2017), p. 33.

134 Nogueira (2008), 152.

135 Epstein (2005), p. 16.

136 Sica (2013), p. 448.

137 Zimmermann (1996), p. 770.

depending on the object of the violation, in terms of its extent and transience. Therefore, unilateral protection may be partial or total, according to the scope of the protection, enforcement or satisfaction provided, and may be definitive or provisional, depending on the persistence of this outcome in favour of the active party.

Regarding the scope of unilateral protection, some preliminary observations are warranted. Firstly, before it is manifested, various acts may be performed, many of which are preparatory in nature, such as notifications, consultations, dialogues, warnings, alerts, notices, recordings, and monitoring. Although these are relevant for contextualising the violated or threatened legal situation, the causality previously asserted should be restricted; that is, there must be a direct implication of the act with the attainment of legal protection.[138] The answer is guided by the following question: What is the act or set of acts that directly produced the protection, enforcement, or satisfaction of the interest? Secondly, unilateral protection may not be achieved because the conduct did not fulfil its intended purpose. As a result of the previous observation, the actions taken may be insufficient for unilateral protection, even if they were initially intended for this purpose. For example, a private individual's actions in legitimate defense might be unable to repel an attack against them, or the actions of the Public Administration may be inadequate to prevent the entry of a medicinal product into national territory without regulatory approval. Third, the conduct of the active party will not always be one-sided. The same An act can provide unilateral protection in its favor while also offering third-party protection to another party. For instance, possessory protection initiated by one owner concerns their legal sphere, as well as that of other holders of title who, for various reasons, did not act; or, the removal, blocking, or restriction of a user on a social network by the provider, which protects its interests regarding ethical organization in the digital environment, might also safeguard the interests of those who were victims of the unlawful acts that led to these consequences.

One of the ways identified by legal systems, in Dedek's words, to "bridge the gap between the abstract discourse of norms and the reality of their application" is unilateral protection.[139] In this regard, the distinction between partial and total self-help considers both the authorized scope of action of the active party and the effectiveness of their conduct. These two factors are evaluated based on the factual circumstances of the violation or threat. Upon review, it will be necessary to determine whether there is room to act, if the acts are within legal boundaries, and whether they can protect, enforce, or satisfy, in whole or in part.

Thus, unilateral protection will be either total or partial when the situation the legal remedy seeks to address is entirely or partly compatible with self-help. These criteria help determine whether, and to what extent, it is suitable for resolving the dispute. Two examples illustrate these classifications. A neighbor whose land is encroached upon by tree roots and branches may cut them, thereby ending the harmful situation through their own actions; this is an example of executive self-help that entirely removes the problem of infringement. The police arrest individuals caught in the act

[138] Riehm (2017), pp. 355–356.

[139] Dedek (2010), p. 65.

of drug dealing in a specific location and seize the narcotics. Although the illegal act has stopped, a penalty can only be imposed through proper criminal procedures, so the administrative action offers only partial and limited protection, given the complexity of the typical offense. The examples used thus far clearly demonstrate the configuration of self-help, but its presence can also be found in less obvious and more straightforward situations.[140] The motivation to act unilaterally may arise in circumstances that do not necessarily warrant judicial protection. Suppose the different degrees or levels of legal protection are also measured by the scope of action granted to the active party. In that case, this framework may reveal that certain behaviors can amount to self-help, even though the conflict does not give rise to a legitimate interest in seeking judicial protection. The scenarios discussed by Beurskens illustrate this spectrum of everyday actions that, while simple, can afford some protection, such as closing windows to prevent the intrusion of unwanted barbecue smells from a neighbouring property, or a viewer choosing to change the channel when confronted with abusive advertising.[141] Thus, the scope of self-help may not coincide with that of other forms of legal protection, not only for the reasons mentioned above—ineffectiveness or impossibility of the conduct—but also because the interest to be protected is only partially compatible with one or some of these forms.

Regarding transience, some preliminary observations are also necessary. The stability of legal remedies is typically assessed in relation to judicial decisions, focusing on the extent to which they become unassailable.[142] Unilateral action places the active party in the role of deciding when, why, and how to act, but this does not guarantee that their actions will be beyond challenge, whether because they are subject to later review, lack a direct normative source of stability, or because of the changing behavior of the parties involved in the conflict. The primary goal of self-help is not to achieve stable results, but to establish a sense of protection, fulfillment, or satisfaction that is independent of external factors.[143] However, these statements should not be viewed as conflicting with the division of self-help into provisional and definitive types, since the connection between stability and unilateral action—which might seem incompatible with the idea of a solution imposed by one party at first glance— manifests in the tension between legal certainty and due process law.[144] Therefore, is it possible for unilateral protection to become stable even if it is a solution imposed by one party to the conflict? Additionally, since the stability of judicial decisions is evaluated in subjective, objective, and temporal dimensions, it is essential to consider whether these concepts apply to unilateral protection. Or, in other words: stability in what sense?

Provisionally, as susceptibility to reversal or change, characterizes unilateral protection for various reasons,[145] as exemplified by: broad oversight of conduct;

140 Rodrigues (2023), p. 188.

141 Beurskens (2017), p. 17.

142 Eid (2024), p. 411.

143 Landmann (1975), pp. 45–47.

144 Criscuolo (2023), p. 48.

145 Benedetti (2011), pp. 43–45.

changes in the actions of the passive party, who may, at different times, repeat infringements against the interests of the active party; subsequent ineffectiveness of the protection, fulfillment, or satisfaction; alteration of the factual situation established by the active party; non-compliance by the passive party, etc. Some examples include cases where the active party exercises legitimate self-defense, repelling attacks at that moment but later faces renewed assaults; or efforts to have a digital platform remove a profile used to disseminate hate speech, which is then recreated through other fake profiles controlled by the same individual.

Precariousness or transience is, therefore, inherent to unilateral action.[146]Is evident in the traits currently valued in self-help, such as speed, reduced bureaucracy, and efficiency. Therefore, stability is neither a planned nor an expected outcome; it is a fortunate element. Unlike judicial protection, which is generally intended to lead to finality, unilateral protection—lacking comprehensive debate on the conflict and relying on the judgment of the active party—is only incidentally related to stability. The finality of the solution is evident, for example, in the case of the passive party's complete submission and their inertia in contesting self-help; in the statute of limitations for damages claims; in the forfeiture of rights to change the legal position established by unilateral protection; due to the factual impossibility of changing this legal situation, and so on. The superiority of certain forms of protection over others does not only depend on how they are enforced but also on how predictable the stability of such enforcement is.

2.2.3 *Absence of a Third-Party Adjudicator*

The final feature that characterizes self-help is the absence of the need for a third-party adjudicator. Unilateral adjudication occurs when the active party takes the initiative to protect their infringed or threatened rights. It is the active party that promotes protection, enforcement, or satisfaction. However, this does not exclude the possibility of third-party involvement or participation. Although they are not responsible for providing legal protection, third parties may, for example, act as certifying agents or consultants regarding the occurrence of an unlawful act, serve as cooperation agents, custodians, or delegates of powers, among other roles. This distinction is essential for differentiating unilateral protection from bilateral or an adjudication provided by a third person, for defining the roles involved, and for determining the applicable legal framework.[147] Therefore, analyzing self-help with third-party involvement is relevant because it can encourage, legitimize, facilitate, and organize unilateral efforts for protection.[148]

Unlike the classifications used in other types of dispute resolution, the relationship between third parties and self-help is characterized by significant variation and

[146] Mezzanotte (1995), p. 37.

[147] Matri (2017), pp. 22–24.

[148] Adler and Fromer (2019), pp. 1493–1496.

ambiguity, as a third party is anyone who is neither the active nor the passive subject. This emphasizes the need to evaluate, in specific terms, both their functions and the boundaries of their involvement. The variety of roles they may assume can, for example, require impartiality and neutrality, adherence to contractual obligations, oversight of unilateral acts, and so on. Due to this complex involvement, it is necessary to maintain and define self-help to ensure that a third party cannot serve as the judge of all the infringing or threatened legal issues.[149]

Several examples highlight the importance of such agents: a dispute review board certifying the occurrence of a contractual breach and supporting one of the contracting parties in exercising the right of retention or suspending performance of their obligations based on the *exceptio non adimpleti contractus*; the active party who files an evidentiary action to demonstrate facts, based on which he will exercise his self-help; the appointment of a custodian for financial resources intended to guarantee contingencies in performance contracts; and digital platforms offering mechanisms for users to protect themselves against others users.

While this variety does not allow for strict categorization of third-party functions, it also highlights their importance, for example, in expanding the scope of the active party's conduct or supervising the process established for self-help. Although self-help is characterized by the active party's exclusive discretion over their actions, third parties may temper this discretion by being designated to determine, wholly or partly, the existence of the factual basis that justifies unilateral protection, or by participating in the process to enhance the legitimacy of unilateral decisions and the methods used to subject the passive party.[150]

Self-help is also compatible with using or creating mechanisms to achieve the outcome desired by the active party. These are mediated or instrumental forms of exercising power, such as defensive devices, weapons, or animals for property protection, or more recently, technological tools like algorithms for enforcing contractual rights, controlling unlawful acts, and so on. Unlike involving third parties, mediated self-help is characterized by using some instrument to carry out unilateral protection.[151] These relate to how self-help is implemented, as these tools serve to turn a potential action into an actual one. Various reasons, such as the inability to act personally, the optimization and efficiency of power, and the complexity and dynamics of the legal relationship between active and passive parties, justify their use.

The importance of this classification lies in determining whether the methods used are appropriate and, therefore, whether unilateral protection is lawful. Two examples demonstrate the intended utility: Article 25 of the Brazilian Penal Code states that a person acts in legitimate defense when they use "moderate and necessary means" to repel an unlawful attack; according to Article 368 of the Brazilian Civil Code, if two people are simultaneously creditor and debtor to each other, the obligations are extinguished by set-off, which can take various forms. One form involves a financial institution using its electronic system to directly deduct the difference from the

---

149 Machete (1992), p. 71.

150 Verkuil (2005), pp. 969–970.

151 Bell (2003), p. 746.

current account of the passive party, the account holder. Therefore, Duden's summary is timely in recognizing the use of mechanisms for self-help and explaining the range of physical and digital means available for this purpose.[152] These instruments become part of the analysis concerning the admissibility, appropriateness, and legitimacy of unilateral action remedies.

2.3 Self-Help Within the Framework of Dispute Resolution Mechanisms

With clarifications on the configuration, delimitation, and structure of self-help, the analysis now focuses on its role within dispute resolution mechanisms. The topic has gained notable prominence in Brazilian legal scholarship, originating from a specific understanding of the term "multi-door justice."[153] According to this school of thought, Sander's ideas are believed to have developed: Originally, courts were seen as providing more than one type of resolution besides adjudication (multi-door courthouse). Therefore, before the Judiciary, there were different forms of settlement, resulting from the adoption of what were then called alternative dispute resolution methods.[154] Now, regardless of judicial proceedings, multiple avenues would be available to resolve disputes, considering the arrangement and relationship of legal institutions for this purpose, involving both state and private entities—not as alternatives, but based on the appropriateness of each. For some authors, self-help is included in this multi-door justice system, as it relates to a broad perspective on access to justice.[155]

Underlying these conclusions are two key issues: whether proceduralists should examine self-help and, if so, what methodology should be used in such analysis. Epistemological questions like these have occupied procedural law literature for many years, and reflection on the subject of the jurist's study remains current in various branches of Law.[156] In the present case, the peculiarity lies, on one hand, in the expanding tendency of the Theory of Procedure as a starting point for any dispute resolution method—despite the obstacles to developing self-help already discussed—and, on the other hand, in the need to adopt a different theoretical paradigm related to a theory of dispute resolution mechanisms.[157] The following question explores this duality: Are the statements, concepts, and classifications of the Theory of Procedure sufficient to analyze, in general, any means of dispute resolution and, specifically, self-help?

---

[152] Duden (2023), p. 322.

[153] Didier Jr. (2024), pp. 113–114. Navarro (2023), pp. 11–13.

[154] Sander (1979), pp. 65–87.

[155] Didier Jr. (2024), pp. 213–237. Navarro (2023), pp. 388–389. Barona Vila (2024), p. 24.

[156] Ávila (2013), pp. 181–204. Rodrigues Jr. (2023), pp. 17–20.

[157] Yarshell (2020), p. 146.

The answer is negative. Although many dispute resolution mechanisms include procedural features, this is not a trait shared by all of them. There is not always a requirement to initiate adversarial proceedings for resolution or settlement in different situations. This does not mean that the outcomes are necessarily worse for the parties. It does, however, mean that protection of interests can occur even without a formal legal relationship, either because it is not necessary or because the factual circumstances prevent it. Simple examples, such as a settlement where parties quickly agree on the terms, the wrongdoer submitting to the other party's claim and ceasing their conduct, or the legitimate defense of a third party, illustrate this reality.

Some conclusions need to be drawn from this premise.

The first is the relevance of the Theory of Procedure to any situation involving a procedural legal relationship, understood as the legal relationship composed of rights, duties, capacities, burdens, and powers related to a procedural context.[158] The proposal presented in this study, concerning public and private spaces for dispute resolution, also applies here, as procedural legal relationships may exist in both spheres.

The second point is to recognize that legal remedies and procedural features do not share the same scope, as the former extends beyond the capabilities that the latter provides. In this regard, both the need for a theory capable of integrating common elements of legal remedies—whether preceded by a procedural legal relationship—and, on a doctrinal level, linking it to the horizontal and vertical effectiveness of fundamental rights, is essential for a systematic analysis of various dispute resolution methods. This analysis aims to assess their suitability, their admissibility limits, and the scope of protection, satisfaction, and fulfillment within the context of the Brazilian legal system.

The third point is to recognize that this theory neither opposes nor conflicts with the Theory of Procedure or the concept of the justice system, as it serves a broader purpose: to provide the means and forms of obtaining protection for interests recognized by the Rule of Law. Once again, examining the division of public and private responsibilities in dispute resolution shows the dispersion of avenues for both third-party adjudication and party settlement, making it relevant to shift from a model of alternativity—centered on state jurisdiction—to a model of suitability and interaction, which accepts the coexistence and interrelation of these avenues.[159]

Finally, the fourth conclusion is to recognize the expansion of the proceduralist's field of study. If not, it means that being endowed with procedurality can provide legal protection; it is appropriate to accept that the proceduralist should also examine conflicts and the legitimate means for resolving them. This epistemic observation has been signaled for several decades in Brazil,[160] and, at present, it seems inevitable, whether due to the theoretical and practical emancipation of dispute resolution

---

158 Didier Jr. (2024), p. 345.

159 Silva (2008), p. 104.

160 Watanabe (1988), pp. 130–132.

models that are not centered on the state's jurisdiction, or because of the relational structure of these mechanisms.[161]

Given these considerations, the theory introduced earlier also deserves some reflection. Although interest in dispute resolution mechanisms isn't new, there's still no agreement on the best way to define their core elements, concepts, and methods.[162] The attempt to organize them around a multi-door justice system should also be approached with caution. The use of the term "justice" is not particularly clarifying, as it suggests selecting means that achieve a regulatory ideal whose meaning is highly debated. This implies that only those means capable of delivering justice should be studied. In the literature, there is generally an emphasis on mechanisms such as arbitration, state judicial proceedings, mediation, conciliation, and, for some, self-help.[163] Why should self-help be connected to the idea of justice? Or: what does it mean for justice to be employed?

The lack of clarity in these criteria excludes various configurations of third-party adjudication in both public and private spheres that fall outside these frameworks. To cite a few examples, consider the role played by the Oversight Board, created by Facebook, Inc., established as a private tribunal composed of independent experts from different countries, tasked with adjudicating appeals submitted by platform users in matters involving freedom of expression[164]; the group of users registered on an electronic gaming platform, responsible for assessing allegations of cheating by professional players and imposing sanctions such as bans, suspensions, or access restrictions; the Loss Compensation Mechanism (MRP), maintained by the Brazilian stock exchange, intended to compensate for specific losses suffered by investors as a result of acts or omissions by intermediaries or their agents; the role of the Central Bank of Brazil as an active agent in the extrajudicial liquidation of financial institutions, with broad powers of intervention and realisation of assets in favour of creditors; or, indeed, the chair of the general meeting or collegiate decision-making body of a company who fails to count a vote cast in contravention of a duly filed shareholders' agreement. In other words, various forms of dispute resolution are not limited to these figures or those that fall outside the framework of a National Judicial Policy for Dispute Resolution,[165] but should be taken into account by a theory whose object is legal protection, regardless of what is understood by justice.

Furthermore, the argument linking access to justice is also unconvincing. For reasons like those already explained, limiting the theory solely to the means of achieving this guarantee is inadequate. First, there are many disagreements about the scope of this principle, as well as ongoing tensions between advocating for broader access to the judiciary and, on the other hand, supporting more restricted access.[166]

---

[161] Didier Jr. (2024), pp. 121–123.

[162] Silva (2021), pp. 15–16. Calmon and Andrade (2024), pp. 10–12. Navarro (2023), pp. 11–13. Didier Jr. (2024), pp. 113–114.

[163] Didier Jr. (2024), pp. 213–237. Navarro (2023), pp. 388–389.

[164] Klonick (2020), pp. 2428–2430.

[165] According to Resolution No. 125/2010 of the *National Council of Justice*.

[166] Gabbay et al. (2019), pp. 155–158.

Secondly, there is no consensus on the essential core of the fundamental right to access justice, which determines which dispute resolution mechanisms may enshrine it.[167] Making the relevance of these mechanisms dependent on a specific purpose can create significant uncertainties and prevent a comprehensive examination with legal protection. Thirdly, although the Brazilian State has increasingly expanded the availability of alternatives to state jurisdiction, it is not possible to include self-help within this framework based on a broad interpretation of Article 5, XXXV, of the Brazilian Constitution of 1988. As discussed, private self-help is an expression of individual freedom of self-help.

In contrast, public self-help is a power limited by legality, so both are used to pursue unilateral actions.[168] For this reason, Sinel's observation is pertinent, as "self-help, properly understood, is not an alternative to the civil justice system. It is a privilege to act *vis-à-vis* another person in a certain way, when certain circumstances exist."[169]

It is thus understood that self-help should be incorporated into a Theory of Dispute Resolution Mechanisms, which aims to classify the types of interest protection and the methods of achieving them within the Rule of Law, whether through state or private initiatives. The foundations of this theory can be summarized as follows: (a) the constitutional basis that legitimizes various forms of interest protection, considering the limits of direct action by the disputing parties and the different formats of third-party adjudicator involvement; (b) the segmentation into heteronomous protection, resulting from resolution by a third party, bilateral or multilateral protection, arising from the parties' convergence to resolve the dispute, and unilateral protection, as a solution imposed by one of the parties; (c) the criteria of suitability to determine which mechanisms can provide legal protection for specific types of disputes; (d) the criteria regulating the relationship and control among different dispute resolution mechanisms; (e) the identification of mechanisms capable of ensuring effective access to justice and those that, despite being legitimate, do not serve this purpose; and (f) the relationship between substantive law and procedural law, given the numerous procedural and non-procedural configurations of these mechanisms. Based on these points, it follows that self-help does not relate to Article 5, XXXV, of the 1988 Federal Constitution, and it is therefore mistaken to oppose it to the right of action or to support a state-based dispute resolution model predominantly reliant on judicial heteronomous protection. Besides the questions raised above, it is concluded that various forms of legal protection are rooted in different fundamental rights, and it is the responsibility of procedural experts to examine the requirements for legitimizing these different dispute resolution mechanisms.

---

[167] Kötter (2016), p. 285.

[168] Saturno (1995), p. 249.

[169] Sinel (2017), p. 34.

2.3.1 Substance and Procedure in Self-Help

Over the centuries, jurists have aimed to define the role of their time. Savigny stated that he lived in the era of legislation and the science of law.[170] Later, Picardi claimed to be within the jurisdictional age.[171] This concern could be applied to Procedural Law with the following question: What is the current purpose of this area of legal science? One way to address this is to revisit the relationship between law and procedure, considering the points made earlier. This relationship is at the core of modern procedural studies[172] and, although influenced by distinct approaches, three well-defined phases can be identified.[173]

The first is marked by the pursuit of making procedural law independent from substantive law, with the dividing line being the distinction between the right of action and the right that is the subject of the claim. During this period, the concept of the procedural legal relationship and its prerequisites was introduced as a key idea to support this separation. This development occurred in the late nineteenth and early twentieth centuries, primarily through the work of German doctrine.[174]

The second emphasizes the importance of ensuring that procedures align with the needs of substantive law, a perspective that is advocated as a method.[175] This period was marked by a proliferation of procedural techniques, solutions for acceleration, the creation of new procedures, debates on the relation between the Constitution and Procedural Law, tensions between public and private interests, and legislative reforms across many countries aimed at achieving these goals. Not only at the legislative level but also mainly in academic doctrine, there was a prolific output concerning the relationship between law and process. To give a few examples, this topic occupied a significant portion of studies conducted throughout the twentieth century and early twenty-first century, with numerous theoretical proposals regarding how and to what extent the process of adaptation should evolve.[176] Unlike the first, the second phase was not halted by the passage of time, as it remains a flexible agenda that adapts to the specificities of social evolution.

The third phase is characterized by a more advanced understanding of the role of procedural norms. Besides governing how decisions are made, procedural norms are now understood as the rules that govern the resolution of issues.[177] And as the subject of agreements.[178] These scenarios extend beyond the narrow view of just procedural rules, assigning them the role of regulating significant legal problems. However, this

---

[170] Savigny (1892), pp. 82–90.

[171] Picardi (2011), pp. 41–72.

[172] Pisani (2008), pp. 1–5.

[173] Habscheid (1977), pp. 120–121.

[174] Simhäuser (1965), pp. 22–37.

[175] Carnelutti (1958), p. 33.

[176] Fazzalari (1957), pp. 109–112. Binder (1969), pp. 239–250. Henckel (1970), pp. 61–64. Silva (2006), pp. 57–60. Oliveira (2006), pp. 286–289. Bedaque (2022), pp. 27–29.

[177] Braga (2015), pp. 167–169.

[178] Cabral (2022), pp. 83–86.

study does not use the term "materialization" in reference to these cases, for two reasons. The first is connotative: the term has a particular historical and semantic meaning, linked to the contrast between formalization and materialization, used to evaluate the criteria of substantive justice in legal relations. The term is used in German legal scholarship (*Materialisierung*) with this meaning, although there are disagreements about its scope.

An example is the debate sparked by Canaris.[179] and Auer[180] on contractual justice and the materialization of the contract as a means of moving beyond a purely formal analysis of freedom, considering the individual and the proper exercise of their autonomy. The second reason is denotative, related to the use of the term in Civil Procedural Law, as well as in German scholarship, where the concept was developed. As Kehrberger points out, the term opposes a formalist conception, sometimes as the influence of substantive law on procedure, and sometimes as the need to apply ethical, social, and economic values to the process,[181] none of which align with the focus discussed in the third phase.

When considering certain forms of legal protection, it is possible to argue for a fourth phase, involving the instrumental function of substantive norms. Just as procedural rules may serve as the law applicable to the legal position at hand, substantive rules may also act to protect, or remedy violated or threatened interests. This represents the enforcement of substantive law through the application of substantive law itself. The numerous examples discussed above demonstrate an approach different from the traditional one, which limits substantive law to regulating substantive legal situations. In contrast, procedural law is confined to managing how conflicts are resolved. This view is criticized by Konzen, who points to the dogma of separation (*Trennungsdogma*) between substantive and procedural rules, as the latter also serve as sources of rights, duties, powers, and burdens that exist before, during, and after the legal process.[182] In Brazilian scholarship, Sarno notes that it is "inevitable to recognize that the rule defining the criterion for proceeding may serve as a criterion for adjudication, and vice versa."[183] The goal here, therefore, is to clarify the instrumental purpose of legal norms, especially substantive norms.

By instrumental, one understands the role of serving to obtain legal protection. Contrary to what is often argued regarding the semantic meaning of protection provided by substantive law, it is a synonym for legal regulation.[184] The instrumental perspective of substantive norms, whether statutory or conventional, involves a different analysis—namely, their usefulness in protecting an injured or threatened interest at the substantive level. One purpose of these rules is to empower the active subject to defend their interests. They thus offer the means to exercise this power. It is

179 Canaris (2000), pp. 276–277.

180 Auer (2005), pp. 23–24.

181 Kehrberger (2019), p. 25.

182 Konzen (1976), p. 40.

183 Braga (2015), p. 170.

184 Marinoni (2020), p. 98.

through these rules that substantive acts are carried out until some degree of protection, realization, or satisfaction of the interest is achieved. For example, Article 644 of the Brazilian Civil Code grants the depositary the authority to retain the deposit until payment of the due remuneration or compensation for losses suffered, thereby indicating the existence of a rule that safeguards such interests. A similar situation is found in Article 6 of Law No. 6360/1976, which grants the Public Administration the authority to seize and require modifications to the formulas of products that are harmful to health or do not meet legal standards.

Even when cases of self-help are proceduralized, the instrumental function of substantive norms remains intact,[185] as it remains the source of power ultimately exercised through the implementation of procedural guarantees.[186] Tavormina made a similar observation based on two key points: substitutivity, identified as a feature of jurisdiction, also exists in self-help as the realization of an interest through substantive law; when examining the coercive enforcement of a subjective right, the author highlights cases where the creditor directly performs the obligation, based on the powers granted by the substantive legal relationship with the debtor. This characteristic of substantive rules is not exclusive to self-help. It is also evident in bilateral or multilateral remedies, where the solution results from the convergence of wills.[187] The example of settlement helps demonstrate the scope of the contract in preventing or resolving disputes (Article 840 of the Brazilian Civil Code). The substantive legal relationship governed by such a contract is not limited, for instance, to the disposition of assets or the creation of rights or duties. Still, it encompasses all these elements with the specific aim of protecting the interests of the parties in view of a conflict between them.

Instrumentality does not change the fundamental nature of the rule, as it will still govern an equally significant legal situation. It is defined by its purpose, which considers the goal of conferring powers, providing techniques, or regulating situations aimed at safeguarding the interests that are infringed or threatened. Returning to the question raised at the start of this section, one of the current roles of Procedural Law is to reevaluate its various principles to adapt them to a field of study that encompasses multiple methods of dispute resolution. One such revision involves a broader classification and a more comprehensive understanding of substantive law. The instrumentality of legal rules supports the criticism already made about the issues of the dichotomous formalism between law and procedure. Therefore, the criterion of purpose not only helps identify the procedural rule as the law applicable to the judge's decision but also allows the substantive rule to serve as a means of securing the protection of interests.

[185] Chizzini (2018), pp. 36–37.

[186] Vermeule (2016), p. 1926.

[187] Pérez Ragone (2018), p. 269.

2.3.2 Self-Help and its Relationship with other Means of Dispute Resolution

The inclusion of self-help within dispute resolution mechanisms requires an understanding of certain key concepts. First, it is essential to understand it in relation to the concept of conflict. Although some points have already been addressed, the goal here is to show that unilateral protection depends on the existence of a dispute to be established. Second, the criteria for determining the appropriateness of self-help are evaluated. While the current stage involves moving beyond viewing these mechanisms as merely alternative, the criteria for appropriateness must be objective. Third, it is crucial to understand how self-help relates to other legal protection mechanisms in the context of this appropriateness assessment. These three pillars help define the scope of the institute's application and the potential ways it may interact with other forms of legal protection.

The element of conflict, dispute, or controversy used in this study is legal and clearly defined. There is no intention to confuse it with sociological perspectives, which have been criticized in procedural doctrine.[188] This element exists in any situation involving a violation or threat to a legally protected interest. Legal remedies, as mentioned, extend beyond these limits. Legal protection may be provided to achieve or satisfy a right, the limitation of which is set by the legal system or by the impossibility of direct action by the claimant. .

All of this shows that this element is crucial for defining the scope of self-help.[189] Considering private self-help, the usual exercise of a right is broad enough to include rights of self-help, which are characterized by the unilateral action of the right-holder to counter an infringement or threat. Self-help is, therefore, a specific situation where the claimant acts to protect their infringed or threatened interests.[190] Once again, the example of the express resolutive clause illustrates the distinction between the situation in which it is invoked by the creditor to terminate the contractual relationship without reacting to any unlawful act, and the situation in which the creditor invokes it as a remedy in response to the debtor's default. In public self-help, it is also necessary to include the element of conflict to define the State's actions in pursuing unilateral protection. Although it results from self-executing authority, the concept of a public square has no direct connection to the exercise of police powers, such as seizing counterfeit or smuggled goods. Viewing self-help as a means of conflict resolution is not merely a methodological choice, but a genuine reflection of its theoretical independence and its specific purpose.

Given this, it is crucial to understand what is meant by the perspective of adequacy.[191] As Twining explains, as the State began to incorporate conflict resolution methods beyond third-party adjudication, it no longer made sense to view them

[188] Yarshell (2020), p. 32.

[189] Silva (1967), p. 13.

[190] Cordeiro (2018), p. 449.

[191] Martín Diz (2024), pp. 78–79.

as alternatives, since they underwent a growing phase of institutionalization.[192] This institutionalization is seen as the State's encouragement of these methods, whether through the creation of specific laws or the adoption of public policies. One result of this process of incorporation is typification, which involves the adoption of models of dispute resolution, such as arbitration, mediation, and conciliation. It is common for studies to rely not only on institutionalized mechanisms but also to focus on typified models to describe potential forms of conflict resolution. This perspective has been adopted in Brazil and influences how adequacy is analyzed,[193] both by dismissing atypical forms and by ignoring the division of public and private responsibilities for protecting infringed or threatened rights interests.

From this perspective, it is also common to overlook self-help due to the ongoing difficulties in defining its scope and the lack of clarity regarding the limits of legitimate action by the interested party. Nonetheless, adequacy should prevail for any means capable of providing legal protection,[194] since one of its purposes is to establish a relationship of preference or quality between one means and another. There are at least three criteria for its assessment: (a) the possibility of submitting the conflict to a given means; (b) the quality of the outcome considering the characteristics of the conflict; and (c) the maintenance of the outcome for the interested parties.

The applicability of self-help to different types of conflicts is broad. As a form of private or public unilateral action, its restrictions depend on two factors: whether it can be used to protect a violated or threatened legal right, and the limits set by the legal system to do so lawfully. The characteristics of the conflict indicate a qualitative preference for the outcome achieved through one method over another.[195] Family disputes brought before the judiciary require an impartial third party to provide a solution, which could, under more suitable circumstances, be reached by the parties themselves. Although the court is available, it tends to be less appropriate than a consensual solution, such as in determining child custody or support. While perceptions of quality are subjective, they can be objectively measured by the ability to prevent harm or threats, the protection offered to the party whose interests have been infringed or threatened, and the lesser sacrifice imposed on the perpetrator of the unlawful act. Self-help also fits within this context. It would be difficult to ignore its advantages when weighing the quality of the outcome,[196] despite characteristics such as precariousness, unilateralism, and subjection.[197] Examples where it is used to prevent immediate danger are illustrative, such as property destruction by someone in a state of necessity. The measures taken to eliminate the risk proved to be more effective for their purpose than the time required for potential judicial intervention.[198]

---

[192] Twining (1993), p. 391.
[193] Silva (2021), pp. 15–16.
[194] Salles (2006), p. 782.
[195] Zekoll (2016), pp. 350–351.
[196] Taylor (1998), pp. 847–851.
[197] Stănescu (2015), pp. 14–16.
[198] Landmann (1975), pp. 46–47.

References

Addis F (2021) Autotutela contrattuale. Enciclopedia del Diritto. Giuffrè, Milano
Adler A, Fromer JC (2019) Taking Intellectual Property into Their Own Hands. Calif Law Rev 10(5):1455–1530
Alexy R (1995) Individuelle Rechte und kollektive Güter. In: Recht, Vernunft, Diskurs: Studien zur Rechtsphilosophie, Frankfurt am Main, Suhrkamp
Amorim Filho A (1960) Critério científico para distinguir a prescrição da decadência e para identificar as ações imprescritíveis. Revista Dos Tribunais 49(300):7–37
Alland D (2001) Justice privée (Droit de se faire justice à soi-même). Droits 34:2
Almeida FDM (2012) Contrato administrativo. Quartier Latin, São Paulo
Auer M (2005) Materialisierung, Flexibilisierung, Richterfreiheit: Generalklauseln im Spiegel der Antinomien des Privatrechtsdenkens. Mohr Siebeck, Tübingen
Augsberg I (2021) Theorien der Grund-und Menschenrechte. Mohr Siebeck, Tübingen
Ávila H (2013) Constituição, liberdade e interpretação, 2nd edn. Malheiros, São Paulo
Bachman G (2006) Private Ordnung. Mohr Siebeck, Tübingen
Barona Vila S (2024) ¡Los MACS existen! Son medios de acceso a la justicia. In: Barona Vilar S (ed) MASC, to be or not to be? Medios adecuados de solución de conflictos en la justicia. Tirant Lo Blanch, Valencia
Bedaque JRS (2022) Direito e processo: influência do direito material sobre o processo, 7th edn. Malheiros/Juspodivm, São Paulo
Bell TW (2003) Free Speech, Strict Scrutiny, and Self-Help: How Technology Upgrades Constitutional Jurisprudence. Minnesota Law Review, 743–778
Bensey G (1835) Beiträge zur Lehre von der Selbsthülfe nach Römisch-justinianischem Rechte. Göttingen, Neues Rheinisches Museum für Jurisprudenz
Beltran AP (1996) A autotutela nas relações de trabalho. LTR, São Paulo
Benedetti AM (2011) Le autodifese contrattuali. Artt. In: Schlesinger P, Busnelli FD (eds) Il codice civile commentario. Giuffrè, Milano, pp 1360–1462
Betti E (1959) Autotutela (dir. priv.). In: Enciclopedia del diritto, vol. IV. Milano, Giuffrè
Beurskens M (2017) Privatrechtliche Selbsthilfe, Rechte, Pflichten und Verantwortlichkeit bei digitalen Zugangsbeschränkungs- und Selbstdurchsetzungsbefugnissen. Mohr Siebeck, Tübingen
Binder J (1969) Prozess und Recht. Ein Beitrag zur Lehre vom Rechtsschutzanspruch. Scientia Verlag Aalen, Leipzig
Blomeyer A (1982) Substantive Law and Judicial Remedies. In: Cappelletti M (ed.) International Encyclopedia of Comparative Law, vol XVI (Civil Procedure), Ch. 4, Types of Relief Available (Judicial Remedies). Tübingen, Mohr Siebeck; The Hague, Nijhoff
Bomfim NL Fidalgo CB (2008) Releitura da autoexecutoriedade como prerrogativa da Administração Pública. In: Direito administrativo e seus novos paradigmas. Belo Horizonte, Fórum
Bongiorno G (1984) L'autotutela esecutiva. Giuffrè, Milano
Bötticher E (1964) Gestaltungsrecht und unterwerfung im privatrecht. Walter De Gruyter & Co., Berlin
Braga PS (2015) Norma de processo e norma de procedimento: o problema da repartição de competência legislativa no Direito Constitucional brasileiro. Salvador, JusPodivm
Cabral ADP (2022) Da instrumentalidade à materialização do processo, as relações contemporâneas entre direito material e direito processual. In: Cruz e Tucci JR et al (eds) Estudos em homenagem a Cândido de Rangel Dinamarco. Malheiros, São Paulo
Cabral ADP (2024) Repensando a autotutela, conceito e limites no direito brasileiro. In: Eid EP (ed.). Ensaios sobre autotutela. Londrina, Thoth
Calmon P and Andrade AKS (2024) Teoria geral dos meios de solução de conflitos. Brasília, Gazeta Jurídica
Canaris CW (2000) Wandlungen des Schuldvertragsrechts Tendenzen zu seiner "Materialisierung". Archiv für die civilistische Praxis 200(3/4):273–364

Cannata C A (2011) Violenza fittizia e violenza reale nelle strutture primigenie del processo privato romano. In: Scritti scelti di Diritto Romano, vol. I, a cura di Letizia Vacca. Torino, Giappichelli
Carnelutti F (1958) Direito e processo. Morano, Napoli
Carvalhosa M (2004) Eficácia e execução específica do acordo de acionistas. Revista Da EMERJ 7(26):125–132
Chizzini A (2018) La tutela giurisdizionale dei diritti (art. 2907). In: Busnelli F (ed) Il Codice Civile–Commentario. Giuffrè, Milano
Comoglio LP (2000) Mezzi alternativi di tutela e garanzie costituzionali. Revista de Processo 99:262–265
Cordeiro AM (2018) Tratado de Direito Civil, vol V, 3rd edn. Almedina, Lisboa
Couto e Silva AD (1997) Os indivíduos e o Estado na realização das tarefas públicas. Revista de Direito Administrativo 209:43–70
Couto e Silva AD (2011) Perspectivas atuais da "teoria geral do processo". In: Calmon P, Carneiro AG (eds) Bases científicas para um renovado Direito Processual. JusPodivm, Salvador
Criscuolo A (2023) Rimedi unilaterali e poteri negoziali. Edizione Scientifiche Italiane, Napoli
Cretella Júnior J (1972) Da autotutela administrativa. Revista De Direito Administrativo 108:47–63
Dagnino A (1983) Contributo allo studio dell'autotutela privada. Milano, Giuffrè
D'Acunto L (2020) Self-help in civil matters and state justice. Diritto Mercato Tecnologia, Roma
Dedek H (2010) The relationship between rights and remedies in private law, a comparison between the common and the civil law tradition. In: Sharpe R, Roach K (eds) Taking remedies seriously. Canadian Institute for the Administration of Justice, Montreal
Dedek H (2018) Zur "Legalisierung des Natürlichen", Subjektives Recht und Gewalt. In: Fischer-Lescano A, Franzki H, Horst J (eds) Gegenrechte, Recht jenseits des Subjekts. Mohr Siebeck, Tübingen
Delgado Castro J et al (2017) Autotutela, solución adecuada del conflicto y reposesión, revisión y propuesta. Revista de Derecho de la Universidad Católica del Norte 24:2
Didier F Jr (2024) Do que se ocupa um(a) processualista? Civ Proced Rev 12(3):119–127
Dinamarco CR (2013) A instrumentalidade do processo, 15ª edn. São Paulo, Malheiros
Duchstein M (2015) Die Selbsthilfe. Juristische Schulung (JuS) 2:105–109
Duden K (2023) Digitale Sachherrschaft. Mohr Siebeck, Tübingen
Eid EP (2024) A autotutela na teoria geral do processo. In: Yarshell FL et al (eds) 50 anos da Teoria Geral do Processo no Brasil. Thoth, Londrina
Epstein RA (2005) The theory and practice of self-help. J Law Econ Policy 1(1):1–31
Fairén Guillén V (1992) Teoría general de derecho procesal. Universidad Nacional Autónoma de México, Mexico
Fazzalari E (1957) Istituzione di diritto processuale. Padova, CEDAM
Feldman R (2020) Der possessorische Besitzschutz und sein Verhältnis zum petitorischen Recht. Mohr Siebeck, Tübingen
Follieri L (2016) Dall'esecuzione forzata all'autotutela esecutiva nel terzo millennio. Nuovo Diritto Civile, anno VI(4):35–66
Fonseca RG (2012) O fundamento da autotutela executiva da Administração Pública, contributo para a sua compreensão como problema jurídico-político. Almedina, Lisboa
Fornaciari M (1999) Situazione potestative, tutela costitutiva, giudicato. Giappichelli, Torino
Franchini L (2012) Alle origini di negozio e processo; l'autotutela rituale. In: Garofalo L (ed) Il giudice privato nel processo civile romano, omaggio ad Alberto Burdese. CEDAM, t. I, Padova
Gabbay D et al (2019) Acesso à justiça no Brasil, reflexões sobre escolhas políticas e a necessidade de construção de uma nova agenda de pesquisa. RBSD–Revista Brasileira de Sociologia do Direito 6(3):152–181
Geri L B (1971) L'occupazione d'azienda come possibile forma di autotutela. In: Rapporti giuridici e dinamiche sociali, principi, norme interessi emergenti. Milano, Giuffrè
Gil y Gil JL (1994) Autotutela privada y poder disciplinario en la empresa. Centro de Publicaciones del Ministerio de Justicia, Madrid
Goldman E (2021) Content moderation remedies. Mich Technol Law Rev 28:1

Goode R (1988) The codification of commercial law. Monash Univ Law Rev 14:3
Gordillo A (2011) Tratado de Derecho Administrativo. Buenos Aires, Fundación de Derecho Administrativo, 10th edn. Fundación de Derecho Administrativo (F.D.A.), Argentina
Grinover AP (2018) A inafastabilidade do controle jurisdicional e uma nova modalidade de autotutela (parágrafos únicos dos artigos 249 e 251 do Código Civil). Revista Brasileira de Direito Constitucional–RBDC 10:13–19
Guerra S, Palma JB (2018) Art. 26 da LINDB–Novo regime jurídico de negociação com a Administração Pública. Revista de Direito Administrativo, Edição Especial 2018:135–169
Gutmann T (2011) Die Grenzen staatlicher Gewalt. In: Gutmann T, Pieroth B (eds) Die Zukunft des staatlichen Gewaltmonopols. Nomos, Baden-Baden
Habscheid WJ (1977) As bases do direito processual civil (relatório-geral apresentado ao Congresso Internacional de Direito Processual, em 1977, Grand/Bélgica). Revista de Processo 3(11/12):117–135
Haferkamp H (2003) §§ 226-231. Ausübung der Rechte, Selbstverteidigung, Selbsthilfe. In: Schmoeckel M et al (eds) Historisch-kritischer Kommentar zum BGB, Band I, Allgemeiner Teil §§ 1–240. Mohr Siebeck, Tübingen
Hamburger P (2014) Is administrative law unlawful? The University of Chicago Press, Chicago
Hattenhauer C (2011) Einseitige private Rechtsgestaltung. Mohr Siebeck, Tübingen
Helmreich H (1967) Das Selbsthilfeverbot des französischen Rechts und sein Einfluß auf Gestaltungs- und Gestaltungsklagerecht. Duncker und Humblot, Berlin
Henckel W (1970) Prozessrecht und materielles Recht. Verlag Otto Schwarz & Co., Göttingen
Hensler DH (2014) The private in public, the public in private, the blurring boundary between public and private resolution. In: Zekoll J et al (eds) Formalization and flexibilization in dispute resolution. Brill, Leiden
Isensee J (1983) Das Grundrecht auf Sicherheit. Zu den Schutzpflichten des freiheitlichen Verfassungsstaates. Walter de Gruyter, Berlin
Jhering RV (1866) Geist des römischen Rechts auf den verschiedenen Stufen seiner Entwicklung, vol I. Breitkopf und Härtel, Leipzig
Kaiser R (1983) Selbsthilfe und Gewaltmonopol Königliche Friedenswahrung in Deutschland und Frankreich im Mittelalter. Zeitschrift Frühmittelalterliche Studien 17:1
Kehrberger RF (2019) Die Materialisierung des Zivilprozessrechts. Mohr Siebeck, Tübingen
Kelly J (1967) M. Causam Dicere. Irish Jurist 2:1
Klingbeil S (2019) Die not- und Selbsthilfe, eine dogmatische Rekonstruktion. Mohr Siebeck, Tübingen
Klonick K (2020) The facebook oversight board, creating an independent institution to adjudicate online free expression. Yale Law Rev 129:8
Kneis B (2005) Verfassungsfragen des so gennannten staatlichen Gewaltmonopols am Beispiel des österreichischen Rechts. Der Staat 44:2
Konzen H (1976) Rechtsverhältnisse zwischen Prozessparteien. Duncker und Humblot, Berlin
Kötter M (2016) Better access to justice by public recognition of non-state justice systems? In: Collin P (ed) Justice without the state within the state. Judicial self-regulation in the past and the present. Vittorio Klostermann, Frankfurt am Main
La Torre M (2011) The Ancients' and the Moderns' Constitutionalism – Constitution, 'State of Exception', and the Public Monopoly of Violence. In, Die Zukunft des staatlichen Gewaltmonopols. Baden-Baden, Nomos.
Lampis M (2019) Autotutela pubblica e privata. In: Pubusa F, Puddu S (eds) Procedimento, provvedimento e autotutela, evoluzione e involuzione. ESI, Napoli
Landmann V (1975) Notwehr, Notstand und Selbsthilfe im Privatrecht. Schulthess Polygraphischer Verlag, Zürich
Leão MT (2023) O direito fundamental de economizar tributos. São Paulo, Malheiros
Lepore A (2019) Autotutela e autonomia negoziale. Edizione Scientifiche Italiane, Napoli
Lichtman DG (2004) How the law responds to self-help. John M Olin Program Law Econ Work Pap 232:I–XX

Loterstein A (2013) Law-enforcement officers and self-help repossession. State-Action Approach Mich Law Rev 111:7
Luzzatto G (1956) Von der Selbsthilfe zum römischen Prozeß. Zeitschrift der Savigny Stiftung für Rechtsgeschichte 73:29–67
Machete RC (1992) A execução do acto administrativo. Direito e Justiça 6:65–88
Majo AD (2001) La tutela civile dei diritti, terza edizione. Giuffrè, Milano
Marino FPDCM (2020) Revisão contratual, onerosidade excessiva e modificação contratual equitativa. Almedina, São Paulo
Marino S (2021) Selbsthilfe als Konfliktlösung. In: Grotkamp N, Seelentag A (eds) Konfliktlösung in der Antike. Springer, Heidelberg
Marinoni LG (2020) Técnica processual e tutela dos direitos, 7th edn. Editora Revista dos Tribunais, São Paulo
Martín Diz F (2024) Modelo de justicia contemporáneo con solución extrajudicial de litigios integrada, adecuación, condiciones y límites. In: Barona Vilar S (ed) MASC, to be or not to be? Medios adecuados de solución de conflictos en la justicia. Tirant Lo Blanch, Valencia
Martins-Costa J (2005) Reflexões sobre o princípio da função social dos contratos. Revista Direito GV 1(1):41–66
Matri D (2017) Covenants and third-party creditors. Empirical and law & economics insights into a common pool problem. Springer, Switzerland
Maurer H (2000) Allgemeines Verwaltungsrecht, 11 Auflage edn. C. H. Beck, München
Mccall J (1973) The past is prologue, a history of the right to repossess. South Calif Law Rev 47(58):58–81
Medauar O (2021) A processualidade no direito administrativo, 3rd edn. Fórum, Belo Horizonte
Medicus D (1974) Anspruch und Einrede als Rückgrat einer zivilistischen Lehrmethode. Archiv für die civilistische Praxis 174:313–332
Mezzanotte L (1995) Il diritto di ritenzione. Dall'autotutela alla pena privata. Edizione Scientifiche Italiane, Napoli
Miragem B (2021) Causas de justificação do comportamento causador do dano na responsabilidade civil. In: Simão J F and Pavinatto T (eds). Liber Amicorum Teresa Ancona Lopez – Estudos sobre Responsabilidade Civil. São Paulo, Almedina
Moreira Neto DF (2008) Quatro paradigmas do direito administrativo pós-moderno, legitimidade, finalidade, eficiência e resultados. Fórum, Belo Horizonte
Motto A (2012) Poteri sostanziali e tutela giurisdizionale. Giappichelli, Torino
Mouzalas R (2024) Autotutela privada no direito brasileiro. Londrina, Thoth
Navarro T (2023) Justiça multiportas. Editora Foco, Indaiatuba
Nerson M (1969) R. Rapport introductive. In: Travaux de L'association Henri Capitant des amis de la Culture Juridique Française, t. XVIII, nul ne peut se faire justice à soi-même. Paris, Dalloz
Nivarra L (2018) La tutela giurisdizionale dei diritti: Prolegomeni. Giappichelli, Torino
Nogueira PHP (2008) A teoria da ação de direito material. Salvador, Editora Juspodivm
Nomos Medauar O (2018) Direito administrativo moderno. Belo Horizonte, Fórum
Noronha CS (2016) Repensando a tutela dos direitos. Revista da Faculdade de Direito da UFRGS 1(32):76–97
Oliveira CA (2006) Direito material, processo e tutela jurisdicional. In: Machado F, Amaral GR (eds) Polêmica sobre a ação, a tutela jurisdicional na perspectiva das relações entre direito e processo. Livraria do Advogado, Porto Alegre
Pérez Ragone A (2018) El impacto del diálogo entre derecho substantivo y derecho procesal. Revista Derecho del Estado 41:255–283
Petrone M (1997) La compensazione tra autotutela e autonomia. Giuffrè, Milano
Picardi N (2011) La crisi del monopolio statuale della giurisdizione e la proliferazione delle Corti. Rivista italiana per la scienza giuridica 2:43–78
Pinto CADM (2005) Teoria geral do direito civil, 4th edn. Coimbra Editora, Coimbra
Pisani AP (2008) I rapporti fra diritto sostanziale e processo. In: I diritti e le tutele. Napoli, Edizione Scientifiche Italiane

Popineau-Dehaullon C (2008) Les remèdes de justice privée à l'inexécution du contrat. Étude comparative. LGDJ, Paris
Ragazzo M (2006) L'autotutela amministrativa. Principi operativi e ambiti applicativi. Giuffrè, Milano
Raimo RD (2018) Autotutela satisfattoria e giustizia "volontaria". Rivista Diritto Costituzionale 3:67–85
Ricciardoni ADS (2011) L'autotutela civile. Jovene, Napoli
Riehm T (2017) Rechtsgrund–Pflicht–Anspruch. Zur Dogmatik des Schuldverhältnisses. In: Auer M et al (eds) Privatrechtsdogmatik im 21. Jahrhundert. Festschrift für Claus-Wilhelm Canaris zum 80. Geburtstag. De Gruyter, Berlin
Rodrigues AB (2023) Em defesa da legítima defesa. Um olhar sobre os limites da justificação na dogmática civil moderna. Revista da Faculdade de Direito da Universidade de Lisboa 1(1):183–239
Rodrigues OL Jr (2023) Direito Civil contemporâneo: estatuto epistemológico, Constituição e direitos fundamentais, 3rd edn. Forense Universitária, Rio de Janeiro
Romano S (1958) L'atto esecutivo nel direito privado. Milano, Giuffrè
Romano S (2021) Introduzione allo studio del procedimento giuridico nel direito privato. ESI, Napoli
Salles CAD (2006) Mecanismos alternativos de solução de controvérsias e acesso à justiça, a inafastabilidade da tutela jurisdicional recolocada. In: Nery N Jr et al (eds) Processo e Constituição, estudos em homenagem ao professor José Carlos Barbosa Moreira. RT, São Paulo
Salles RBDO (2019) Autotutela nas relações contratuais. Editora Processo, Rio de Janeiro
Samuel G (2001) Law of Obligations and Legal Remedies, 2nd edn. Cavendish Publishing Limited, London
Sander FEA (1979) Varieties of Dispute Processing. In, The Pound Conference: Perspectives on Justice in the Future: Proceedings. Saint Paul, West Publishing Co
Saturno A (1995) L'autotutela privata. I modelli della ritenzione e dell'eccezione di inadempimento in comparazione col sistema tedesco. Edizione Scientifiche Italiane, Napoli
Savigny FC (1892) Vom Beruf unserer Zeit für Gesetzgebung und Rechtswissenschaft. Freiburg, J. C. B. Mohr
Schauer F (2015) The Force of Law. Harvard Law Press, Massachusetts
Schimpfhauser EM (2009) Das Gewaltmonopol des Staates als Grenze der Privatisierung von Staatsaufgaben. Peter Lang, Frankfurt am Main
Schirato VR (2011) Repensando a pertinência dos atributos dos atos administrativos. In: Medauar O, Schirato VR (eds) Os caminhos do ato administrativo. Editora Revista dos Tribunais, São Paulo
Schmidt E (1973) Der Zwecke des Zivilprozesses und seine Ökonomie. Athenaeum, Frankfurt am Main
Schmidt-Aßmann E (2006) Das allgemeine Verwaltungsrecht als Ordnungsidee. Grundlagen und Aufgaben der verwaltungsrechtlichen Systembildung, 2. Auflage. Berlin, Springer-Verlag
Schoueri LE et al (2021) Legalidade tributária e o Supremo Tribunal Federal, uma análise sob a ótica do RE. IBDT, São Paulo
Schünemann W (1985) Selbsthilfe im Rechtssystem, eine dogmatische Studie am Beispiel der §§ 227–229 ff. BGB. Tübingen, J.C.B. Mohr (Paul) Siebeck
Sica HVM (2013) Velhos e novos institutos fundamentais do direito processual civil. In, 40 anos da teoria geral do processo no Brasil: passado, presente e futuro. São Paulo, Malheiros
Silva OB (2006) Direito material e processo. In, Polêmica sobre a ação: a tutela jurisdicional na perspectiva das relações entre direito e processo. Porto Alegre, Livraria do Advogado
Silva PC (2008) O acesso ao sistema judicial e os meios alternativos de resolução de controvérsias: alternatividade efectiva e complementaridade. Revista De Processo 33(158):104
Silva VA (2013) Na encruzilhada liberdade-autoridade: a tensão entre direitos fundamentais e interesses coletivos. In, Direito Público em evolução: estudos em homenagem à Professora Odete Medauar. Belo Horizonte, Editora Fórum

Silva VA (2014) Direitos fundamentais: conteúdo essencial, restrições e eficácia. São Paulo, Malheiros
Silva PE (2021) Resolução de disputas: métodos adequados para resultados possíveis e métodos possíveis para resultados adequados. In, Negociação, mediação, conciliação e arbitragem: curso dos métodos adequados de solução de controvérsias. Rio de Janeiro, Forense
Simhäuser W (1965) Zur Entwicklung des Verhältnisses von materiellem Recht und Prozerecht seit Savigny. Verlag Ernest und Werner Gieseking, Bielefeld
Sinel Z (2009) Causes of Action and Self-Help Remedies. Restitution Law Review 17:122–132
Sinel Z (2017) De-ciphering self-help. Univ Tor Law J 67:1
Smith SA (2019) Rights, wrongs, and injustices, the structure of remedial law. Oxford University Press, Chicago
Stănescu CG (2015) Self-help, private debt collection and the concomitant risks. a comparative law analysis. Springer, Heidelberg
Stănescu CG, Gikay A (2017) The reluctance of civil law systems in adopting the UCC article 9 'without breach of peace' standard—Evidence from national and international legal instruments governing secured transactions. J Civ Law Stud 10:1
Sundfeld CA (2003) Direito administrativo ordenador. São Paulo, Malheiros
Smorto G (2015) Il linguaggio dei direitos e il linguaggio dei rimedi. In, Categorie e terminologie del direito nella prospettiva della comparazione. Milano, Giuffrè
Talamini CAG and Cardoso (2022) Smart contracts, "autotutela" e tutela jurisdicional. In: Bellizze MA et al (eds) Execução civil, novas tendências. Editora Foco, Indaiatuba
Tango G (2014) Autotutela individuale del lavoratore, analisi approfondita sul tema. Edizione Accademiche Italiane, Roma
Taylor CR (1998) Self-help in contract law, an exploration and proposal. Wake For Law Rev 33(4):839–908
Theodoro Jr. H (2023) Desjudicialização da execução, autotutela executiva, pacto comissório e pacto marciano. Revista Magister de Direito Civil e Processual Civil 18(4):5–21
Titze H (1897) Die Notstandsrechte im deutschen bürgerlichen Gesetzbuche und ihre geschichtliche Entwickelung. Veit & Comp, Leipzig
Twining W (1993) Alternative to what? Theories of litigation, procedure and dispute settlement in anglo-American jurisprudence, some neglected classics. Mod Law Rev 56(3):380–392
Vallemaresco A (1926) La justice privée en droit moderne. Libraire de Jurisprudence Ancienne et Modern, Paris
Verkuil PR (2005) Privatizing due process. Adm Law Rev 57(4):963–994
Vermeule A (2016) Deference and due process. Harv Law Rev 129(7):1890–1931
Von Tuhr A (1888) Der Nothstand im Civilrecht. Carl Winters Universitätsbuchhandlung, Heidelberg
Wach A (1885) Handbuch des deutschen Civilprozessrechts. Erster Band. Leipzig, Duncker und Humblot
Watanabe K (1988) Acesso à justiça e sociedade moderna. In, Participação e processo. São Paulo, Revista dos Tribunais
Watanabe K (2012) Acesso à Justiça e Meios Consensuais de Solução de Conflitos. In: Tribunal Multiportas, investindo no capital social para maximizar o sistema de solução de conflitos no Brasil. Rio de Janeiro, Editora FGV
Wendelstein C (2021) Pflicht und Anspruch. Zugleich ein Beitrag zur Bedeutung subjektiver Rechte im Privatrecht. Mohr Siebeck, Tübingen
Werner O (2000) Staatliches Gewaltmonopol und Selbsthilfe im Rechtsstaat. Hirzel Verlag, Leipzig
Yarshell FL (2006) Tutela jurisdicional, 2nd edn. DPJ Editora, São Paulo
Yarshell FL (2020) Curso de Direito Processual Civil. São Paulo, Marcial Pons
Yarshell FL (2022) O processo como instrumento de solução não adjudicada de conflitos, novas perspectivas para o direito processual? In: Cruz e Tucci JR et al (eds) Estudos em homenagem a Cândido de Rangel Dinamarco. Malheiros, São Paulo
Yoshikawa EH (2008) Da autotutela (2008). RDDP 66:19–32

Zamora y Castillo NA (2000) Proceso, autocomposição e autodefesa. Contribuição ao estudo dos fins do processo. Mexico D. F., UNAM
Zimmermann R (1996) The law of obligations. Oxford Press, Oxford
Zekoll J (2016) Online Dispute Resolution: Justice Without the State? In, Justice without the State within the State. Judicial Self-Regulation in the Past and the Present. Frankfurt am Main, Vittorio Klostermann

Chapter 3
Instrumental Function of Self-Help

Having established the concept of self-help and its role among dispute resolution methods, we now examine the instrumental aspect of unilateral protection. This involves its presence in various legal relationships created by private parties and the State, serving as an instrument for enforcing, protecting, and satisfying infringed or threatened interests. To organize this approach, two perspectives directly impact the scope of actions available to the active party: contractual and non-contractual relationships. In each case, there are different levels of freedom and limitations regarding the subjection of the passive party. This segmentation is further highlighted by the increasing use of technology, which has proven to be a key mechanism for enhancing self-help, as will also be discussed.

3.1 Private and Public Conducts in Contractual and Non-Contractual Contexts

The starting point for understanding the instrumental function is identifying its scope.[1] By scope, one refers to the extent to which the active party is authorized to act. It has been demonstrated that the basis for such authorization differs between the State and private individuals. For the former, the principle of legality applies, and for the latter, the principle of freedom. This initial distinction does not exhaust the subject, given the specificities of the Brazilian legal system in organizing both principles for this permissive purpose.

The motivations behind these two agents' actions are driven by different factors: the typicality and atypicality of instrumental power, the existence of both general and specific powers of unilateral protection, and, most importantly, the unique aspects

[1] Klingbeil (2017), pp. 18-19.

E. Pierre Eid, *Self-Help as Method of Conflict Resolution*,
https://doi.org/10.1007/978-3-032-13905-4_3

of each type of unilateral protection. Therefore, it is crucial to distinguish how self-help is applied in non-contractual and contractual legal relationships, considering the different impacts each has on this scope.[2] The influence of legality and freedom varies in the contractual and non-contractual spheres when defining the scope of self-help, as many forms of unilateral protection stemming from the autonomy of contracting parties would be forbidden if deemed non-contractual conduct.

The power of self-help includes both typical and atypical aspects of situations.[3] The importance of the type in the normative sense lies in providing a class of conduct with paradigmatic and interpretative objectives,[4] to categorize and designate a model.[5] This function serves two primary purposes: to define what is accepted by the norm and to ensure security by pre-establishing expected behavior and its consequences. The logical counterpart to this statement is the recognition of atypicality as something that falls outside this categorization.[6] Atypical conduct includes actions that are not classified under standard categories, whether due to the specific facts involved or the teleological criterion. According to Glazel, the typicality-atypicality dichotomy is balanced by standards set by the law norm,[7] so that the consequences of classification under each of these standards can vary.

It is essential to understand how the principles of legality and freedom function within this dichotomy. Discussing strict legality and, consequently, the principle of typicality, highlights the absence of a factual basis and legal consequence for atypical conduct, as seen in Criminal Law or Tax Law. When considering the principle of freedom, atypical conduct can be admitted and assigned a lawful legal consequence, as in private law. This duality is reflected in the power of self-help[8], as evidenced by these observations. These observations highlight that public self-help is governed by the legal framework of public law, where legality determines when and how the State can act to enforce, protect, and satisfy interests unilaterally. The connection between self-executing authority and legality is evident in situations where unilateral protection is permissible; beyond this scope, the behavior of the active party must be considered unlawful.[9] Private self-help coexists with many typical forms as an expression of the specific normative provision of this power, but this does not prevent unilateral protection through atypical actions, whether they arise from contractual provisions or are exercised within the limits of lawful exclusions when non-contractual.[10]

[2] Schimpfhauser (2009), pp. 70-71.

[3] Larenz (1997), p. 670.

[4] Beduschi (1992), p. 115.

[5] Bombelli (2020), p. 304.

[6] Schauer (1988), p. 519.

[7] Glazel (2006), p. 35-36.

[8] Yarshell (2006), pp. 55-56.

[9] Carvalho Filho (2011), p. 79.

[10] Saturno (1995), pp. 215-216.

The rejection of private self-help based on the interpretation of Article 345 of the Brazilian Penal Code should be reconsidered, taking into account these explanations. The legal text establishes the offence known as "arbitrary exercise of one's own rights", classified among crimes against the administration of justice. It is characterized by the conduct of "taking justice into one's own hands" with the specific intent of "satisfying a claim" without legal authorization. Consequently, much of the legal scholarship assumes the necessity of a legal provision for the lawfulness of private self-help, applying, in this context, the logic of strict legality.[11] To challenge this deeply ingrained premise and support the reasoning presented here, it is essential to understand the legal interest protected by the criminal statute and to evaluate whether the outcome mainly supported can indeed be derived from this statute.

Bechara emphasizes that criminal liability cannot arise solely from the formal classification of conduct as an offence, "it is necessary, above all, to assess its social significance, through the harm or risk to a protected legal interest."[12] The legal interest protected by Article 345 of the Brazilian Penal Code is considered the essential function of the administration of justice, namely the monopoly over the protection, satisfaction, and enforcement of infringed or threatened rights and interests.[13] It should not be forgotten that this provision originates from the Brazilian Penal Code and reflects the values of an era in which hardly any form of legal protection other than state jurisdiction was considered. Referring back to Hungria's commentary, this is clearly the inspiration, as the aim is to prevent the resolution of "private disputes" without "recourse to judicial authority.".[14] Case law discusses how this offence is characterized in situations, such as when a creditor seizes the debtor's property to satisfy an outstanding debt, [15] enters a property to retrieve a vehicle that was impounded due to administrative irregularities,[16] or uses firearms to coerce a contracting party and seize their assets to recover losses from defective service provision. [17]

Relying on this legal provision to universally prohibit private self-help is fraught with contradictions. Firstly, criminal protection of a person and their property is already provided for by a range of offences, such as homicide, theft, robbery, and criminal damage, among others. Actions undertaken to satisfy claims by illegitimate means will constitute more serious offences,[18] which will absorb the offence set out in Article 345 of the Brazilian Penal Code (as well as the minor offence known as

[11] Cintra et al. (2015), p. 44. Yoshikawa (2008), pp. 24-25. Salles (2019), p. 46.

[12] Bechara (2014), p. 147.

[13] Bittencourt (2018), p. 472.

[14] Hungria (1959), p. 490.

[15] STJ, REsp No. 1.860.791/DF, Justice Laurita Vaz, Sixth Chamber, judged on 9/2/2021.

[16] STJ, AgRg in AREsp No. 2.347.053/SC, Justice Ribeiro Dantas, Fifth Chamber, judged on 3/10/2023.

[17] STJ, RHC No. 33.166/RN, Justice Jorge Mussi, Fifth Chamber, judged on 28/8/2012.

[18] Mañalich (2009), pp. 95-98.

"assault" – Article 21 of Brazilian Decree-Law[19] No. 3,688/41).[20] Secondly, just as with private individuals, public officials can also commit criminal offenses if they exceed or refuse to exercise self-enforcing powers for public self-help, such as offenses like malfeasance, corruption, homicide, excessive exaction, etc. This means that the constraints from criminal liability and administrative sanctions also apply to public officials who unlawfully exercise unilateral protection; however, this does not justify a general ban on public self-help.[21] Thirdly, doctrinal and case law analysis shows that much of the concern about the offense of arbitrary exercise of one's rights focuses on the use and application of unlawful means of self-redress, including when private individuals substitute the State in using force to, for example, satisfy a debt. Private self-help may not always be of an executive nature. When it is, there must be a legitimate reason for private acts of self-redress to prevent them from being deemed unlawful, just as there must be valid grounds for executive acts by the Public Administration for the same purpose.[22] Fourthly, it is not coherent to argue that the legal interest protected by Article 345 of the Brazilian Penal Code is violated if a private individual is authorized to infringe upon the personal or proprietary domain of the victim, just as the Public Administration must be authorized by law, agreement, or if the conduct is not criminally relevant. Although the text mentions "law," the many instances of private executive self-help stemming from agreements between parties should not be disregarded.[23] Fifthly, even when private self-help is allowed, any excesses may lead to civil and criminal liability, just like any other dispute resolution method that can have such consequences (e.g., strict liability in interim relief, judicial corruption, judicial error resulting in wrongful conviction and imprisonment of the defendant, etc.).

In the interaction between the principles of legality and freedom, particularly in typical and atypical cases, the instrumental role of self-help is shaped by the provision of specific powers and the existence of general powers. Powers are those derived from legality, meaning the legislator's effort to define the conditions under which self-help is permissible. This is exemplified when the power of public self-help is regulated in a strict manner of legality,[24] as well as when a legal provision addresses private self-help within a specific context, constituting a typical example of private self-help (e.g., Article 1,210 of the Brazilian Civil Code)[25] The specific power, therefore, reflects how typicality functions within the public and private regimes of self-help. In contrast, the general power should be viewed as a prerogative to use unilateral remedies in cases beyond the typical instances. As discussed in the previous chapter, the principle of freedom grants recognition of a general power for private

[19] A Decree-Law is a sort of normative act issued by the federal executive branch. With the Brazilian Federal Constitution of 1988, it is no longer possible to enact it.

[20] Greco and Leite (2022), pp. 141–142.

[21] Souza (2023), pp. 134-135.

[22] Pertence Júnior (2023), p. 411.

[23] Purpura (2020), pp. 193-194.

[24] Medauar (2014), pp. 22-23.

[25] Mouzalas (2024), p. 127.

self-help in both non-contractual and contractual relationships. In non-contractual relationships, this general power is guided by grounds for excluding unlawfulness, ensuring the legitimacy of the active party's actions when exercising a regular right, acting in legitimate defense, or in a state of necessity. Although it is more challenging to define the boundaries between lawful and unlawful conduct in this area, it is possible to identify, for example, actions covered by rights of resistance,[26] such as conscientious objection or refusals by a particular group confronted with policies that violate fundamental rights, like the right to self-determination of peoples. There is also a general power stemming from the autonomy of will, based on which parties can agree on various atypical forms of self-help as legitimate methods of dispute resolution. In this context, the instrumental power can be strengthened by including authorizing clauses, for example, for acts of unilateral subrogation, which may lead to personal or proprietary limitations,[27] that would constitute civil and criminal offenses if performed outside of contractual obligations relationships.

These observations lead to another issue, also part of the debate on the scope of authorization for public and private self-help, concerning the relationship between unilateral remedies and coercion. This is the subject to be addressed in the following section.

3.1.1 Self-Help and Imperium

The concept of *imperium* is closely linked to that of self-help.[28] From an evolutionary perspective, the power of coercion shaped the idea of the State's monopoly on the use of force.[29] This concept has a historical aspect, resulting from two movements: the concentration of state powers aimed at replacing individuals, among other reasons, in pursuing their claims; and the removal of these powers from individuals under the justification of protecting them, preserving social order, and asserting sovereignty through an "unassailable power of coercive will". [30] There is also a normative dimension resulting from both the evolution of fundamental rights and a framework of rules that grant this power in various forms, such as public security, administrative oversight, control of freedoms, or enforcement.[31] The monopoly on the use of force also affects how responsibilities are divided between the State and private individuals.[32] Determining what belongs to each in terms of the coercive imposition of conduct

---

26 Miranda (2020), p. 519.

27 Aiwanger (2021), pp. 16-17.

28 Sica (2018), pp. 372-375.

29 Kelsen (1992), p. 40.

30 Dallari (2011), p. 86.

31 Jarrosson (1991), p. 253.

32 Schimpfhauser (2009), pp. 19-20.

when interests are infringed or threatened shows how imperium is expressed today. [33]

The scope of the concept of imperium must be clarified in this context. By *imperium merum*, it is meant the authority to use force to suppress unlawful acts, impose sanctions, invade the debtor's private or personal domain, or other actions that involve subjugation to satisfy, protect, or realize an interest.[34] This imposition, sometimes accompanied by the use of force, lies at the core of the aforementioned state monopoly. In carrying out the judicial function, it is reflected in the expected result inherent to enforcement proceedings, which is, "the judge produces or enables the satisfaction of one person's right at the expense of another's assets, whether with the latter's consent, regardless of it, or even against it." [35] For this reason, the substitutive nature of jurisdiction is also demonstrated through the granting of judicial powers of coercion and subrogation, which are usually withheld from the creditor.

Tavormina notes that, chronologically, the use of state apparatus for coercive action against debtors came before the development of mechanisms designed to rationalize such acts of personal or proprietary aggression, which were later formalized through proceedings on the merits.[36] This observation is crucial for understanding the connection between *imperium merum* and self-help.

In the context of public law, this means of dispute resolution is readily observable, such as when the Public Administration uses force to enforce its acts, particularly in cases involving police powers. This is evident in cases such as seizing illegal goods, closing businesses, and demolishing private buildings on public land, among others. This aspect of the state's power of compulsory enforcement is not limited to the judiciary but also includes public officials authorized to carry out administrative acts within the scope of public authority self-help[37]. Added to this is the importance of procedural guarantees in administrative activities, as a requirement to strengthen the cognitive aspects that precede the enforcement of compulsory acts.

In the context of private law, however, other factors must be considered. Although enforcement proceedings are viewed as a legitimate means of satisfying private interests through force, they have not eliminated extrajudicial and unilateral actions by individuals. As Pugliatti noted, the connection between the coercive realization of rights, enforcement proceedings, and state intervention through acts that intrude on the debtor's legal sphere lies in the dogmatic justification for transferring assets from one party to another or for personal obligations.[38] In other words, enforcement proceedings serve to legitimize the compulsory transfer or to provide identical or equivalent means for such personal realization, which would be unlawful if carried out by the individual acting alone.

[33] Laher (2017), pp. 345-347.

[34] Johnston (1997), pp. 98-99.

[35] Dinamarco (2024), p. 34.

[36] Tavormina (2003), p. 75.

[37] Maurer (2000), pp. 241-242.

[38] Pugliatti (1978), pp. 116-118.

However, this observation—supported by some as a punitive view of enforcement proceedings[39] — should not lead to ignoring the existence of *imperium merum* in the hands of the individual.[40] There are many ways in which this power is exercised, not always involving physical force or violence against a person or their property. This power manifests at different levels of imposition or subjugation, as it is inherent to private self-help. After all, if the remedy is unilateral, its effectiveness depends on the ability to subject the passive party to the outcome. Even if the form of unilateral remedy is not enforcement-based, there is still an exercise of power, sometimes confined to the legal sphere, as seen in constitutive or declaratory actions remedies.[41]

Private *imperium merum* will appear in executive self-help in different forms, so the suspicion surrounding this relationship should be viewed with some caution reservation,[42] especially by those in the doctrine who view it as a foundation for the deterioration (or erosion) of the Rule of Law.[43] One such form is through specific powers, as the actions of the active party are legitimized by legal authorization, which removes the *prima facie* unlawfulness that would otherwise attach to the conduct.[44] Numerous examples throughout the legal system demonstrate executive self-help. Besides those already discussed in this study, such as the right of repurchase as a remedy for contractual default (Article 505 of the Brazilian Civil Code), the enforcement of fiduciary guarantees (e.g., Decree-Law No. 911/69 and Laws Nos. 9.14/97 and 10.931/2004), or forced sale by the company of actions from the defaulting shareholder (Article 107, II of Law 6,404/1976), another approach involves general powers through atypical forms. These may allow for executive self-help either via contractual provisions or conduct permissible within lawful limits. Santana's example illustrates this: the lawfulness of the landlord's actions in directly repossessing a residential property abandoned by the tenant is upheld, either because no personal force is used against the individual or because such power derives from the right of ownership. [45]

These developments lead us to conclude that the connection between imperium and self-help is also part of the division between public and private spheres for resolving disputes. [46] The use of force, whether limited to the legal sphere or of a proprietary or personal nature, does not constitute a state monopoly when considering the enforcement of infringed or threatened interests, given the coercive or mandatory nature of unilateral private remedies.[47]

The granting of specific powers related to private and public executive self-help also reflects de-judicialization, meaning that when the law provides such powers, the State signals a preference for self-help in satisfying certain obligations, especially

[39] Dinamarco (2024), p. 32. Zavascki (2004), pp. 67-70.

[40] Bongiorno (1988), pp. 461-462.

[41] Terra and Schenk (2019), p. 5.

[42] Mezzanotte (1995), pp. 38-39.

[43] Paulus (2000), p. 296.

[44] Follieri (2021), pp. 39-40.

[45] Santana (2024), pp. 371-372.

[46] Zoppini (2019), pp. 58-59.

[47] Tesheiner (2007), p. 380.

in economic contexts.[48] However, this is not the only way enforcement can happen outside the Judiciary. General powers, especially those held by private parties, can lead to various unconventional forms of credit satisfaction through unilateral remedies. This is evident in many contracts made in digital environments, where the user authorizes and provides their credit card details to the software company to offset or self-satisfy monthly payments for services used but not voluntarily paid, or for imposed payment penalties.

For all these reasons, the presence of *imperium merum* in self-help has come to be seen as an advantage, even when used alongside other dispute resolution methods that lack such coercive power, such as arbitration. [49] This complementarity may be twofold: while the absence of a cognitive phase in self-help may encourage interested parties to seek fact-finding mechanisms, means not endowed with *imperium merum* may be combined with self-help to enable interested parties to achieve the satisfaction, realization, or protection of their interests.

3.1.2 Division of Powers Between the State and Private Parties for Unilateral Remedies

From the perspective of the division of tasks between the State and private parties in exercising *imperium merum,* there are several significant consequences: (i) to assess the grounds for granting specific powers of private self-help based on legislation; (ii) to consider why enforcement is no longer carried out through the Judiciary and is instead executed by public self-help; and (iii) to examine the core of the judicial reserve argument, often invoked when the constitutionality of extrajudicial enforcement is challenged. To analyze these issues, it is crucial to relate them to the instrumental power grounded in legality and freedom.

The first of these outcomes is shown in the increased opportunities for private executive self-help through explicit legislative provisions. This option highlights the state's interest in allowing private parties to independently and directly fulfill their credit claims.[50] It is essential to note that this is not an isolated occurrence in any particular country. Due to economic factors, there has been an increase in this legislative option, which has been called the "privatization of enforcement". [51]In the field of security interests,[52] in banking relationships[53], and in commercial relations.[54] The reasons for the State to promote such incentives are clear. While these relationships are built around the principles of speed and dynamism, few dispute

[48] Theodoro and Andreade (2021), p. 112.

[49] Schinemann (2023), pp. 123-124. Leite (2024), pp. 431-432.

[50] Andrade et al. (2021), pp. 455-456.

[51] Zado (2013), p. 136. De Belvis (2018), pp. 171-172.

[52] Levada (2022).

[53] Gabrielli (2017), p. 1,725.

[54] Murino (2018), pp. 228-231.

resolution methods can meet these demands other than self-help, despite its flaws. It might be possible to include in these discussions the supranational pressures for legal remedies to be available without the delays of the Judiciary or the reliance on the parties' wills for consensual agreement solutions.

An example of this global expansion is the legislative reforms that have been implemented to allow for extrajudicial enforcement of security interests, in some cases by the creditor through the Marcian Pact,[55] the collection of usufructs derived from the asset, or even the management of the asset to extract economic benefits capable of remedying the default.[56] When discussing a global phenomenon, there is a clear concern among countries in the European, Asian, and African blocs, as well as the longstanding traditions in the United States and England, regarding the modification and adaptation of their respective legal frameworks to facilitate commercial transactions.[57] This encouragement is not just a coincidence among these countries: the guidelines outlined in model laws presented by both the European Bank for Reconstruction and Development (EBRD) and the United Nations Commission on International Trade Law (UNCITRAL)—both influenced by the United States' Uniform Commercial Code (UCC)—reflect this concern not only to make the enforcement of security interests extrajudicial but also to enable creditors to take direct action to realize them.[58]

In Brazil, besides the well-known examples of fiduciary transfer of real estate[59] and other self-executing warranties, [60] the enactment of Law No. 14,711/2023 has advanced the issue of executive self-help by granting the creditor powers to locate, seize, and dispose of movable property given as security, as well as powers to enforce a mortgage through extrajudicial sale at public auction. [61]The enhancement of such specific powers demonstrates the State's role in promoting self-help as a means of dispute resolution, in assigning the Judiciary the role of oversight body for irregularities, and in providing an environment in which swift mechanisms monitor credit relationships. The accepted standards for expanding executive self-help include security measures such as adopting the Marcian Pact, providing judicial recourse to remedy or prevent abuse during the extrajudicial phase, and implementing procedural guarantees that involve the debtor's participation and right to respond during the extrajudicial stage. This framework is understood to strike a balance between procedural guarantees and the effectiveness of executive self-help. It is one of the criteria for its legitimacy, as discussed in the following chapter.

---

[55] Matos (2006), pp. 85-87. Cipriani (2000),pp. 182-184 . Luminoso (2017), pp. 20-21. Russo (2017), pp. 67-68. Terra and Guedes (2017), pp. 70-71. Monteiro Filho (2017), pp. 120-122. Theodoro Jr. (2021), pp. 8-12.

[56] Stănescu (2015), pp. 69-70.

[57] Mooney Jr. (2021), pp. 25-26.

[58] Beale (2019), pp. 9-10.

[59] Conti (2022), pp. 55-58.

[60] Levada (2022), pp. 257-277.

[61] Oliveira and Tartuce (2024), pp. 63-64.

In the field of public self-help, the executive modality draws less surprise and fewer concerns.[62] To use an obvious example, expropriation, even when it is done with consent, remains a form of taking private property through the direct use of state power, both legally (such as encumbering the asset) and physically, by removing persons and items. As a tool for self-satisfaction, this practice extends to various areas, including enforcing warranties in administrative contracts to satisfy penalties imposed on private parties, executing monetary or personal sanctions by regulatory bodies that are also responsible for oversight, and so on. However, it is essential to recognize how the exercise of public self-help can also challenge the traditional notion of the state's monopoly on the use of force in unilateral enforcement.

This proposal relates to the delegation of state powers to private parties, as discussed in administrative law doctrine concerning the delegation of police powers, for example.[63] The longstanding idea that the State possesses powers that would only be available to private parties if they had an extrajudicial enforcement title[64] is undergoing significant reformulation beyond all the considerations already outlined in this study. As these instrumental powers of self-execution are transferred to private parties, inevitable consequences arise, such as the imposition by one private party on another within the limits of strict legality (and thus only with specific powers), since delegation must be formal and legal act;[65] The state begins to transfer some of its coercive powers, further reinforcing the division of tasks in this area and thereby weakening the claim of a monopoly on the use of force. A public regime of self-help may be present when exercised by a private party against another.[66]

Therefore, it cannot be claimed that extrajudicial enforcement is a new concept. The exercise of public and private authority to fulfill obligations outside the Judiciary, including forms of executive self-help, has been an everyday activity conducted by both the State and private individuals for a long time.[67] The point raised by national procedural scholarship appears to address a different issue: it pertains to recognizing the expansion of situations where legislation grants specific powers, and increases opportunities for satisfaction of performance interests through the creditor's direct initiative, within a context where the literature adopts a restrictive view of self-help.[68] This is confirmed by the fact that "the ill-famed extrajudicial enforcement enshrines a form of self-help, repudiated in the Rule of Law, except in exceptional cases."[69] That is, the problems usually raised regarding the admissibility of extrajudicial enforcement carried out by private parties stem from criticisms generally based on the view of self-help as an act of barbarism or unrestrained conduct aggression.

[62] Fonseca (2012), pp. 343-345.

[63] Schwind (2014), pp. 131-134.

[64] García de Enterría and Fernández (2022), pp. 777-778.

[65] Klein (2022), pp. 342-343.

[66] Zago (2010), pp. 48-49.

[67] Romano (1958), pp. 55-56.

[68] Yoshikawa (2010), pp. 112-115. BRESOLIN (2013), pp. 170-174.

[69] Grinover (1987), p. 82.

Hence, the argument of judicial exclusivity, often used to challenge the constitutionality of extrajudicial enforcement, [70] must be critically examined. In this context, judicial exclusivity refers to the Judiciary's exclusive authority to carry out enforcement activities. [71] At least in terms of civil enforcement, this assertion does not hold. First, although a broad regulatory framework governs judicial enforcement, no known constitutional or infra-constitutional provision explicitly establishes this exclusive function. This observation is also important to reaffirm that the alleged monopoly of enforcement power does not support such exclusivity. Second, the performance of extrajudicial enforcement, which results from the instrumental power of public and private self-help, is justified both by legality and by freedom, so the division of functions between the State and private parties in this area has already been well demonstrated through the concept of *imperium merum*. Third, the legislator's decision to subject enforcement to either judicial or extrajudicial regimes, beyond being a political choice, is protected by the guarantee of due process of law, the implications of which for self-help will be discussed in the next chapter. Therefore, the judicial and extrajudicial regimes of civil enforcement must coexist and operate together, both to uphold the constitutional principles of legality and freedom, and to connect them through mechanisms of control and effectiveness.

3.1.3 Impossibility of Subjection by Certain Forms of Unilateral Protection

The instrumental power of self-help may not always be suitable or effective in compelling submission. These limitations refer to the impossibility of the conduct of the active party producing the intended result, due to its unenforceability against the party infringing or threatening their interest. The ineffectiveness of legal remedies is widely addressed in procedural scholarship, [72] and it is worth examining how it manifests in unilateral protection. Suppose the premise of this form is the imposition of a result through subjection. In that case, this may not occur due to the impossibility of achieving it solely by the initiative of the active party. For specific disputes, the solution must be provided through settlement or autonomous protection, due to the insufficiency of unilateral action.[73]

This scenario highlights the limitations of self-help in certain disputes and demonstrates that unilateral protection is ineffective. In such cases, no matter how much the active party wants to act, complete legal protection can't be achieved without the consent of the party causing the harm or threat, or without an authoritative decision by a third party. To illustrate this with two examples, one only needs to consider

[70] STF, RE 860.631, Justice Luiz Fux, Plenary, adjudicated on 26.10.2023.

[71] Rangel (1997), p. 27.

[72] Auletta (1999), pp. 123-124. Besso (1997), pp. 247-248. Pereira (2024). Puigvert (2011), pp. 115-117. Martins (2012), pp. 138-146. Cruz and Tucci (2020), p. 223.

[73] Motto (2012), pp. 79-82.

the necessity of invalidating a legal act carried out against the interests of the active party,[74] or the need to address legal uncertainty caused by objective doubt regarding the existence of a specific legal relationship.[75] On their own initiative, the active party would not be able to undo such an act—assuming that another performed it—nor resolve the uncertainty with binding effect—based on the same causal premise. To understand the ineffectiveness of unilateral remedies in such cases, it is important to consider both substantive and procedural aspects.

From a substantive perspective, a possible solution could involve the responsible party ceasing its conduct. This party would revoke the legal act or eliminate the uncertainty it caused, on its own initiative, which is separate from the unilateral remedy discussed in this study. In this scenario, the person who caused harm or a threat chooses to eliminate or interrupt it. There is no obligation, but rather a stance that can range from acquiescence to the active party's demand or, without any provocation, simply acknowledging the illegality of the situation and deciding to correct it.[76] Although this may result in the claimant's interest being satisfied, it is not the claimant who has obtained the adjudication. This occurs, for example, when the Public Administration ex officio invalidates its own unlawful acts, or when a supplier admits that it never entered a legal relationship with a consumer, despite initially indicating that a service contract had been concluded.

From a procedural perspective, the inadequacy of unilateral remedies highlights the need for either self-settlement or third-party adjudication. In the case of the former, the intended effectiveness stems from *pacta sunt servanda,* due to the binding nature of the bilateral or multilateral outcome. For the parties involved, the expected effects occur precisely because the object is enforceable. The binding force is a crucial element in this analysis, because not all heteronomous adjudication will have such effectiveness[77]. The ability to impose the outcome on interested parties stems from a source of binding power capable of removing uncertainty[78] or exercising a formative right. This source must be the decision of a third party, vested with the authority to impose the outcome substitution.[79]

Thus, it is confirmed that subjection is a key feature of self-help, as it mirrors the binding effect seen in other legal remedies. In self-settlement, the sign of subjection, which is the enforceability of the outcome, comes from the parties' deliberate commitment. In heteronomous adjudication, this enforceability results from a third party's power to impose the outcome so.

---

[74] Sassani (1999), pp. 34-35.

[75] Menchini (1987), pp. 59-61.

[76] Fonseca (2021), pp. 332-333.

[77] Talamini (2011), pp. 136-137.

[78] Pisani (2008), pp. 36-37.

[79] Liebman (1984), pp. 17-19.

3.2 Influence of Technology and the Automation of Legal Relationships

A significant part of the recent interest in studying self-help is due to the rise of technology and digitization in law relationships.[80] The perception that technological tools have come to promote and instrumentalize the power of unilateral remedies has followed profound transformations in various canons Law.[81] It is accurate to say that self-help mechanisms mediate a significant portion of current disputes in the digital sphere.

To give a few examples, one only needs to consider the significant and growing debates about controlling freedom of expression on social networks and digital platforms; controlling fake profiles and the spread of false information; the growth of e-commerce and managing relationships between platforms, traders, and consumers; the large electronic gaming market and the rules imposed on players to prevent cheating; how users, workers, and platforms interact in ride-hailing and delivery apps; how sports betting sites use mechanisms to maintain bettor trust; and so on. All of this indicates that self-help is becoming an increasingly integral part of people's lives and institutions.[82]Addressing from a technological perspective, it is not just a methodological choice, but a necessity resulting from the rising use of this instrument of power.[83]

The reasons for the connection between technology and self-help arise from various factors. The speed and dynamics at which events happen in this context are, in most cases, incompatible with other dispute resolution methods. Although unilateral remedies may have certain limitations, utilizing this instrumental power of legal protection proves to be the most suitable approach in this reality due to its immediacy. [84] Obstacles such as territorial jurisdiction limits and state bureaucracy are factors that separate many dispute resolution methods from the characteristics of digital disputes, including deterritorialization and dematerialization.[85] Many of these digital environments are characterized by self-regulation, whereby self-help acts as a governance mechanism for the agents operating within them, particularly due to the regulatory challenges posed by new technologies. In this context, unilateral self-help is seen as a form of internal control, unconstrained by borders, which aims to organize legal relationships and uphold the authority of certain agents.[86]

---

[80] Raskin (2017), pp. 333-337. Poncibò and Dimatteo (2019), pp. 125-126. Paulus and Matzke (2017), p. 770. Möslein (2018), p. 220. Riehm (2019), pp. 92-93. Duden (2023), pp. 321-323. Santisteban Castro (2023), pp. 596-597. Yarshell and Rodrigues (2021), p. 422. Cabral (2022), p. 35. Talamini and Cardoso (2022), pp. 196-199. Salles and Faleiros Júnior (2024), pp. 231-234.

[81] Nieva-Fenoll (2023), pp. 41-43.

[82] Koulu (2018), p. 54.

[83] Flor (2010), pp. 400-403.

[84] Pellegrini (2019), pp. 875-876.

[85] Laux (2023), pp. 291-2295.

[86] Müller (2018), pp. 33-34.

For this reason, self-help should also be classified as Online Dispute Resolution (ODR). Despite the semantic variation and ambiguity of this term, it can be argued that it encompasses any dispute resolution method influenced or shaped by technology and conducted in the online sphere.[87] Classifying them as ODR does not create an independent category but describes how this mechanism is presented with technological tools. In this case, it is not just a transfer from the physical world to the digital realm. Instead, there is an expansion of self-help methods enabled by this technological infrastructure, involving algorithms, blockchain, the Internet of Things, and the automation of numerous legal relationships. The following sections demonstrate how technology has been instrumental in expanding and realizing the power under discussion here.

3.2.1 *Algorithms and Automation*

Although the term "algorithm" has gained popularity only recently due to the rise of social networks, it is much older than this invention. Mathematicians have studied algorithms for centuries, as they are simply a precise sequence of instructions designed to produce an expected result as a solution to a problem.[88] Not infrequently, in specialized literature, an algorithm is compared to a cake recipe. If this recipe (sequence of information) is followed, the expected result is the creation of the dessert (a solution to the problem). The somewhat ambiguous relationship between algorithm and technology stems from the fact that the former serves as a set of instructions for executing a program. For example, the word processing software used to write this work is built with algorithms that enable all its functions to be performed based on the information it contains.

From these very basic notions, which are nonetheless sufficient for present purposes, it is clear that algorithms serve to automate the execution of patterns on specific information. This process occurs in several stages: the input of data to feed the algorithm, the algorithm's processing of this data, and the output of this data to a specific destination.[89]

This operation is complex. Depending on the algorithm's purpose, the tasks it performs will vary. The connection between algorithms and artificial intelligence shows how these processes can mimic patterns rooted in human experience.[90] Artificial intelligence, driven by algorithms, is a branch of engineering that focuses on making machines intelligent—that is, capable of making decisions. Most work in artificial intelligence involves exploring the problems posed by the world.

Within this range of possibilities, the intersection of algorithms, artificial intelligence, and self-help takes place. Programming a sequence of instructions, along with

[87] Callies and Heetkamp (2019), pp. 2-3.

[88] Dasgupta et al. (2010), p. 2.

[89] Martini (2020), p. 100.

[90] Cui (2020), pp. 5-6.

the learning gained by artificial intelligence from data, can be aimed at practicing unilateral self-help. In the digital realm, this is a common aspect of governance and control of legal relationships.[91] To provide different examples, consider the email account user who uses a spam filter to avoid reading repeated offensive messages from a specific sender or to prevent banking fraud attempted via links sent by a scammer; or the social network user who activates a feature provided by the platform to block comments, many of which are racist or homophobic. Algorithms shape digital presence and, in many cases, are driven by artificial intelligence; therefore, these mechanisms inevitably influence the actions taken in this environment. [92]

To understand the significance of technology in self-help studies, it is helpful to note that much of the current debate about the control of freedom of expression, fake news, the role of digital platforms in democracy in the digital age, and the regulation of these business activities is directly related to the practice of unilateral decision-making in self-help. [93]Besides being a common topic in recent elections in many countries,[94] national experience has shown concern regarding the operation of algorithms, not only in terms of programming for the visibility and dissemination of such content, but above all, in their removal.[95]

The debate addressed in themes 533 and 987 of general repercussion (RE 1.037.396/SP and RE 1.057.258/MG) concerns the liability regime applicable to providers of applications or internet tools for user-generated content, as well as the possibility of removing content that may infringe on personality rights, incite hatred, or spread fraudulent news. In both cases, the court will examine the constitutionality of Article 19 of Law No. 12,965/14 (the Brazilian Civil Rights Framework for the Internet), which requires a specific court order for the removal of unlawful third-party content as a condition for civil liability. The core issue extends further: if the requirement for a court order is waived and liability arises from the mere existence of unlawful content, application providers would be compelled to exercise ongoing self-regulation to remove content that breaches their terms of use and the national legal order.[96] Based on the previously accepted premises, this discussion again focuses on the division of powers between the State and private parties in resolving disputes. In this context, the trend of using civil liability to force platforms to increase their control over such content is paired with the judicial system's inability to address these issues promptly.

Reinforcing the instrumental role of self-help, algorithms can function in different ways, both as tools provided by the platform and in support of the user. [97]This observation considers that unlawful acts are often multidirectional, meaning they violate terms of use, participants' rights, and more. For example, a post containing hate

---

[91] Kaminski et al. (2021), pp. 2,005-2,008.

[92] Douek (2022), pp. 546-550.

[93] Goldman (2021), pp. 21-25.

[94] Syed (2017), pp. 346-347.

[95] Frazão (2022), p. 592.

[96] Manne et al. (2021), pp. 15-16.

[97] Laux (2024), pp. 162-163.

speech targeting a specific ethnic group can lead to several responses: the platform might censor the post; depending on the situation, the profile could face restrictions, such as limitations in third-party searches; the offended user might block the profile responsible for the post, among other options. Overall, these functions show how technology can create new forms of self-help and support its use in different situations. The following sections will review some applications discussed in the literature that confirm this conclusion.

3.2.2 *Internet of Things: Self-help and Digital Tangible Assets*

The Internet of Things refers to a physical asset, or in civil law terms, a tangible asset, that is connected to the internet through devices or sensors embedded in it.[98] According to this category, internet connectivity is no longer limited to computers or mobile phones, but extends to any tangible asset that serves as a means of one of its functionalities. Today, people are surrounded by such assets (also called smart devices), including televisions, light bulbs, household appliances, watches, virtual assistants, vehicles, and more. Everyday objects gain "intelligent life," access data broadly, interconnect, are monitored, and enable remote access and interaction. The physical and digital worlds converge into a single asset.

This innovation has had a significant impact on legal relations. Currently, issues such as changes in consumer relationship profiles, contractual complexity due to the inclusion of the cloud provider in relationships between people and assets, civil and criminal liability for accidents caused by autonomous vehicles, revisions to the concept of possession due to sharing and reliance on third parties for many functionalities, personal data protection, and the legal framework for smart cities are all being discussed in various contexts countries.[99] In Procedural Law, issues involving the Internet of Things are starting to emerge. For example, the 2nd Criminal Chamber of the Regional Court of Regensburg, Germany, admitted as evidence the audio recording by the virtual assistant Alexa during a woman's homicide, which her former partner committed. Despite extensive debate about whether this type of evidence is lawful, without this audio recording, the accused's presence in the victim's apartment at the time of the crime would have remained uncertain. Additionally, the content allowed the prosecution to link the accused to the voice of the former partner through other forensic evidence. [100]

Self-help is not immune to this technological evolution. The connectivity of these tangible assets to the internet allows for the exercise of unilateral protection from a distance. This analysis has gained traction among US scholars, who have referred to

[98] Allen (2016), p. 71.

[99] Diega (2023), pp. 11-15.

[100] LG Regensburg, Decision of 16.12.2020 – Ks 103 Js 28875/19.

such measures as technological self-help or remote self-help[101]. The interest in using the Internet of Things for this purpose has a practical basis: case law surrounding Section 9-609 of the Uniform Commercial Code interprets any acts involving aggression, injury, or moral or physical offense to the debtor as a breach of the "without breach of peace" clause. The potential for remote access to enforce the creditor's interests—without the personal confrontation often seen in repossession—has become an appealing feature that would enable the exercise of this right to self-help, [102] reducing some of the interpretative obstacles raised by the courts. [103]

The scope of remote access for exercising self-help is examined from different perspectives. The debtor's default could result in the blocking of certain functions of the asset, such as access to applications, the deactivation of its vital tasks until payment is made, or the disconnection of the asset from the internet.[104] Furthermore, the removal of physical intermediaries has encouraged the market to invest in these digital unilateral enforcement mechanisms, such as proposals to allow the recovery of vehicles with defaulted financing through autonomous return to the manufacturer's premises or by turning off the vehicle to make it unusable to the debtor. [105]

In analyzing the revision of the concept of possession in consideration of the Internet of Things, Duden notes that these changes have also affected the traditional way self-help over an asset was exercised.[106] Historically, this instrumental power was focused on physical, personal, and direct protection against threats or attacks by others. With the digitization of tangible assets, it becomes necessary to evaluate which interests are protected—that is, whether the measures shift to protecting something immaterial and aim to safeguard (i) the asset itself; (ii) the credit, by influencing the functionalities of the asset as a means of indirect coercion; or (iii) whether there is an extension of powers exercised materially over the asset to defend contractual positions, such as the exception of non-performance regarding the obligation to provide streaming services.[107]

In Brazil, there is still no specific regulation governing self-help related to the Internet of Things. However, some guidelines can be highlighted for further examination. The first is Decree No. 9,854/2019, issued by the President of the Republic, which established the National Internet of Things Plan. Some of its guiding principles, such as promoting efficiency gains in services (Article 3, Item I) and increasing the productivity and competitiveness of Brazilian companies in this sector (Article 3, Item III), suggest that maintaining these digital relationships based on tangible assets will require regulation to prevent unilateral enforcement. It is also known that a significant portion of these relationships is consumer-based and, therefore, must also comply with the Brazilian Consumer Protection Code. The second guideline

---

[101] Crootof (2024), pp. 9-12.

[102] Roditti (1995), pp. 452-456.

[103] Moringiello (2022), pp. 575-577.

[104] Beurskens (2017), pp. 298-299.

[105] Raskin (2017), pp. 333-337.

[106] Duden (2023), p. 322.

[107] Crootof (2024), pp. 13-14.

is to interpret Article 1,210 of the Brazilian Civil Code in a manner that adapts it to a reality where the asset is connected to the internet and possession protection is carried out through digital means, which are not always immediate. The third guideline involves adding rules to the Civil Code, with the draft reform creating a "Digital Civil Law" book. There are important benchmarks to guide the application of self-help in this context, such as respect for privacy and personal and proprietary data; the inviolability of intimacy, honor, private life, and image; and the guarantee of digital rights security.

3.2.3 Smart Contracts and Self-Enforcement

Smart contracts are agreements that are self-executing due to their programming code. [108]Generally, a smart contract is seen as a technological code created to facilitate, verify, or execute the negotiation or performance of transactions between parties, allowing them to conduct reliable, traceable, and irreversible transactions, especially when blockchain technology is employed.

The general objectives of smart contracts are to fulfill contractual clauses (such as payment terms, confidentiality, and performance), minimize the effects of breaches, and reduce the need for third-party intervention to resolve disputes arising from these relationships. Smart contracts are, therefore, computer-automatable and executed based on software code. They not only define the contractual rules but also automatically and coercively enforce these obligations. [109]

This self-execution happens through the pre-programming of information within these coded systems. The reason for using the term "smart contracts" is that it translates contractual clauses into programming code, ensuring that the provisions are automatically enforced. The lack of human intervention in executing these clauses confirms the automation and the technological mediation aimed at reducing the issues identified as obstacles. [110]

Examples of certain commercial contracts already implemented as smart contracts highlight the importance of such programming. The interest rate on some goods transport financing arrangements may vary based on the actual risk of cargo loss, whether due to external factors like weather or the nature of the freight itself. In these cases, financial institutions automatically program the calculation and collection of the rate, depending on the risk as it occurs, determined through applications and sensors that provide real-time information on the cargo's condition when it arrives at its destination.

The automatic enforcement of contractual clauses has led legal scholars to consider smart contracts as a potential form of self-help. For some, the mere existence of programmed enforceability would be enough to generalize the presence of

---

[108] Werbach and Ornell (2017), pp. 338-339.

[109] Kuhlmann (2019), pp. 119-120.

[110] Poncibò and Dimatteo (2019), p. 123.

unilateral protection in any situation, even when only the performance of an obligation is involved. [111] This, however, should be reevaluated. The fact that these are contracts with obligations that are automatically fulfilled does not change the previous considerations regarding the characterization of self-help. Therefore, the criticism by Talamini and Guskow is well-founded.[112] It is accurate to say that not everything automatically executed in smart contracts counts as self-help.[113] Nor should automation be seen as a method to prevent, for example, default.[114]

The line between exercising rights, performing duties, and self-help must be more clearly defined in this context. Some automated functions might also fall under this type of legal protection. Möslein's observation is relevant, as it emphasizes the importance of evaluating how the smart contract is designed and how self-execution is intended on a case-by-case basis.[115] It is not possible to generalize the link between these contracts and self-help, just as such a link cannot be generalized in any other contractual context model.

Remedies automatically applied to address contractual breaches for the benefit of the injured party may be considered cases of self-help. [116] The application and self-enforcement of penalty clauses in case of a breach by one of the contracting parties, the programmed retention of amounts previously allocated for this purpose, or immediate set-off in cases where there is a reciprocal creditor and debtor relationship between the parties, are some examples of the scope for unilateral protection in smart contracts.

The debate may center on how much the smart contract model enables unlawful self-help.[117] After all, such automatic programming would, in theory, prevent the passive party from reacting, which might be necessary to prevent or reduce losses caused by proprietary or personal restrictions resulting from the enforcement of unilateral action protection.[118] There is, however, an important observation: although the systems underpinning smart contracts aim to be stable and ongoing, it is not possible to ignore the inherent flexibility in programming them. To assume beforehand that self-help in these contracts is unlawful, simply because performance is automatic, overlooks the various possible models, including those that may be adapted to meet judicial requirements for the regularity of unilateral protection of interests.

---

[111] Raskin (2017), pp. 333-337. Santisteban Castro (2023), pp. 596-597. Cabral (2022), p. 35.

[112] Talamini and Cardoso (2022), pp. 186-187.

[113] Didier Jr. and Fernandez (2024), p. 202.

[114] Schumann Barragán (2021), pp. 317-318.

[115] Möslein (2018), p. 220.

[116] Yarshell and Rodrigues (2021), p. 422.

[117] Sklaroff (2017), p. 300.

[118] Paulus and Matzke (2017), p. 770.

3.2.4 Cyberattacks and Self-Defence

A cyberattack can be defined as the "use of code, malicious computer or electronic signals to alter, disrupt, degrade, or destroy computer systems or networks, or the information or programs contained therein," [119] or, more succinctly, as "any action taken to impair the functions of a computer network for political or national security purposes."[120]

Such an attack can be executed through various methods, including hacking, espionage, and the deployment of viruses. However, to be considered cyber in nature, its goal must be to impair or disrupt the functioning of a computer network.[121] Warfare can be classified according to the forms of attack, such as kinetic (conventional, physical) warfare, biological warfare, chemical warfare, nuclear warfare, artificial intelligence-based warfare, or network-based warfare.

The use of technology in attacks by nations, violations, or threats to security and sovereignty has influenced the understanding of self-defense. Determining the scope of the powers derived from this right in such situations requires, first, an evaluation of the requirements for legal protection, and second, an assessment of the conduct that should be accepted to prevent or avoid harm.

In international relations between States, the right of self-defense is guaranteed by Article 51 of the Charter of the United Nations, but the text does not provide enough specificity to determine what measures would be necessary in the event of a cyberattack: "Nothing in the present Charter shall impair the inherent right of individual or collective self-defense if an armed attack occurs against a Member of the United Nations." The question arises as to the extent to which this type of attack constitutes an armed attack and what response is possible.[122]

Some challenges faced by scholars in applying international law to cyberspace include attributing responsibility for attacks, defining the type of attack, and determining the appropriate form of defense and permissible retaliation. The Charter of the United Nations states that all members "shall refrain in their international relations from the threat or use of force against the territorial integrity or political independence of any State, or in any other manner inconsistent" (Article 4 [2]). To address these issues, NATO experts on cyber conflict have developed the Tallinn Manual, a non-binding document that offers interpretations of international law to guide *jus ad bellum* and *jus in bello*.[123]

Rule 68 of the Manual addresses the threat or unlawful use of force. The explicit or implicit threat must be communicated to the recipient, as it is understood that the use of force is not permitted without such a warning. A state possessing the capability to conduct cyber operations against another does not in itself constitute a threat. This only occurs if there is communication regarding these cyber-attack

[119] Waxman (2013), p. 109.

[120] Hathaway et al. (2012), p. 826.

[121] Tsagourias (2012), p. 230.

[122] Hayward (2017), pp. 401-402.

[123] Schmitt (2017), pp. 9-10.

capabilities. This connection creates challenges in determining how to characterize the threat of harm if a state, without the capacity to carry out a cyber operation, issues a warning. This is an important point, as if the criterion is cumulative, it requires that much confidential information, such as national security matters, be assessed before exercising self-defense, since it is often not possible to ascertain the existence of such a capability.[124]

Rule 69 outlines the prohibition on the use of force. A cyber operation counts as a use of force if it targets a State's territorial integrity or political independence. Item 4 of this rule states that "the armed forces of a State need not conduct an act qualifying as use of force." This means that a cyber operation would qualify as a use of force if carried out by the armed forces, but it will also be considered as such if performed by State entities or private actors.[125]

To help classify a cyberattack as an armed attack, Rule 69 of the Manual considers the effects produced as use of force. Eight effects are identified for this classification: (i) gravity: this carries the most weight in characterizing a cyber operation; (ii) imminence: a swift and unannounced attack makes peaceful conflict resolution more difficult, thus making it easier to classify a cyber operation with immediate consequences as an armed attack; (iii) directness: the greater the causal link between the cyber operation and its effects, the easier it is to determine the need for intervention; (iv) invasiveness: this refers to how much a State's cyber operations intrude into another; (v) quantification of effects: assessing the results and damage caused by the attack; (vi) military character: if a cyber operation is a military activity, it increases the likelihood of it being classified as use of force; (vii) illegitimacy: under international law, the use of force is illegitimate unless it is a permitted act, in the absence of treaties or an explicit prohibition under customary law; and (viii) involvement of the State: the State must be the responsible agent for the operation and the attack.

This discussion aims to demonstrate that the effects of technology are evident in various settings where self-help is employed.[126] In international relations, self-defense, as an extension of the principle of reciprocity, is also influenced by this context and must be adapted to a reality where physical and in-person attacks coexist with virtual ones. This point is also relevant to the overall concept of self-defense—that is, understanding how not only states in their interactions but also private individuals can defend themselves and the lawfulness requirements when facing harm or threats in the digital arena environment.

---

[124] Andrade et al. (2021). Cabral (2022). Cintra et al. (2015). Oorsprong et al. (2023), pp. 224-225.

[125] Tladi (2019), pp. 16-17.

[126] Sharkey (2010), p. 105. Flor (2010), pp. 400-403.

References

Aiwanger F (2021) Kohlhaas' kapsel oder: Private vollstreckung zwischen selbsthilfe und selbstjustiz. In: Croon-Gestefeld J, Korsch S, Kuschel L, Sarel R, Scholz P (eds) Das private im privatrecht. Nomos, Baden-Baden

Allen AL (2016) Protecting one's own privacy in a big data economy. Harv Law Rev 130(71):71–78

Andrade E et al (2021) Autonomia privada e solução de conflitos fora do processo: autotutela executiva, novos cenários para a realização dos direitos? Rev Processo 46(322):437–476

Auletta F (1999) Nullità e <<inesistenza>> degli atti processuali civili. CEDAM, Padova

Beale H (2019) An outline of a typical PPSA scheme. In: Gullifer L, Akseli O (eds) Secured transactions law reform. Principls, policies, and practice. Hard Publishing, Oxford

Bechara AELS (2014) Bem jurídico-penal. São Paulo, Quartier Latin

Beduschi C (1992) Tipicità e diritto. Contributo allo studio della razionalità giuridica. CEDAM, Padova

Besso C (1997) La sentenza civile inesistente. Giappichelli, Torino

Beurskens M (2017) Privatrechtliche Selbsthilfe: Rechte, Pflichten und Verantwortlichkeit bei digitalen Zugangsbeschränkungs- und Selbstdurchsetzungsbefugnissen. Tübingen, Mohr Siebeck

Bittencourt CR (2018) Tratado de Direito Penal, 12th edn. Saraiva, v, São Paulo, p 5

Bombelli G (2020) Appunti sui concetti di "tipo", "tipicità" e "atipicità". JUS 2-3:293–325

Bongiorno G (1988) Profili sistematici e prospettivi dell'esecuzione forzata in autotutela. Riv Trimest Dirit Proced Civ 42(2):444–484

Bresolin UB (2013) Execução extrajudicial imobiliária, aspectos práticos. São Paulo, Atlas

Cabral ADP (2022) Da instrumentalidade à materialização do processo, as relações contemporâneas entre direito material e direito processual. In: R C e TJ et al (eds) Estudos em homenagem a cândido de rangel Dinamarco. Malheiros, São Paulo

Callies G, Heetkamp SJ (2019) Online dispute resolution, conceptual and regulatory framework. TLI Think! Pap King's Coll 22:2–22

Carvalho Filho JDS (2011) A autoexecutoriedade e a garantia do contraditório no processo administrativo. Revista do Ministério Público. Rio Jan 39:75–97

Cintra ACA et al (2015) Teoria geral do processo, 31th edn. São Paulo, Malheiros

Cipriani N (2000) Patto commissorio e patto marciano. Proporzionalità e legittimità delle garanzie. Edizioni Scientifiche Italiane, Napoli

Conti BCTD (2022) Garantías fiduciarias. São Paulo, Almedina

Crootof R (2024) Remote repossession. DePaul Law Rev 73:3–26

Cruz e Tucci JR (2020) Limites subjetivos da eficácia da sentença e da coisa julgada civil. São Paulo, Marcial Pons

Cui Y (2020) Artificial intelligence and judicial modernization. Springer and Shanghai People's Publishing House, Singapore

Dallari DA (2011) Elementos de teoria geral do Estado, 30ª edn. São Paulo, Saraiva

Dasgupta S et al (2010) Algoritmos. AMGH, Porto Alegre

De Belvis E (2018) L'esecuzione privatizzata. Edizione Scientifiche Italiane, Napoli

Didier Jr F, Fernandez L (2024) Autotutela e smart contracts. In: Eid EP (ed) Ensaios sobre autotutela. Thoth, Londrina, pp 179–204

Diega G (2023) Internet of things and the law: legal strategies for consumer-centric smart technologies. New York, Routledge

Dinamarco CR (2024) Instituições de direito processual civil, 5th edn. Malheiros, v. IV, São Paulo

Douek E (2022) Content moderation as systems thinking. Harv Law Rev 136(2):528–607

Duden K (2023) Digitale Sachherrschaft. Mohr Siebeck, Tübingen

Flor R (2010) Tutela penale e autotutela tecnologica dei direitos d'autore nell'epoca di internet. Padova, CEDAM

Follieri L (2021) Dall'esecuzione forzata all'autotutela esecutiva nel terzo millennio. Nuovo Diritto Civile, anno VI, n. 4:35–66

Fonseca AT (2021) Da recusa de cumprimento da obrigação para tutela do direito de crédito, em especial na excepção de não cumprimento, no direito de retenção e na compensação. Almedina, Lisboa
Fonseca RG (2012) O fundamento da autotutela executiva da Administração Pública, contributo para a sua compreensão como problema jurídico-político. Almedina, Lisboa
Frazão A (2022) Julgamentos algorítmicos, a necessidade de assegurarmos as preocupações éticas e o devido processo legal. In: Colombo C et al (eds) Tutela jurídica do corpo eletrônico. Editora Foco, Indaiatuba
Gabrielli E (2017) Una garanzia reale senza possesso. Riv Giuridica Ital 7:1715–1754
García de Enterría E, Fernández TR (2022) Curso de derecho administrativo. Civitas, v. I, Madrid
Glazel LP (2006) La forza normativa del tipo. Pragmatica dell'atto giuridico e teoria della categorizzazione, Quodlibet, Macereta
Goldman E (2021) Content moderation remedies. Mich Technol Law Rev 28:1
Greco L, Leite A (2022) Concurso de delitos, uma primeira tentativa de reorientação. Rev Inst Ciênc Penais 7(1):131–158
Grinover AP (1987) Deformalização do processo e deformalização das controvérsias. Rev Processo 12:46
Hathaway O et al. (2012) The law of cyber-attack. Cal L Rev, 100:817–885
Hayward R (2017) Evaluating 'imminence' of a cyber attack for purposes of anticipatory defense. Columbia L Rev, 117:399–434
Hungria N (1959) Comentários ao Código Penal, arts. 250 a 361. Rio Jan Rev. Forense IX, p 490
Jarrosson C (1991) Réflexions sur l'imperium. In: Études offertes à Pierre Bellet. Litec, Paris
Johnston D (1997) The general influence of roman institutions of state and public law. In: Carey D et al (eds) The civilian tradition and Scots law, Aberdeen quincentenary essays. Duncker & Humblot, Berlin, pp 98–99
Kaminski M et al (2021) The right to contest AI. Columbia Law Rev 121(7):1957–2048
Kelsen H (1992) Reine rechtslehre, 2 Auflage edn. Österreichische Staatsdruckerei, Wien
Klein AL (2022) Poder de polícia e poderes privados. In: Klein AL, Marques Neto FPA (eds) Funções administrativas do Estado. Editora Revista dos Tribunais, São Paulo
Klingbeil S (2017) Privatrechtliche Selbsthilfe, Rechte, Pflichten und Verantwortlichkeit bei digitalen Zugangsbeschränkungs und Selbstdurchsetzungsbefugnissen. Mohr Siebeck, Tübingen
Koulu R (2018) Law, technology and dispute resolution. Privatization of coercion, Routledge, London
Kuhlmann N (2019) Smart enforcement bei smart contracts. In: Fries M, Paal B (eds) Smart contracts. Mohr Siebeck, Tübingen
Laher R (2017) Imperium et jurisdictio en droit judiciaire privé. Mare & Martin, Paris
Larenz K (1997) Metodologia da Ciência do Direito, 3ª edn. Fundação Calouste Gulbekian, Lisboa
Laux FDM (2023) Redes sociais e jurisdição, 2ª edn. Editora Revista dos Tribunais, São Paulo, pp 291–295
Laux FDM (2024) A moderação de conteúdo em redes sociais sob a ótica da autotutela. In: Eid EP (ed) Ensaios sobre autotutela. Thoth, Londrina
Leite CFL (2024) Execução arbitral sob perspectiva da Análise Econômica dos Métodos de Solução de Conflitos. Rev. Processo 49:349
Levada FAM (2022) Garantias autoexecutáveis. Editora Revista dos Tribunais, São Paulo
Liebman ET (1984) A autoridade da coisa julgada. In: Eficácia e autoridade da sentença. Forense, Rio de Janeiro
Luminoso A (2017) Patto commissorio, patto marciano e nuovi strumenti di autotutela esecutiva. Riv Dirit Civ 63:1
Mañalich RJP (2009) Autotutela del acreedor y protección penal del deudor. Ediciones Juridicas de Santiago, Santiago de Chile
Manne G et al (2021) Who moderates the moderators? A law and economics approach to holding online platforms accountable without destroying the internet. Law Econ. Cent. George Mason Univ. Scalia Law Sch. Res. Pap. Ser 22-040:1–67

Martini M (2020) Regulating algorithms. In: Ebers M, Navas S (eds) Algorithms and law. Cambridge University Press, Cambridge, p 100
Martins SG (2012) Processo, procedimento e ato processual, plano da eficácia. Campus Jurídico, Rio de Janeiro
Matos IAD (2006) O pacto comissório, contributo para o estudo do âmbito da sua proibição. Almedina, Lisboa
Maurer H (2000) Allgemeines Verwaltungsrecht, 11 Auflage edn. C. H. Beck, München
Medauar O (2014) Poder de polícia, origem, evolução, crítica à noção, caracterização. In: Medauar O, Schirato VR (eds) Poder de polícia na atualidade. Forum, Belo Horizonte, pp 13–26
Menchini S (1987) I limiti oggettivi del giudicato civile. Giuffrè, Milano
Mezzanotte L (1995) Il diritto di ritenzione. Dall'autotutela alla pena privata. Edizione Scientifiche Italiane, Napoli
Miranda J (2020) Direitos fundamentais, 3rd edn. Almedina, Coimbra
Monteiro Filho CEDR (2017) Pacto comissório e pacto marciano no sistema brasileiro de garantias. Editora Processo, Rio de Janeiro
Moringiello JM (2022) Automating repossession. Nev. Law J. 22(2):564–603
Möslein F (2018) Rechtliche grenzen innovativer finanztechnologien (FinTech), smart contracts als selbsthilfe? Z Bankr Bankwirtsch. 30(4):208–221
Motto A (2012) Poteri sostanziali e tutela giurisdizionale. Giappichelli, Torino
Mouzalas R (2024) Autotutela privada no direito brasileiro. Thoth, Londrina
Müller MW (2018) Mapping paradigms of European internet regulation – The example of internet content control. In: Krönke C et al (eds) paradigms of internet regulation in the European Union and China. Nomos, Baden-Baden, pp 33–34
Murino F (2018) L'escussione. In: Gabrielli E (ed) I contratti di garanzia finanziaria. Giuffrè, Milano, pp 228–231
Nieva Fenoll J (2023) Inteligência artificial e processo judicial. Juspodivm, Salvador
Olveira CE, Tarturce F (2024) Lei das garantias (lei 14.711/2023). Forense, Rio de Janeiro
Oorsprong F et al (2023) Cyber-attacks and the right of self-defense, a case study of the Netherlands. Policy Des. Pract 6(2):217–239
Paulus CG (2000) Die Privatisierung der Zwangsvollstreckung – oder, Wie der Rechtsstaat an seinem Fundament erodiert. Z Rechtspolit 33(7):296–297
Paulus CG, Matzke R (2017) Digitalisierung und private Rechtsdurchsetzung. Relativierung der Zwangsvollstreckung durch smarte IT-Lösungen? Computer und Recht. Z Prax Rechts Inf 13: 12:769–778
Pellegrini T (2019) Prestazioni auto-esecutive. Smart contract e dintorni. Comp dirit civ 3:843–880
Pereira CFB (2024) Revisitando a fonte de normas processuais. In: Yarshell FL et al (eds) 50 anos da Teoria Geral do Processo no Brasil. Thoth, Londrina, pp 195–218
Pertence Júnior CM (2023) Autotutela e execução fiscal, os Projetos de Lei 4.257/2019 e 2.488/ 2022. Rev Processo 346(48):403–430
Pisani AP (2008) I rapporti fra diritto sostanziale e processo. In: I diritti e le tutele. Edizione Scientifiche Italiane, Napoli, pp 2–35
Poncibò C, Dimatteo L (2019) Smart contracts. contractual and noncontractual remedies. In: The Cambridge handbook of smart contracts, blockchain and digital platforms. Cambridge University Press, Cambridge, pp 119–134
Pugliatti S (1978) Esecuzione forzata e diritto sostanziale. Edizione Scientifiche Italiane, Napoli
Puigvert S (2011) La ineficacia de los actos procesales, sistematización y clarificación de conceptos. Marcial Pons, Madrid
Purpura A (2020) Autonomia privata, responsabilità e attuazione coattiva del credito. Giappichelli, Torino
R C e TJ (2020) Limites subjetivos da eficácia da sentença e da coisa julgada civil, 2nd edn. São Paulo, Marcial Pons
Rangel PC (1997) Reserva de jurisdição, sentido dogmático e sentido jurisprudencial. Universidade Católica Portuguesa – Editora, Porto

Raskin M (2017) The Law and Legality of Smart Contracts. Georget Law Technol Rev 304:305–341
Riehm T (2019) Smart contracts und verbotene eigenmacht. In: Fries M, Paal BP (eds) Smart Contracts. Mohr Siebeck, Tübingen, pp 85–98
Roditti E (1995) Is Self-Help a Lawful Contractual Remedy? Rutgers Comput Tech Law J 21(2):431–459
Romano S (1958) L'atto esecutivo nel diritto privato. Giuffrè, Milano
Russo D (2017) Oltre il patto marciano. Edizione Scientifiche Italiane, Napoli
Salles RBDO (2019) Autotutela nas relações contratuais. Editora Processo, Rio de Janeiro
Salles RBDO, Faleiros Júnior JLDM (2024) Autotutela em plataformas digitais, estudo de caso do algoritmo 'content ID' e de seus contornos contratuais. In: Eid EP (ed) Ensaios sobre autotutela. Thoth, Londrina, pp 223–246
Santana TCD (2024) Reflexões sobre o direito do locador ao exercício da autotutela para retomada de imóvel residencial urbano abandonado pelo locatário. In: Eid EP (ed) Ensaios sobre autotutela. Thoth, Londrina, pp 361–383
Santisteban Castro M (2023) La incidencia de la autotutela en los smart contracts. In: J P i J (ed) Aspectos críticos del derecho procesal. Diálogos hispano-italianos en homenaje a Angelo Dondi. Barcelona, JM Bosch
Sassani B (1999) Impugnativa dell'atto e disciplina del rapporto. Contributo allo studio della tutela dichiarativa nel processo civile e amministrativo. CEDAM, Padova
Saturno A (1995) L'autotutela privata. I modelli della ritenzione e dell'eccezione di inadempimento in comparazione col sistema tedesco. Edizione Scientifiche Italiane, Napoli
Schauer F (1988) Formalism. Yale Law J. 97(4):519
Schimpfhauser EM (2009) das gewaltmonopol des staates als grenze der privatisierung von staatsaufgaben. Peter Lang, frankfurt am main
Schinemann CB (2023) Arbitragem e execução, divisão de competências, poderes do árbitro e limites subjetivos. Editora Revista dos Tribunais, São Paulo
Schmitt MN (2017) Tallinn manual 2.0 on the international law applicable to cyber operations. Cambridge University Press, Cambridge
Schumann Barragán G (2021) Smart contracts y tutela judicial. La incidencia de los contratos autoejecutables en la tutela judicial de los derechos y los intereses materiales de los justiciables. Rev Derecho procesal 2:309–338
Schwind RW (2014) Particulares em colaboração com o exercício do poder de polícia. O procedimento de polícia. In: Medauar O, Schirato VR (eds) Poder de polícia na atualidade. Fórum, Belo Horizonte, pp 139–155
Sharkey CM (2010) trespass torts and self-help for an electronic age. NYU Law Econ Res Pap 10:07
Sica HVM (2018) Os conceitos de "imperium" e "iurisdictio" no direito romano. In: Bedaque JR et al (eds) Estudos de direito processual civil em homenagem ao professor José Rogério Cruz e Tucci. Juspodivm, Salvador, pp 367–397
Sklaroff JM (2017) Smart contracts and the cost of inflexibility. Univ Pa Law Rev 166(1):263–303
Souza LA (2023) Crimes contra a Administração Pública, 3rd edn. Editora Revista dos Tribunais, São Paulo
Stănescu CG (2015) Self-help. Private debt collection and the concomitant risks. A comparative law analysis, Springer Cham, Heidelberg
Syed N (2017) Real talk about fake news, towards a better theory for platform governance. Yale Law J 127(337):337–357
Talamini E (2011) Objetivação do controle incidental de constitucionalidade e força vinculante (ou "devagar com o andor que o santo é de barro"). In: Nery N Jr et al (eds) Aspectos polêmicos e atuais dos recursos cíveis e assuntos afins. Editora Revista dos Tribunais, São Paulo, pp 135–166
Talamini E, Cardoso AG (2022) Smart contracts, "autotutela" e tutela jurisdicional. In, Bellizze M A et. al. (eds) Execução civil, novas tendências. Editora Foco, Indaiatuba
Tavormina V (2003) Il processo come esecuzione forzata. Jovene, Napoli

Terra AMV, Guedes GSC (2017) A apropriação do objeto da garantia pelo credor, da vedação ao pacto comissório à licitude do pacto marciano. Rev Fac Direito UFMG 70:51–77
Terra AMV, Schenk LF (2019) Inafastabilidade da jurisdição e autotutela, o exemplo da cláusula resolutiva expressa. Rev Eletrônica Direito Process 13(20–3):1–19
Tesheiner JMR (2007) Jurisdição, execução e autotutela. In: Instrumentos de coerção e outros temas de direito processual civil – estudos em homenagem aos 25 anos de docência do Professor Dr. Araken de Assis. Forense, Rio de Janeiro, pp 379–384
Theodoro Jr H (2021) Desjudicialização da execução, autotutela executiva, pacto comissório e pacto marciano. Rev Magister Direito Civ Process Civ 18(4):5–21
Theodoro Jr H, Andreade E (2021) Novas perspectivas para atuação da tutela executiva no direito brasileiro, autotutela executiva e "desjudicialização" da execução. Rev Processo 46(315):109–158
Tladi D (2019) The use of force in self-defense against non-state actors, decline of collective security and the rise of unilateralism, whither international law? In: Self-defense against non-state actors. Cambridge University Press, Cambridge, pp 14–89
Tsagourias N (2012) Cyber-attacks, self-defense, and the problem of attribution. J Confl Secur Law 17(2):229–244
Waxman MC (2013) Self-defensive force against cyber attacks, legal, strategic and political dimensions. Int Law Stud. 89(109):109–122
Werbach K, Ornell N (2017) Contracts ex machina. Duke Law J 67(313):313–382
Yarshell FL (2006) Tutela jurisdicional, 2nd edn. DPJ Editora, São Paulo
Yarshell FL, Rodrigues VS (2021) Contratos inteligentes e execução civil, diálogo possível e útil? In: Cabral TNX et al (eds) Tecnologia e justiça multiportas. Editora Foco, Indaiatuba, pp 417–425
Yoshikawa EH (2008) Da autotutela, vol 66. RDDP, São Paulo
Yoshikawa EH (2010) Execução extrajudicial e devido processo legal. Atlas, São Paulo
Zado J (2013) Privatisierung der Justiz zur Bedeutung und verfassungsrechtlichen Zulässigkeit von Privatisierungen in Rechtsprechung, Strafvollzug, Zwangsvollstreckung und Handelsregister. Duncker & Humblot, Berlin
Zago MF (2010) O dogma da indelegabilidade do poder de polícia defrontado com os casos do Código de Trânsito Brasileiro. Fórum Adm 10:111
Zavascki T (2004) Processo de execução, parte geral, 3rd edn. Revista Dos Tribunais, São Paulo
Zoppini A (2019) L'effettività in-vece do processo. In: Grisi G (ed) Processo e tecniche di attuazione dei diritti. Omaggio a Salvatore Mazzamuto a trent'anni dal convegno palermitano. Jovene, Napoli, pp 53–69

Chapter 4
Limits to Self-Help

Two companies entered into a contract for the supply of medicines and other health products. After receiving €337,596.00, the supplier stopped delivering the products and retained this amount, claiming it would cover losses allegedly caused by the other contracting party's unlawful conduct, as one of its managers was diverting clients, which, up to that point, had resulted in a verified loss of €855,000.00. In reviewing the case, the Supreme Court of Justice of Portugal characterized the supplier's conduct as precautionary self-help (direct action) in the form of seizure but considered it unlawful due to disproportionality, since it did not meet the requirements outlined in Article 336 of the Portuguese Civil Code: (a) the existence of a legitimate right; (b) the impossibility of resorting to judicial or administrative enforcement measures in due time; (c) the action being necessary to prevent the practical frustration of the right; (d) the absence of excess in preventing the loss; and (e) the direct action not resulting in the sacrifice of interests that are more important than those the agent seeks to protect.[1]

A French financial institution leases electric cars. Under the contract with the consumer, it was stipulated that, after fourteen days of default, the vehicle's battery would be remotely deactivated using blockchain technology. A consumer organization filed a lawsuit to prevent the financial institution from invoking this clause and disabling the battery that powers the vehicle. The case was brought before the German Federal Court of Justice (*Bundesgerichtshof* – BGH), which ruled that the company's self-help measure was unlawful. Even though the deactivation was performed remotely, the court applied, among other laws, § 307, paragraphs (1) and (2) of the BGB, recognizing that the clause imposed an unjustified disadvantage on the consumer and shifted the business risk to them, since the battery would make a product of greater value than the debt unusable. This decision was also made since the consumer had no alternative available in the market other than to use a battery from a specific manufacturer. It was further noted that the financial institution should

[1] *Supreme Court of Justice, Review* 6524/18.9T8LRS-A. L1.S1, Justice Ilidio Sacarrão Martins, 7th Section, judged on 08/04/2021.

E. Pierre Eid, *Self-Help as Method of Conflict Resolution*,
https://doi.org/10.1007/978-3-032-13905-4_4

have sought a court order for the payment of the outstanding amounts or included a provision in the contract for an advance deposit to mitigate business risks.[2]

A company uses an e-commerce platform to sell its products to consumers. The amounts from these transactions are deposited with a financial institution associated with the platform. The account holder may be prevented from withdrawing these funds if the platform's terms of use or trading rules are violated, such as by advertising goods that infringe on industrial property rights or with the intent to deceive the public. After learning that access to its current account had been blocked, the company sought clarification from the platform but was unsuccessful. It decided to take legal action to regain access to the account, release the deposited funds, and seek damages for the days without access and for delays in delivering products to consumers. In its analysis, the São Paulo Court of Justice (TJSP) ruled that the blocking was unlawful because the platform failed to prove any violation of the rules governing the digital environment.[3]

Law No. 13,606/2018 added Article 20-B, §3, item II to Law No. 10,522/2002, authorizing the Public Administration to "register, including electronically, the certificate of tax liability with the registries of assets and rights subject to seizure or attachment, making them unavailable." The constitutionality of this provision was challenged through a concentrated review via ADI 5,881, as it allegedly violates Article 146, item III, subparagraph b of the 1988 Federal Constitution. It was argued that a supplementary law should set general rules on tax obligations, assessment, credit, limitation, and prescription. Among other points, it was emphasized that the provision infringed principles of substantive due process, the reservation of jurisdiction, and the principle of proportionality by restricting the right to property. The Federal Supreme Court (STF) reviewed the arguments and concluded that there is no formal unconstitutionality, since the matter is not reserved to supplementary law. It also upheld the constitutionality of registering the certificate of tax liability in asset and rights registries before beginning tax enforcement proceedings. However, it declared unconstitutional the part of the provision that addresses the administrative unavailability of assets, because that power failed the proportionality test, given that less restrictive methods, such as fiscal precautionary measures, exist to protect taxpayers' fundamental rights. Since it interferes with the property right, such unavailability must be subject to judicial review, with adversarial proceedings and complete defense guaranteed. [4]

The examples above show that both national and foreign courts are hesitant to accept self-help measures, as well as the challenges faced by the party trying to implement them properly. On the one hand, this may limit the potential of the mechanism, as such uncertainties tend to discourage its use. On the other side, case law shows substantial variation in legal reasoning, terminology, and standards for defining the limits of the active party's conduct—such as abuse of rights, vulnerability, violation

[2] BGH, 26.10.2022 – XII ZR 89/21.

[3] São Paulo Court of Justice, Appeal No. 1031624–87.2021.8.26.0224, Judge Angela Lopes, 28th Private Law Chamber, judged on 03.02.2023.

[4] STF, ADI 5886, Justice-Rapporteur Roberto Barroso, Full Court, decided on 09/12/2020.

of due process, reservation of jurisdiction, excess of power, or infringement of fundamental rights—which adds to the legal uncertainty mentioned earlier. Unlike systems like German, American, Swiss, and Portuguese law, which set general requirements for using private self-help, Brazil has no rule that, for example, requires first turning to public authorities, prefers third-party adjudication means, or mandates any other precondition.

Suppose this makes it harder to identify clear criteria for justifying and assessing the lawfulness of private actions. In that case, it's important to remember that self-help, like any dispute resolution method, has many features: it can be public or private, occur in civil, administrative, commercial, corporate, consumer, or labor relations, and there may be specific legal provisions governing the conduct of the active party. In short, when unilateral protection affects property, individuals, or legal positions, clear limits must be established so it isn't rendered invalid by a broad application of illegality across its various forms. This chapter aims to outline these limits within the Brazilian legal system and define the criteria for their assessment.

4.1 Due Process of Law and Means of Dispute Resolution

The aspects discussed above lead to the following questions: what are the limits of conduct, whether public or private, for unilateral protection? Are the specific requirements of certain modalities enough, or should others be added? How can consistent treatment be applied to self-help if there are multiple rules concerning the initiative of the active party and a series of principles aimed at protecting individuals and property?

The solution to these issues is far from simply invoking constitutional procedural guarantees to justify, with equal weight, their use in different dispute resolution methods. It is essential to clarify the forms of these mechanisms, determine whether the State acts as a party or adjudicator, understand the role of autonomy of will in setting the boundaries of legal protection, and grasp how these guarantees are applied. Often, to simplify this critical discussion, due process of law is mentioned without further explanation, without questioning how it would work in contexts beyond state judicial proceedings or whether it would need to be adapted to different dispute resolution models. To explore these questions, the following section presents the view of due process of law it adopts, its functions, and how it applies to self-help.

The starting point is to analyze the specificities of Article 5, Section LIV, of the 1988 Brazilian Federal Constitution. As a principle, its ideal states are challenging to define due to the vagueness and indeterminacy of the legal text and the wide variation in what is understood by due process. To understand it, generally in relation to means of dispute resolution and specifically regarding self-help, it is necessary to critically assess the following objectives that are commonly attributed to it: (a) to amalgamate and articulate other fundamental principles applicable to proceedings;

[5] (b) to underpin proportionality in the application of legal norms; [6] (c) to establish different models of protection according to the type of proceedings and legal protection;[7] and (d) to ensure that any procedural legal relationship is permeated by it, even if the intended outcome does not involve restriction of property or liberty.[8]

The current approach to due process of law, seen as a principle from which other procedural rights, such as impartiality, reasoning, adversarial proceedings, and full defense, derive, faces certain limitations in coherence and applicability. First, the 1988 Brazilian Federal Constitution includes autonomous provisions for most fundamental procedural rights typically associated with due process. This not only makes this overarching perspective unnecessary but also limits the individual scope of each of these rights. For example, consider the implications that adversarial proceedings or complete defense can have independently, each varying in significance depending on the context. This approach would make sense if the Brazilian Constitution lacked fundamental procedural rights, with due process serving as a source for legitimizing implicit rights. The German Basic Law exemplifies this well, as it only guarantees adversarial proceedings (*rechtliches Gehör*) as a guarantee in state proceedings, from which the doctrine and case law of the Federal Constitutional Court, over the past seventy years, have developed a broad set of rights principles.[9] Secondly, treating due process as a clause or a "catch-all" for other principles that are already expressly provided for in the constitutional text has intensified the existing difficulty in defining its purpose. Although at first glance such breadth might be assumed to reinforce the guarantee, it is, in fact, a way of making not only its identification but also its scope more difficult. An analysis of Brazilian Supreme Federal Court (STF) case law reveals how the lack of specification undermines the guarantee, for example, by reducing it to a synonym for adversarial proceedings and full defense, a procedural formality, or an exclusively judicial activity.[10] This trivialization is not a problem with the guarantee itself, but instead with the method by which it is applied in specific cases, which can lead to unnecessary restrictions on other fundamental rights or conflicts with different principles, thereby affecting their development.[11]

If the usefulness of due process is reduced when examined in this way, it becomes necessary to determine how to approach it by identifying its core goal of realization. One can start with Ávila's idea of the "ideal of protectiveness" of rights.[12] To go beyond the abstraction of this proposal, it is necessary to take a further step and recognize that, in addition to the ideal of protection, there is an ideal of adequacy of this protection based on the specificities of each intended outcome. This principle allows for a wide range of adaptability depending on the type of protection sought

[5] Mattos (2009), p. 157. Dinamarco (2020), pp. 320–323.

[6] Castro (2010), p. 158.

[7] Moraes (2022), p. 1152.

[8] Braga (2008), pp. 178–179.

[9] Rosenberg et al. (2018), pp. 460–461.

[10] STF, MS 35506, Justice-Rapporteur Ricardo Lewandowski, Full Court, decided on 10/10/2022.

[11] Yoshikawa (2010), pp. 108–112.

[12] Ávila (2008), pp. 55–56.

and the circumstances of its application, rather than being a static model that limits everything to the parameters of state judicial proceedings, for example. Therefore, it is essential to include this perspective as an ideal state of protection tailored to each legal position. Due process in state judicial proceedings has specific features that differ from those of consensual methods or arbitration, and it applies in situations where there is procedural activity without necessarily involving legal protection, such as legislative procedures.

On this basis, this principle aims to establish *specific and adaptable conditions for protecting rights.*

Firstly, this is not an absolute guarantee. It has the capacity to adapt to different configurations of legal protection and procedural activity, based on the interests protected, the parties involved, and the protection needs presented. This adaptability also means imposing different requirements for the constitutionality of various models of rights protection. Furthermore, it demonstrates the ability to shape how legal protections are exercised so they can be consistently implemented. Therefore, it is not about using state judicial proceedings as the benchmark for assessing the constitutionality of other dispute resolution mechanisms, but about determining to what extent these mechanisms can provide some degree of protection within the limits accepted by the Federal Constitution. What may exist is a difference in how strongly guarantees are applied to such protection, and thus, in choosing which means is best suited to protect a right.

Secondly, just as the proceduralization of legal relations heightens the debate on the scope of due process, restrictions, limitations, or satisfactions of rights show how the State and private parties should act. Here, there is a direct link to what Calliess calls "social and legal rationality" in the creation, restriction, protection, and realization of rights.[13] Thus, the characteristics of specificity and adaptability explain how and why the features of the application circumstances must be examined to determine whether, in that model, adequate protection exists. [14]

These conclusions help to dispel the idea that "substantive" due process serves as the basis for proportionality. The criticism from some authors is relevant not only to reject this link but also to show that proportionality is a method for applying principles. [15] It is an obligation that arises from the way principles are handled, not a result of due process. However, this does not mean that these specific and adaptable conditions for protecting rights cannot be procedural or substantive. On the contrary, the impact of due process applies to both spheres.

The consequences of these explanations extend beyond methodological considerations. By defining due process as outlined above, it is evident that many judicial decisions underestimate the scope of this principle, limiting it to a basis for proportionality. If approached as suggested here, case law could have progressed further in clearly defining, for example, the relevance of this principle to different dispute resolution methods, whether or not they are proceduralized. Legal scholarship on

---

[13] Callies (1999), pp. 176–179.

[14] Talamini (2023a), p. 329.

[15] Silva (2002), pp. 31–32.

structuring these methods reveals the adaptable nature of due process, demonstrating that it is not a principle incompatible with other forms of legal protection, but rather one that establishes suitable protection models for various situations. [16] Zanoide de Moraes, for example, when proposing a non-violent criminal process, acknowledges that "(...) it is intended that new procedural guarantees or new spaces within existing guarantees be coherently adapted or even created," since "it is an expansion of the factual basis and the scope of protection of fundamental rights."[17]

The reasoning here defends due process in the examination of self-help.[18] This argument was addressed by the Supreme Federal Court (STF) when analyzing the state or private power of unilateral enforcement. To focus on one example, consider RE 860.631 (topic 982), where the constitutionality of extrajudicial enforcement in fiduciary transfer contracts under Brazilian Law No. 9.514/1997 was upheld. The main argument regarding due process concerns centered on execution against assets "without the participation of the Judiciary and, consequently, without the figure of the natural judge, which would constitute a form of self-help, rejected in the Democratic Rule of Law." It was initially argued that there was an incompatibility between the due process of law and self-help, and therefore that judicial intervention in the enforcement process should be exclusive, implying a reservation of state jurisdiction. The judgment of this extraordinary appeal showed that the STF not only recognized that the principle applies beyond state judicial proceedings but also acknowledged the flexibility of procedural rules that uphold constitutional guarantees such as adversarial procedures, predetermined jurisdiction, and proceedings before a notarial authority—thus removing from the creditor's claim the characterization of "illegitimate form of self-help." [19] This decision offers essential guidance for other cases questioning the constitutionality of extrajudicial enforcement, especially those that may be considered self-help, as it recognizes the possibility of fulfilling obligations outside the Judiciary, provided this is permitted by due process.

The connection between due process and self-help is based on the idea that unilateral enforcement serves as a form of legal protection, where the satisfaction, realization, or safeguarding of interests is carried out by the active party itself, thereby involving the passive party. Both the State and private individuals can act as agents in these processes[20], and for this reason, must follow an appropriate and adapted approach based on the different circumstances in which this power is exercised.[21] Even when considering the Italian constitutional text, Carimini's observation is relevant, as "just protection (...) cannot be exhausted in judicial protection, which, in the modern world, is facing a difficult crisis, and thus cannot be limited by the right of

[16] Talamini (2023b), p. 435.

[17] Moraes (2022), p. 1152.

[18] Yarshell (2024), pp. 138–141.

[19] STF, RE 860,631, Justice Luiz Fux, Full Court, decided on 26/10/2023.

[20] Salles (2019), pp. 49–50.

[21] STJ, REsp No. 2,139,749/SP, Justice Ricardo Villas Bôas Cueva, Third Panel, decided on 27/08/2024

action."[22] In other words, once the monopoly on enforcement or coercion of interests through judicial protection has been broken, due process must be an essential feature of any legal guarantees and any method of obtaining them. [23] From this, it follows that, due to the principle of protecting rights under specific and adaptable conditions, we can discuss effective and fair unilateral enforcement. This enforcement pertains to the interests of the active party and the personal and proprietary sacrifices of the passive party. The unique aspects and adaptations of self-help arise from (a) the reasons behind the active party's actions; (b) the public or private legal regime governing unilateral enforcement; (c) the scope of protection, whether it concerns the person, property, or legal position; (d) how the restriction is imposed on the passive party; (e) the involvement of agents certifying interests or providing assistance to evaluate the conduct's legality; and (f) the level of oversight by other dispute resolution methods that may provide greater guarantees.

4.2 Proportionality and Unilateral Enforcement

Even when discussing limits on self-help, it is often claimed that proportionality is the key point of equilibrium.[24] Usually, this proposal is offered as a solution amidst many variables in the active party's conduct, without clarifying what is meant by proportionality. However, it is implied that this would be a general restriction for both public and private entities' self-help.[25] Case law also uses this term when exercising control over unilateral enforcement, similarly, without additional explanations about its specific meaning in this context.[26]

It is therefore necessary to analyze how proportionality applies, its contribution to this debate, and whether it has been correctly applied in this review context. Two key points should be kept in mind: the distinction between public and private self-protection, considering the specific features of their respective legal regimes, and the existence of rules—and not just principles—that govern the exercise of unilateral protective measures powers.

Unilateral protection, like any other form of legal protection, must be appropriate to achieve the goals of the party whose interests have been harmed or threatened. This involves establishing a relationship between the available means and the desired outcomes, specifically an assessment of the proportionality between means and ends. It is common to refer to this as proportionality. In the study of judicial protection, it appears as a relationship between means. It ends in enforcement actions, infringement of the debtor's personal or proprietary rights, and benefits in favor of

[22] Carimini (2018), p. 46

[23] Comoglio (2000), pp. 262–263.

[24] Bauer (2023), p. 26. Jouannaud (2023), p. 42. Saturno (1995), pp. 284–285. Cipriani (2000), pp. 184–185. Lepore (2019), pp. 65–72. Cabral (2024), pp. 52–53. Mouzalas (2024), pp. 257–260.

[25] Fonseca (2012), pp. 676–679. D'Acunto (2018), pp. 45–49.

[26] STJ, REsp No. 1,766,116/RS, Justice Sérgio Kukina, First Chamber, judged on 6/4/2021.

the creditor.[27] However, there is also another way of addressing proportionality, not as a relationship between means and ends, but as a method for applying principles, [28]when, for example, the admission of unlawfully obtained evidence is allowed to give precedence to life, freedom of movement, and other similar considerations.[29]

Among these uses, the second situation reflects what legal scholarship has called the rule or postulate of proportionality. [30] This is a method used to determine the dominance of one principle over another through a test based on three stages: suitability, necessity, and proportionality *stricto sensu.* Because principles are derived from certain norms, this is the way to handle their conflict and relationship. However, legal protection is not always guided by principles alone; often, it is driven by rules that specify what actions should be taken. In such cases, the term "proportionality" is commonly used as a synonym for the reasonable match between the rule and the conduct. When a judge is allowed to enforce atypical measures against a debtor without a specific rule detailing what these measures are, how they should be executed, or their consequences for the debtor, principles and the proportionality test are used to determine what is an appropriate measure.[31] The situation differs when the rule requires a specific conduct but does not specify the extent of enforcement. What actions are permissible for a contracting party relying on the *exceptio non adimpleti contractus*? How far can someone go in self-defense? What is the scope of the Public Administration's authority to dismiss a civil servant for misconduct?

These questions are of undeniable practical importance in examining self-protection. First, improper use of the proportionality test could lead to the conclusion that a rule granting unilateral protective power might be set aside or overridden by applying a principle, thus reducing the scope for safeguarding interests. Second, there is little debate about applying fundamental rights in legal relationships involving self-protection, which is often used to justify generalizing the proportionality test, assuming that in any scenario, everything can be resolved by balancing principles at the expense of rules. Third, even if the proportionality test is generalized, specific normative criteria exist for various methods that regulate how actions should be taken. In this regard, proportionality could weaken other methods for assessing the unlawfulness of conduct, such as review based on objective good faith and legal boundaries. Fourth, many issues related to whether the active party's conduct is appropriate stem from executive self-protection—understood as unilateral protection to fulfill obligations—not from any form of self-protection, highlighting the inadequacy of this review criterion to determine whether, how, and to what extent a party should act, especially given concerns over the legitimacy of enforcement outside legal bounds. [32]

[27] Didier Jr. (2009), pp. 30–31, 2009.

[28] Ávila (2013), pp. 182–184.

[29] Armenta Deu (2011), pp. 182–183.

[30] Klatt and Meister (2012), pp. 8–9.

[31] Minami (2020), pp. 270–272.

[32] Paulus (2000), p. 296.

For this reason, more than a semantic issue, there is a problem concerning the outcomes of the choices made about the review method. Accepting that proportionality is the approach for working with principles through a test based on suitability, necessity, and proportionality stricto sensu, and that this should not be confused with the relationship of suitability between means and ends for implementing rules, the premises of this work are as follows: (a) the application of fundamental rights in legal relationships between private parties and the State is direct, [33] and this imposes greater limits on public self-protection; (b) the application of fundamental rights in relations between private parties is indirect, so legal and contractual rules should be regarded as filters or mediators for the realization of these rights,[34] which indicates greater flexibility for private self-protection; (c) the proportionality test may be applied, but it is not a universal rule for all contexts of self-protection; (d) the relevance of the relationship between means and ends is crucial for implementing the rules governing the power of unilateral protection, so that violating this relationship could lead to outcomes such as abuse of rights or abuse of power; and (e) due process of law is a principle that applies whenever there is insufficiency, insecurity, or omission regarding the means of protecting rights within a particular form of legal protection. The goal is to both preserve the infra-constitutional framework and ensure the effectiveness of the rules, while also highlighting the mistake of relying on proportionality as an absolute criterion of control. [35]

Two examples can illustrate these assertions. Article 6, §3, item II of Brazilian Law No. 8987/95 provides for discontinuing services due to user default, with prior notice. The law does not distinguish between essential and non-essential services, between current or past defaults, or regarding the characteristics of the service recipient. These omissions also appear in Article 6, item VII of Brazilian Law No. 13,460 (Public Service User Protection Code), highlighting the regulatory gaps in this form of self-help. This lack of protection often leads to the supplementary application of fundamental rights to address these issues. In this context, case law recognizes the unlawfulness of the concessionaire's conduct if the electricity supply is cut off in a manner that affects the user's right to health or physical integrity, 40 if it impacts a healthcare facility, 41 or if the debt relates to a period before the month of consumption. A different situation occurs with the revocation of a mandate due to the agent's disloyalty: in this case, the principal acts by expressing their will and terminates the legal relationship. This scenario does not present significant concerns, as the rule in Article 682, item I of the Brazilian Civil Code, sufficiently regulates the situation, and because unilateral protection ends with the dissolution of the bond between the parties. Therefore, proportionality is not in question here, since the suitability relation between means and ends is clear and direct.

Considering these factors, it is essential to establish general criteria that can legitimize self-protection—whether to support the active party in their actions or to guide later review of conduct. The challenges of this proposal extend not only to balancing

[33] Canotilho (2003), pp. 1255-1257.

[34] Duque (2019), pp. 209–210.

[35] Ascensão (2013), p. 95.

unilateral action and legal protection, but also to addressing the types of conduct involved. This is the purpose of the following discussion.

4.3 Criteria for the Control of Unilateral Protection

The proposal of general criteria for controlling self-protection assumes material, formal, objective, subjective, and temporal limits, considering the variables involved in this analysis. These aspects are evaluated in consideration of previous criticisms, as well as how unilateral action is addressed by law. International legal experience shows that the general criteria set by statute also face issues of applicability, interpretation, and scope—whether because they are relativized in specific cases, constructed around vague concepts, or lack a unified approach to self-help.

The clause 'without breach of peace,' used in section 9–609 of the Uniform Commercial Code of the United States, demonstrates substantial jurisprudential controversy,[36] over the meaning of this restriction, which ranges from the prohibition of using physical force against the debtor to the banning of forced entry into the home, personal injury to the debtor, damage to property other than that pursued by the creditor, or excessive zeal in conduct.[37] The condition imposed by § 229 of the BGB authorizes self-protection when assistance from authorities cannot be obtained promptly and if there is a risk that exercising the claim will be significantly obstructed or hindered without immediate action. [38] The most recent scholarship varies regarding the scope of this provision, with some opinions advocating assessing objective circumstances to determine whether it would be reasonable to perform public actions authorities,[39] the insignificance of such limitations in light of the principle of autonomy of will[40] and the reconsideration of these conditions within the context of modern situations, different from those in which the article was written initially conceived.[41]

Although it can be said that there is no general rule in Brazil governing the control of self-protection by public and private entities, but rather a set of norms to be combined for this purpose, it is necessary to assess how these norms regulate unilateral conduct. Such acts are unilateral because they depend solely on and consist only of the expression of will by the party issuing them. Self-protection constitutes a form of unilateral protection because it represents the safeguarding of interests that have been infringed or threatened, dependent solely on the manifestation of the active party, with the characteristic that it projects itself into the legal sphere of another, who is thereby subjected to it. This relationship between the unilateral nature of legal

[36] Winship (2019), pp. 31–35. Brandon et al. (1984), pp. 916–919.

[37] Mcrobert (2012), pp. 588–591. Korybut (2014), pp. 273–275.

[38] Repgen (2019) § 229, p. 953.

[39] Larenz and Wolf (2004), pp. 345–348.

[40] Beurskens (2017), pp. 298–299.

[41] Möslein (2018), p. 220.

protection and its effects on the passive party must be permeated by the guarantees that only due process of law can ensure, so that the criteria set out below represent the specific and adaptable conditions of this guarantee as applied to self-protection.

Despite the advantages already highlighted regarding the unilateral nature of legal protection, it also presents several drawbacks. The assessment of whether an interest has been infringed or threatened is usually made exclusively by the active party, who is therefore responsible for ascertaining these facts to decide on the measures to be adopted. The absence of a phase for verifying and certifying the facts increases the risk of arbitrary conduct and, consequently, diminishes the legitimacy of unilateral protection.[42] The imbalance of power between the active and passive parties, marked by asymmetries or vulnerabilities, may confer greater powers of protection on the former to the detriment of the latter. All of this is associated with the intended outcome, which is to impose the result of such legal protection on the passive party.

Furthermore, one must not overlook the suspicion surrounding unilateral action, which manifests itself in various ways.[43] It has served to distance individuals from the State, because only the latter would have the power to act directly. At the same time, the former could not enforce their acts because "they should submit them to judicial authority for consideration". [44] It is a criterion for identifying the nullity of contractual clauses in consumer relations, as outlined in Article 51, items X, XI, and XIII of the Brazilian Consumer Protection Code. It also affects the assessment of invalidity and the evaluation of evidence produced with the participation of only one interested party.

Therefore, for all the benefits of self-protection to be realized, it must be tied to a legitimate means of dispute resolution. When the active party takes responsibility for enforcing, coercively, the protection, realization, or satisfaction of infringed or threatened rights interests, [45] their conduct may be classified under common characteristics.[46] By virtue of the same purpose, which is to obtain legal protection, this serves as the foundation for establishing criteria for controlling self-protection. It presents two assumptions previously discussed in Chapter 1. One is the occurrence or potential for an unlawful act. The infringement or threat to an interest is essential for characterizing the power of unilateral protection and distinguishing it from other types, such as normative, managerial, or supervisory powers. Therefore, the active party must be aware of this condition to prearrange their actions and identify the nature of the power being exercised. The other is the possibility of unilateral action. In other words, given the type of infringement or threat, there must be room for unilateral protection; otherwise, the action would be improper from the start. Thus, under the material criterion, the discussion focuses on how unilateral protection should be exercised. Under the formal criterion, it concerns what constitutes and shapes the exercise of unilateral protection. Under the objective criterion, it relates to

---

[42] Hanau (2004), pp. 100–101.

[43] Lucca (2024), pp. 309–310.

[44] Cretella Júnior (1963), pp. 17–18.

[45] Kelsen (1992), p. 40.

[46] Loterstein (2013), pp. 1372-1373.

the extent to which unilateral protection will be used. Under the subjective criterion, it considers against whom unilateral protection is directed. And under the temporal criterion, it addresses when it will be employed.

4.3.1 *Material Criterion: Correlation Between the Type of Infringement or Threat and the Form of Unilateral Protection.*

The first criterion for self-protection involves examining the link between the intended unilateral protection and the type of infringement or threat faced by the active party. [47] Using the example of state judicial proceedings, congruence requires the judge to decide within the limits of what has been requested, which, in most cases, allows for an objective comparison between the subject matter of the proceedings and the subject matter of the decision.[48] Congruent judicial relief is that which resolves the disputed matter as defined. In arbitration, the arbitrator is likewise required to limit their decision to the dispute as presented by the parties.[49] In consensual dispute resolution, it's unlikely that the parties will agree on issues outside the scope of the dispute, which, although possible in theory, would distort or go beyond the bilateral or multilateral nature of such processes. [50]

This brief overview demonstrates that legal remedies must be proportionate to both the extent of the harm or threat identified and the means of resolving the dispute. In cases of unilateral relief, the need for correlation comes not only from comparing it with other forms of legal protection but also from the requirements of the legal system, which sets boundaries for individuals' actions and the State, [51] such as fundamental rights, the requirement for proportionality between means and ends in applying rules, the adaptive nature of due process of law, and the supplementary use of provisions from the Brazilian Code of Civil Procedure concerning the enforcement and satisfaction of interests. Correlation is, therefore, a rule specifically relevant to legal remedies and, more broadly, a fundamental principle of the Theory of Dispute Resolution.

This correlation in unilateral relief is established between the infringed or threatened interest and the protection, satisfaction, or realization that the active party must

[47] Dagnino (1983), pp. 94–95.

[48] Siqueira (2021), p. 92.

[49] Dinamarco (2022), pp. 216–221.

[50] Godinho (2022), pp. 180–181.

[51] A decision of the Supreme Court of Justice of Portugal has recognised retention as a form of self-help for the purpose of securing obligations, as follows, which is relevant to the argument advanced in the text: " *This does not, however, preclude the* ius retentionis *of the defendants, given the legal connection between the obligation to deliver and the claim to which they are entitled, both arising from the same legal relationship.*" (Supreme Court of Justice, Case 662/09.3TVPRT. P1. S1, Rapporteur António Piçarra, 7th Section, decided on 14/12/2016).

provide through their actions in relation to the passive party. It must be kept in mind that certain forms of self-help may skip a cognitive phase and, for this reason, constitute acts of enforcement of the claim.[52] Thus, two factors are essential in this assessment: the characteristics of the harm or threat involved and the nature of the relief sought. Unlike other types, unilateral relief heavily depends on the specific circumstances that manifest these factors, due to the lack of a general normative framework governing such actions. Therefore, these should be regarded as interpretive and evaluative guidelines for the active party's conduct, helping to identify the necessary correlation in practice. This highlights the greater complexity of such an assessment, considering the various implications these requirements may have, as well as the burden on the active party to ensure that their legal rights have not been infringed.[53]

Regarding the characteristics of the harm or threat, it is important to determine whether it affects a person or property, whether it occurs in urgent situations, whether there is a contractual or non-contractual relationship between the parties, or, more generally, what legal consequence it has in relation to the active party's legal rights. Objectively, these characteristics help define the nature of the claim in terms of scope and the need for protection. In this context, it is crucial to establish whether the harm or threat involves rights to performance, formative rights, or other legal positions, which will, in turn, indicate the appropriate course of action for relief. Dinamarco summarized these observations as the connection of "each type of remedy – or each procedural form of relief – with the various situations complained of and the solution provided by substantive law."[54] Although this statement primarily focuses on judicial relief, it does not weaken the criterion under discussion, since the legal consequences of the harm or threat determine the required form of relief, including unilateral relief.[55]

Therefore, correlation is established in this context concerning the type of legal remedy, and in cases of self-help, there are significant consequences for failing to observe this duty. When developing this requirement, it is argued that the dispositive principle would guide the active party's freedom to activate the judiciary. At the same time, the court would be obliged to decide within the scope of the proceedings' subject matter. The duty perspective also appears in unilateral relief, as it reflects the active party's obligation to act within necessary limits to protect the infringed or threatened legal interest. Breaching this duty raises questions about the legitimacy of self-help: correlation may be broken if the active party acts beyond what is necessary to satisfy, protect, or realize the infringed or threatened interest, similar to the phenomenon of an *ultra petita* decision; Another breach involves acting to achieve a result different from the intended purpose of unilateral relief, resulting in a consequence similar to an *extra petita* decision.[56] As highlighted in the first chapter, self-protection coexists with

[52] Murino (2010), p. 4.

[53] Carvalho Filho (2011), pp. 79–80.

[54] Dinamarco (2020), p. 186.

[55] Sinel (2009), p. 131.

[56] Barletta (2012), pp. 14–18.

limitations that may make it appropriate only for resolving part of a dispute, leading to its classification as partial. Therefore, when analyzing the duty of correlation, the behavior of the active subject who seeks to protect only part of the harm or threat does not constitute a violation, either because unilateral protection is not fully applicable or because there is some discretionary margin regarding the extent of legal protections protection.[57]

To illustrate this criterion, consider the following example: a vehicle engaged in unauthorized passenger transport between municipalities was seized by the administrative authority, which required the payment of traffic fines, fees, and removal expenses as a condition for the vehicle's release. When the administrative act was challenged in court, the local court ruled that the requirement was lawful, noting that disembarking passengers would not be enough to fix the irregularity, despite the provision of STJ[58] Precedent 510. This court, when considering the case, applied the precedent to determine that this ground for seizure should not be connected to the payment of those amounts, given the limits of the penalty established by Article 231, item VIII of the Brazilian Traffic Code (CTB).[59] In such cases, the Public Administration, in violation of legality, attempts to use its power of self-enforcement to exceed the legal limits set for sanctions and, as a result, extend public self-protection to the collection of amounts not covered by the prescribed penalty.

Therefore, the combination of rules that impose restrictions and consequences for abusive exercises of the right to self-protection indicates the presence of a substantive criterion embodied in the duty of correlation. This duty requires the active subject to limit unilateral protection both in terms of quantity—using the extent as a parameter—and in terms of quality—according to the intended outcomes—to the nature of the harm or threat suffered.

4.3.2 *Formal Criterion: Procedural Guarantees as an Incentive for Self-Protection*

To address the limitations of self-protection, procedural guarantees serve as a crucial criterion for legitimizing the actions of the active subject. They embody the specific way in which protection is expected to be provided through due process. [60] The concern with the rationality and security offered by procedural guarantees in both state and private functions is longstanding[61]. Still, the central point here is their importance not in preventing, but in encouraging self-protection. At first glance, this analysis might lead to the quick conclusion that procedural guarantees and unilateral

[57] Candeias (2023), pp. 910–911.

[58] The STJ is the highest court for matters of federal law

[59] STJ, AgInt in AREsp No. 1,371,903/SP, Justice Assusete Magalhães, Second Chamber, decided on 7/5/2019.

[60] Medauar (2021), p. 21.

[61] Fazzalari (1975), p. 9.

protection are incompatible, especially when considering this duality in light of the canons already criticized in this study. On the contrary, the goal is to show how procedural guarantees are necessary to legitimize and strengthen the active subject's unilateral efforts to protect infringed or threatened rights interests.[62] The context in which legal protection is exercised, whether or not it involves the State, must be evaluated in light of due process, both from the perspective of adaptation and conformity, considering the realization of protection, satisfaction, or enforcement of a subject's interest against another.[63]

From the perspective of public self-protection, applying fundamental rights directly helps to see procedural guarantees as a way of controlling power, since "state power, in its various forms and manifestations, entails some restriction of individual rights and freedoms."[64] At the core of this type of action is a concept central to this discussion: procedural guarantees are meant to regulate and guide how power is exercised and manifested, often promoting the subjection of others. The procedural guarantees of the Public Administration, established by laws such as Brazilian Law No. 9784/99 and various other regulations that impose limits on state powers for issuing and carrying out administrative acts, should function as a method to control and shape all decision-making activity,[65] Especially when the goal is the unilateral imposition of its content, public self-protection generally comes after the Administration and those affected exercise procedural rights and duties, which enables cognitive activity before legal actions protection.

Recognizing the existence of multiple configurations and objectives of administrative proceedings, many of these are characterized as exercises of self-protection due to the overlap between the adjudicating authority and the authority responsible for safeguarding infringed or threatened interests. Conceived as the method by which an administrative decision must be made and implemented in light of the Rule of Law, with greater rigor, procedural guarantees must be applied to ensure the legitimacy of unilateral actions remedies, [66] through the identification of the competent authority, the occurrence of the unlawful act, the perpetrator, and the appropriate sanction, while guaranteeing the right to defense, adversarial proceedings, and the production of evidence. This constitutional review also serves to determine whether self-help is genuinely suitable for protecting fundamental rights or if another model—primarily based on heteronomous adjudication—should be preferred, considering structural flaws and deficiencies in the exercise of unilateral public power. [67]

When the exercise of power is directed toward legal remedies, it is possible that the same goal of preventing State arbitrariness also applies to limiting private arbitrariness. In other words, procedural guarantees in private activities are essential to legitimize a range of actions, especially those aimed at protecting, satisfying, or

[62] Alexander (1998), p. 21.

[63] Grinover (2018), p. 4.

[64] Marques Neto (2007), p. 264.

[65] Sundfeld (2000), p. 19.

[66] Schirato (2010), p. 17.

[67] Bomfim and Fidalgo (2008), p. 276.

realizing interests based on one's own initiative to the detriment of a passive party.[68]

This does not challenge the idea that fundamental rights can still apply indirectly in private relations. The purpose of proceduralizing these relations is not to exclude rules about self-help power, but to regulate it through proper legal process. This regulation aims to ensure its appropriate use in situations where the law offers limited protection, or to assist litigants in proving unlawful acts and maintaining equal arms.[69] Indeed, for both the State and private parties, procedural guarantees are also essential to help the active party overcome the burden of knowing they are facing a genuine case of harm or threat to interests that justify self-help, as well as to enable the passive party to act and respond in advance or even voluntarily comply with the active party's actions claim.[70]

Thus, although the remedy may be unilateral, this does not mean that the process leading to it must also be characterized by unilateralism.[71] The process from identifying harm or threat, choosing the means to address it, and the moment of action should, whenever possible, be guided by procedural guarantees. Since proceduralizing is a concrete expression of due process of law, it involves giving the passive party the chance to be informed and to respond,[72] including to demonstrate that the facts have been wrongly classified as a case of self-help or to suggest a less burdensome means for their legal sphere.[73]

The combination of these factors helps define the cognitive development needed to strengthen the legitimacy of self-help. The formal criterion of legitimation aims, before any unilateral enforcement, satisfaction, or protection of an interest, to uphold guarantees that have been universalized for other forms of dispute resolution and which, a fortiori, must be present in self-help.[74] The benefits it provides cannot be separated from the balancing effect of protecting rights based on due process of law. That is why many restrictions established by case law originate from the lack of procedural guarantees in implementing unilateral remedies.

From the perspective of insufficient protection by the rules, due process of law operates as a complement in the face of omissions or ambiguities. Interpreting such rules in accordance with the Constitution in these cases enables their application to fulfill the intended purpose, while also ensuring the necessary protections for litigants.[75] It should be noted that the formal criterion analyzed here must be applied proportionally to the imbalance between the active and passive parties. For example, in employment, consumer, or public authority relations, which are characterized by

---

[68] Romano (2021), pp. 219–221.

[69] Renner (2021), p. 492.

[70] Bachman (2006), pp. 126–127.

[71] Lichtman (2004), p. 43.

[72] Yarshell and Rodrigues (2020), p. 370.

[73] Verkuil (2005), p. 968.

[74] Frazão (2022), p. 593.

[75] Hanau (2004), pp. 102–103.

certain inequalities and asymmetries, it is justified to demand, with even greater strictness, the protection provided by procedural guarantees before unilaterally proceeding with remedies.

Looking specifically at the range of rules governing public or private powers of self-help, it becomes clear that such protection is inadequate for exercising unilateral remedies. Although there are instances where the legislator has aimed to guarantee the right of defense, such as in the exclusion of a partner (article 1085, sole paragraph of the Brazilian Civil Code) or a member (article 57 of the same Civil Code), in many other cases, this has not been the case. The numerous rules on retention, for example, are generally not accompanied by the procedures and limits for their implementation, which is why due process is necessary to ensure that the creditor's actions are lawful, often involving procedural steps such as notifying the debtor, thereby enabling a possible response.

Resorting to heteronomous protection characterized by this feature is also a significant alternative. Given the burden on the active party to ensure they are acting within a situation that allows for self-help, the identification of the essential elements of this dispute resolution method can be performed by a third party, thereby ensuring the passive party's participation.

Contrary to what intuitive reasoning might suggest, the role of the third party is not limited to controlling unilateral acts. This impartial and neutral party may also serve as a certifier of the wrongful act and the extent of the damages suffered by the active party, which will guide them regarding the scope for self-help and the appropriate means available. Some of the previously mentioned burdens are reflected in cognitive activities that the active party would be unable to perform or would perform inadequately. Given the uncertainties resulting from cognitive deficiencies, it is in the interests of those involved in the dispute to eliminate doubts about the configuration and nature of the facts that could lead to unilateral protection, which, in many cases, will also trigger other forms of legal protection. In this context, the idea of pre-constituting evidence regarding the facts is relevant not only for determining the admissibility of self-help but also for the admissibility of any other method suitable for resolving the dispute. Therefore, Yarshell emphasizes the importance of such a pre-constitution, as "it enables the parties to identify the relevant aspects of the dispute and consequently seek the best solution" with "an emphasis on party self-determination." [76]

For all these reasons, Article 381 of the Brazilian Code of Civil Procedure plays a crucial role in legitimizing self-help. The early collection of evidence, aimed at supporting the parties regarding the occurrence and extent of wrongful acts, their causes, and those responsible, will be essential in indicating the feasibility of self-help or the preference for another dispute resolution method. Subsection II of this provision introduces a significant change in the regulation of self-help. First, because the interest in pre-constituting evidence and certifying these facts is proportional to the interest in using self-help. Second, because the risks to both the active party and

[76] Yarshell (2009), p. 299.

the passive party are clearly reduced if, in court, the viability of unilateral protection is established, offering them insights into the likelihood of success, including in any future review of the actions taken. Third, because the function of preemptively gathering evidence aligns with the role that a declaratory action could serve in supporting the enforcement of a claim, in whole or in part, through self-help.[77] All of this becomes even more relevant as the use of procedural and certification structures for unilateral protection increases. This includes arbitration, dispute resolution boards, the appointment of third-party certifiers, or certification and fact-recognition clauses. Such developments have led Italian legal scholars to propose the hypothesis of bilateral self-help,[78] but it is nothing more than a declaratory legal act.

However, self-help is not always illegitimate when it occurs without procedural guarantees. In some cases, the formal criteria cannot be met or must be postponed due to situations involving urgency, risk, or danger that justify unilateral action. Examples include self-defense, necessity, and the exercise of police powers that require immediate measures to prevent or address unlawful acts, among others. The existence of these factors justifies reducing or excluding procedural guarantees in favor of immediate unilateral protection, even if persistent issues regarding the understanding of the essential elements remain.[79] A similar logic underpins the reduction of procedural guarantees in favor of granting urgent interim relief. Clearly, such conduct is subject to subsequent review, which is conducted more rigorously to determine whether there was cause and whether the proportionality between means and ends was maintained, or, according to the substantive criterion, whether the correlation was satisfied. This does not mean that the formal criterion will cease to be applied, as it will be examined in light of the objective facts to determine whether its exclusion was justified.

4.3.3 *Objective Criterion: Means Employed to Obtain Unilateral Protection.*

The objective criterion relates to the control of the methods used to achieve unilateral protection.[80] In many cases, this criterion is typically considered part of the proportionality test, which has already been criticized above. Some reasons seem to justify this direct connection, such as the inappropriate adoption of the U.S. doctrine that equates private acts of self-help with public acts through the state action theory, and the confusion of the term "proportionality" with just a simple ratio or a reasonable application of rules based on the specific circumstances case; [81] or, furthermore,

[77] Schinemann (2023), pp. 133–135. Leite (2024), pp. 431–432.

[78] Betti (1959), p. 533. Ricciardoni (2011),pp. 64–67. Montecchiari (2019), pp. 114–115.

[79] Silva (1967), pp. 14–15, Lisbon. Nurra (2022), pp. 35–40.

[80] Gold (2020), pp. 179–180.

[81] Brito (1994), p. 85. D'Acunto (2018), pp. 45–49. Fantini (2024), pp. 1771–78. Mouzalas (2024), p. 127.

a common belief that self-help always requires enforcement and, as a result, will impose personal or proprietary restrictions on the passive party.[82] Although proportionality is important for evaluating the fairness of unilateral remedies, it is not always necessary. As a principle-based approach, it tends to influence the criteria outlined in this chapter where relevant. The idea here is to determine whether the means used by the active party are appropriate for consistently protecting the rights that have been violated or threatened.

Control based on this criterion encounters few issues when self-help relies solely on the active party's expression of will. The action used to secure unilateral protection is the act of declaration itself, which is enough to realize the power. For example, consider the explicit resolutive clause or the revocation of a license by a public authority when an individual fails to meet statutory health requirements. In these cases, the objective criterion is met easily, as the method to protect the interest is the volitional act itself,[83] without prejudice to reviewing any significant acts that follow that declaration. This does not mean the objective criterion loses its significance; it remains relevant and can, for example, support a finding of abuse of right, abuse of power, or bad faith if the declaration does not align with the context of the actual or potential unlawful act, or if the means were not appropriate for the intended result due to some defect present.

The scenario changes if unilateral protection relies on material and specific means for its implementation, especially as seen in self-help involving enforcement actions. As previously noted, many of the rules governing self-help are not comprehensive regarding how such conduct is carried out and with what tools. The result is not only the need to provide procedural guarantees for these actions but also to evaluate them on a case-by-case basis to ensure the objective criteria are met. Therefore, it is important to establish guidelines for reviewing the legality of such conduct. [84] and, in the absence of a general framework for unilateral extrajudicial enforcement, it becomes necessary to consider the rules of the Brazilian Code of Civil Procedure as supplementary or subsidiary parameters in these situations (Article 15), both from the perspective of the active party and the passive party, along with other rules of substantive law that support the logic underpinning procedural law.

Although Article 797, caput, of the Brazilian Code of Civil Procedure emphasizes that enforcement is carried out in the interest of the creditor, Article 805, caput, of the same Code of Civil Procedure requires that enforcement be effected by the least burdensome means, as the "core of the debtor's right." [85] This balance is achieved by authorizing enforcement through the least burdensome methods possible, which should be understood as a general rule applicable to all civil enforcement proceedings, [86] including those that are extrajudicial and unilateral. By selecting very different

[82] Klingbeil (2019), p. 185. Bongiorno (1984), pp. 52–53. Raimo (2018), pp. 68–69. Follieri (2023), p. 97.

[83] Belmonte (2023), pp. 106–107.

[84] Carvalho Filho (2011), p. 81.

[85] Rodrigues (2021), p. 63.

[86] Alves (2004), p. 10.

situations but with a common goal of satisfaction, it is possible to support the idea of carrying out enforcement only through methods that are least burdensome to the passive party, as seen in self-defense, where there is a duty to use only the necessary and proportionate measures,[87] or in accepting the use of the least burdensome means for exercising police powers.[88] The goal of applying the principle of least burdensome means in enforcement is not to avoid, modify, or prevent the outcome desired by the creditor, but to ensure that this outcome is reached without unnecessary sacrifice by the debtor.[89]

The scope of this principle's protection lies in the means, not the end. Therefore, the idea of coherence between means and ends is essential in setting the limits of self-help, especially considering the legal or contractual lack of detail regarding how unilateral remedies are to be carried out. This principle applies to self-help because (i) it reflects a specific aspect of the protection ideals rooted in due process of law, concerning how subjection should be imposed; (ii) it requires the creditor to choose, among equally effective options, those that are least burdensome to satisfy the debtor's claim. In this case, by stating that the judge "shall order" that the process be conducted in the least burdensome way, Article 805 of the Brazilian Code of Civil Procedure mandates that the responsible party—here, the active subject of self-help—who can set these means, must select them based on how much they interfere with the legal rights of the passive subject; (iii) it advances civilizational progress in personal or property enforcement, which must be followed in situations where, generally, there is no impartial third party to verify the legitimacy of executive actions in advance acts;[90] and (iv) it must be required with particular rigor in enforcement proceedings where such means are not pre-defined or specified by law or by agreement between the parties.

Thus, since the objective criterion for controlling self-help is based on the methods used to pursue unilateral protection, the principle of minimizing the burden on the passive subject guides the assessment of the active subject's conduct. These guidelines apply to all actions carried out using means such as objects, legal techniques like set-off or retention, conduct intended to establish the legal position resulting from the non-performance of a contract, acts to protect the public interest in response to unlawful conduct by a private party, and so on. Within this scope, these guidelines serve both an interpretive function, guiding interested parties on the appropriate means to use, and an applicative function, serving as mechanisms to apply the objective criterion when regulating self-help. They can be summarized as follows:

a. The methods used must be legal. The active party cannot resort to illegal means to gain unilateral protection, such as coercion, threats, assaults, or any other improper way of exerting personal or proprietary control over the passive party subject. [91] Illegality may pertain to the means themselves (e.g., a firearm without

---

[87] Miragem (2021), p. 46

[88] Binenbojm (2020), p. 116.

[89] Didier Jr et al. (2017), p. 79.

[90] Dinamarco (2024), pp. 55–56.

[91] Díaz Alabart (2007), p. 23.

proper registration, debt collection teams that harass the debtor, etc.), the method used (e.g., ambushes, falsifications, etc.), or the outcome produced by the means (e.g., harm to physical, psychological, or moral integrity, unlawful restriction of property or liberty, etc.). For instance, tax authorities are prohibited from seizing goods as a means of coercing the taxpayer into paying taxes or for the self-satisfaction of the assessed amount, as reflected in Supreme Federal Court Precedent 323. Similarly, a private individual entering a neighboring property to recover items or animals that happen to be there (Article 1313, II of the Brazilian Civil Code) may not do so by means of breaking, threats, assaults, invasions, or the use of excessive force.

b. The means used must not worsen existing disparities or inequalities in legal relationships that are already marked by an imbalance between the active and passive parties. The active party should not employ methods involving self help as an additional means to increase its power at the expense of the passive party, especially in situations where there is a disparity in information, economic resources, or legal status. This does not mean that self-help is outright prohibited in such legal relationships. Instead, it should be used as a tool that does not deepen the imbalance or even helps promote some level of equality between the parties, such as ensuring the bilateral nature of this power or allowing the weaker party to use self-help against the stronger. And so forth.[92] An example demonstrating the appropriateness of unilateral protection without worsening asymmetries or inequalities is the exercise of the right of withdrawal by the consumer (Article 49 of the Brazilian Consumer Defense Code) when the product or service is defective or faulty.

c. The means used must not be designed to reduce or eliminate the passive subject's ability to respond or defend themselves. Although self-help is a way of resolving disputes by subjugating the passive subject, this does not mean they cannot react, defend themselves, or prevent such subjugation. The means should be suitable to allow unilateral protection without removing all opportunities for the passive subject to act. The focus on procedural guarantees is meant to ensure the passive subject can effectively participate, including preventing their subjugation. Therefore, measures that prevent any form of action, whether before, during, or after the active subject's acts, tend to be inadmissible. [93] For example, one might cite a digital platform that uses algorithms to instantly remove a user for creating a fake profile, without giving the user a chance to be heard or challenge the decision within the same environment. While judicial review of the removal is possible, it does not alter the manner in which the action was taken, particularly since the platform controls the process algorithm.

d. Situations involving urgency, risk, or danger may excuse the above requirements. When the active subject's response is necessary to prevent personal or proprietary harm, the evaluation of means and ends is affected by these circumstances. For

[92] Griener et al. (2017), pp. 1120-1126, 2017.

[93] Matri (2017), p. 25.

example, it may be recognized that the active subject acted in legitimate self-defense to stop an attempted homicide using a firearm that was not registered with the proper authorities. Additionally, a public official required to disperse a crowd, using tear gas, a group linked to a specific organized supporters' group engaged in overtly criminal activities.

e. The active party must follow the means established by law or agreement. This limitation is important because it introduces objectivity in both the conduct and the control of the actions taken. The enforcement process outlined in Brazilian Law 9514/1997 authorizes the creditor to auction the property they hold in accordance with the procedure specified in Article 27, while allowing for any surplus amounts to be preserved in their favor debtor.[94] A similar reasoning applies when the parties contractually specify how unilateral enforcement will be carried out, which is common in highly complex contracts that include custodial entities, mechanisms for dividend redemption, asset deposits, and their use for settling claims. The parties' agreement may regulate these methods, and any restrictions on fundamental rights are subject to the proportionality test. Lastly, the parties' contractual freedom to determine the means of reaching the assets or the person results in a restriction of fundamental rights; therefore, the assessment of suitability here will be subject to the proportionality test due to the conflict between the principles mentioned above.[95]

4.3.4 *Subjective Criterion: Limitation on Personal Submission*

The subjective criterion is directly tied to the limits of submission and personal disposition for enforcing unilateral measures. It is often claimed that the availability of assets is broad, also including property protected by exemption rules seizure. Following the view that these rules have tangible effects [96]and, therefore, would also serve as limits to unilateral enforcement,[97] it is important to consider another perspective regarding acts directed against individuals. One goal in defining the scope of self-help regulations is to prevent excessive personal submission, whether physical or related to fundamental freedoms. There are common cases where the active party acts in these areas to fulfill their claims without adhering to proper standards of conduct, such as in the arbitrary deactivation of users on digital platforms who rely on them for work, like drivers or couriers, or in instances of severe police violence that result in violations of physical integrity during an arrest in progress. The need for a deeper

[94] Yarshell (2024), pp. 138–141.

[95] Silva (2021), p. 120.

[96] Rodrigues (2023a), pp. 12–16.

[97] Follieri (2016), pp. 31–32.

examination of the subjective criterion is also because personal restrictions from self-help are just as common, if not more so, than in judicial contexts of enforcement,[98] not only as a means of inducement or coercion, but also for satisfaction.[99]

Some clarifications are needed regarding the relationship between unilateral enforcement and personal submission. The development of enforcement, considering the attempt to humanize it through patrimonial liability, was neither swift nor absolute.[100] Scholars dedicated to the study of compulsory enforcement have observed, over the centuries, a fluctuation[101] between models that are more or less permissive of personal submission.[102] Currently, the possibility of direct action by the active party against the passive party shows the existence of hybrid models, where both patrimonial and personal elements are present, whether inside or outside of court.[103]

Although patrimonial liability prevails, enforcement actions against the person have not been eliminated. This is illustrated by examples such as direct enforcement to secure the search and seizure of minors, removal of individuals to execute orders for recovering possession, imposition of sanctions that restrict rights in sanctioning proceedings, and indirect enforcement methods, including civil imprisonment or restrictions on freedom of movement through the seizure of passports. [104] In the field of self-help, conduct aimed at satisfying the claim of the active party will, in many situations, involve a human being as the recipient, both to prevent and to remedy harm or threat. In addition to the examples above, others already mentioned reflect the primary goal of preventing or avoiding the actions of the passive party and, consequently, acting upon their personal sphere, which includes physical integrity and non-pecuniary rights, such as personality rights, subsistence rights etc.[105]

Unlike what happens in judicial proceedings, where a variety of proprietary and financial measures may prevent or discourage the offender from committing an unlawful act, the use of such measures in self-help depends on a mutual agreement between the parties, on the active party's desire to induce the passive party to voluntarily fulfill the obligation, or, considering the circumstances, may be impossible. Respecting the extent of the passive party's freedom, the aim to ultimately enforce personal measures through the courts should also be reflected outside the judicial process, based on factual compatibility. This conclusion can be reached through a specific application of the principle of minimal burden in enforcement actions, especially when such actions target the person and the fundamental freedoms of the passive party.[106]

---

98 De Belvis (2018), pp. 171–172.

99 Talamini (2022), p. 34.

100 Moraes (2009), pp. 60–64.

101 Hess (2010), pp. 41–43.

102 Marino (2024), pp. 329–330.

103 Kenett (2021), pp. 36–40.

104 Minami (2020), pp. 242–244.

105 Patterson (2019), pp. 68–69.

106 Alves (2004), p. 15.

The similarity with what has long occurred in the judicial enforcement of obligations to do, not to do, or to deliver a specific item, or, more recently, in indirect enforcement measures for paying a sum, is not coincidental.[107] The proposal of a model or guidelines for interpreting and controlling self-help resulting in personal submission is both a consequence of applying fundamental rights, based on previously established premises, and of infra-constitutional rules related to protecting the passive party. Therefore, the example given by Grinover shows how the objective criterion, with pre-established means, helps fulfill the subjective criterion: the failure to fulfill an obligation to do or not do allows the creditor, in urgent cases, to perform or undo the act themselves or to have a third party do so, both options without any personal interference with the passive party (sole paragraphs of Articles 249 and 251 of the Brazilian Civil Code).[108]

The appropriateness of unilateral personal enforcement must consider the legal interest pursued by the active party, the extent of the personal sphere affected, and the degree of interference required. This approach aligns with the restrictions placed on the passive party and evaluates whether it is necessary to impact their physical integrity or limit their non-pecuniary rights. Therefore, the subjective criterion is mainly guided by proportionality, taking into account both the boundaries accepted for the parties' control over fundamental rights and the limits to direct action when there is no agreement between them. [109]

Since the earliest stages of its development, the issue of personal enforcement has highlighted the limits of when it is acceptable to act on a person in pursuit of another's interests, [110] so that today, the above factors demonstrate the transition from a stage of objectification of the human being to a stage of limitations on freedoms.[111] It is in this context that the guidelines for applying the subjective criterion are set based:

a. Harm to the physical integrity and life of the passive party is exceptional and justified only in specific circumstances that exclude unlawfulness. Permission to act in this way is limited to situations authorized by the legal system, such as self-defense, necessity, or a state of siege, where the only way to prevent or counter the passive party's conduct is to use force against them. Even in such cases, any outcome resulting in injury or death must be consistent with the facts and the active party's lack of alternative actions. Factors such as urgent need for action, urgency, and the inability to clarify the facts due to inherent danger naturally influence the legitimacy assessment of self-help from a subjective perspective, considering the outcome. By demonstrating a fundamental right to personal protection, Roxin and Greco emphasize the importance of legislation that establishes a general objective of prevention by permitting "any necessary

[107] Talamini (2003), p. 274.

[108] Grinover (2007), p. 19.

[109] Adamy (2011), pp. 76–83.

[110] Justo (1993), pp. 277–282.

[111] Peppe (2009), pp. 157–158.

defense," including personal defense, but with limits guided by the "preservation of rights.".[112]

b. The restriction on the passive party's non-pecuniary freedoms must be appropriate to protect the legal interest of the active party. This means that the restriction must be justified by the interest it aims to safeguard, ensuring that the limitation is not more burdensome to the passive party than the benefit gained by the active party. The evaluation of appropriateness is based on an "empirical relationship"[113] Between this restriction and this benefit, as established in judicial proceedings, by limiting the aggressor's freedom to approach or visit the same places as the victim, as provided in Law No. 11.340/2006. In the context of self-help, this can be exemplified by a supermarket chain imposing restrictions on entering into new contracts with defaulting suppliers to prevent future contractual risks, or by excluding a party from a public tender due to irregular tax issues.
c. Preference should be given to proprietary measures or less restrictive personal measures in asymmetric legal relationships. This guideline aims to preserve fundamental non-proprietary freedoms related to the legal relationship. Instead of directly impacting these freedoms and worsening the imbalance favoring the party with self-help power, it is better to use proprietary or milder personal restrictions. For example, blocking or excluding drivers' and couriers' profiles due to infractions illustrates this principle. First, the nature of this work creates dependence on the platform's model. Second, the activity is essential for the worker's livelihood but is largely self-regulated under a specific regime. Third, blocking or excluding users directly affects their work-related freedom, as it is a sanction outlined in the platform's terms of use. To balance this asymmetric relationship, options might include limiting the number of rides per day for a set time or charging a fine based on a reasonable percentage of the economic benefit the worker gains from each ride, without stopping the user's right to challenge the automated decision (Article 20 of the LGPD).[114]
d. Restrictions on non-proprietary freedoms must be evaluated based on subjective interference through the lens of the proportionality test. This guideline is especially relevant when the freedom for self-help stems from a contractual waiver of a fundamental right, in accordance with the binding order between the parties.[115] The goal is to reconcile the authorization for unilateral protection with models where such waiver is paired with varying levels of autonomy for the contracting parties, as seen in different scenarios such as adhesion contracts in consumer relations or commercial contracts between large companies with extensive technical knowledge and broad negotiating power terms.

---

[112] Roxin and Greco (2020), p. 767.

[113] Ávila (2013), p. 187.

[114] STJ, REsp No. 2,135,783/DF, Justice Nancy Andrighi, Third Chamber, judged on 18/6/2024.

[115] Novais (2022), p. 266.

4.3.5 Temporal Criterion: Timing of the Exercise of Unilateral Protection

The temporal criterion helps determine the right time to exercise self-help. It considers both preventive and repressive aspects of unilateral protection to assess whether actions taken prevent or correct the unlawful act. The importance of this criterion lies in identifying when the active party acts in self-help, taking into account the risks of unilateral judgment. The classification of whether the act involves inhibiting or removing the unlawful act or the damage is not limited to judicial protection; it also concerns the categorization of the appropriateness of legal remedies, including unilateral protection. In this context, the criterion is set by pinpointing the moment when the harm or threat to the interest occurred and when the active party took action to address it. [116]

From the perspective of preventive unilateral protection, the active party is required to take specific actions aimed at preventing or reducing the risk of an unlawful act. The challenges associated with this approach mainly relate to identifying the actual risk or threat that justifies protecting an interest. This process is similar to what is needed for repressive protection, but the necessity to foresee potential future events adds an extra layer of difficulty. To justify preventive self-help, there must be clear signs of a potentially harmful intent by the passive party, just as would be necessary if such signs needed to be proven in court.[117]

Therefore, the temporal criterion, when used for controlling preventive protection, will require evidence of this threat context or risk.[118] The certification, which would also be relevant through heteronomous mechanisms as previously mentioned, can be applied in this context. In this context, a reduction in assets that could jeopardize or cast doubt on the contracting party's fulfillment of the obligation gives the other party the right to suspend performance until the situation is resolved or adequate security is provided, as outlined in Article 477 of the Brazilian Civil Code. Many contracts include acceleration clauses that are typically based on demonstrating the debtor's financial inability and act as a preemptive contractual remedy for insufficient assets. The destruction of a building and the imminent risk of collapse authorize a neighbor or the Public Administration to demolish it if the owner remains inactive after being notified to carry out the necessary actions.

Furthermore, the temporal criterion will serve to assess (i) whether there were objective grounds justifying unilateral preventive or repressive actions, and (ii) the possible extent of the conduct when exercised, both in cases of non-compliance with positive duties and negative duties of the passive party. There is also another specific function of this criterion: in certain forms of self-help, immediate action by the active party is required, either because the unlawful act or damage is ongoing, or because it is imminent. The authorization to act in self-defense or in a state of necessity is

[116] Gabrielli (2016), pp. 515–516.

[117] Morato García (2011), pp. 390–391.

[118] Bandeira (2022), p. 37.

based on the premise that the reaction of the active party must be as immediate as the danger faced. [119] If this reaction loses its immediacy, self-help will no longer be characterized, and the conduct will tend to be unlawful. For example, note the concern of the legal text in establishing this emergency and immediate reaction by using terms like "imminent danger" (Article 188, II of the Brazilian Civil Code) or "current or imminent" (Article 25 of the Brazilian Penal Code). Additionally, when public security officers respond with force or violence under the guise of strict legal duty, immediacy of action is necessary due to assaults against them or the current or imminent danger they face.[120]

4.4 Consequences of Non-Compliance With Control Criteria

In dispute resolution mechanisms, the line between lawful and unlawful actions is evident at multiple points: in the examination of procedural nullities, in the limits of an arbitrator's authority, and in conflicts of interest between mediators or conciliators and the parties. However, this does not change the structure of legal protection. Jurisdictional protection remains heteronomous even if it is provided by a corrupt judge or a disqualified arbitrator, just as self-composition occurs if the outcome results from the actions of a mediator or conciliator who was unable to perform that role. The same applies to self-help. There will be unilateral protection exercised by the party whose interest is harmed or threatened, even if the conduct is unlawful. These statements aim to dispel the common idea that self-help can only be discussed if it is lawful.[121]

The issue to be addressed lies elsewhere. The above criteria serve as guidelines for assessing and controlling unilateral acts, to determine whether they were performed within the limits authorized by the law system. [122]The use of self-help can lead to very different outcomes. Actions may result in the passive party's death, but as a reason to exclude unlawfulness, the conduct may be considered lawful. Although the act is lawful, it may still lead to compensation, similar to expropriation cases. Even if no damage occurs, civil liability might arise due to the inherent risk of the activity and breach of duty of care. Even without causing harm or needing to compensate the passive party, the conduct of the active party could still be deemed unlawful. For example, a private individual using a restricted firearm to intimidate and deter threats of invasion of their property, without causing harm to the would-be intruder.

Therefore, although it is important to consider the outcome produced or the existence of liability, these will not always be decisive. The unlawfulness of self-help is

---

[119] Bandeira (2022), p. 37.3–65.

[120] STJ, AgRg in HC No. 826,936/MS, Justice Jesuíno Rissato, Sixth Chamber, judged on 4/3/2024.

[121] Silva (1967), pp. 14–15.

[122] Noronha (2016), p. 93.

multifaceted. It may stem from the conduct, the purpose of unilateral protection, the way the active party carries it out, the aggravated imbalance, the excessive personal or proprietary restriction of the passive party, the violation of fundamental rights, the breach of the limits of correlation, or the use of violent means when not authorized.

References

Adamy P (2011) Renúncia a direito fundamental. Malheiros, São Paulo

Alexander L (1998) Are procedural rights derivative substantive rights? Law Philos 17(1):19–42

Alves JCM (2004) O favor debitoris como princípio geral de direito. Rev Bras Direito Comp. 26:3–23

Andrade E et al. (2021) Autonomia privada e solução de conflitos fora do processo: autotutela executiva, novos cenários para a realização dos direitos? Revista de Processo, 46:322, pp. 437–476.

Armenta Deu T (2011) La prueba ilícita (un estudo comparado), 2nd edn. Marcial Pons, Madrid

Ascensão JO (2013) O direito: introdução e teoria geral, 13ª edn. Almedina, Coimbra

Ávila H (2008) O que é "devido processo legal"? Rev Processo 33(163):50–59

Ávila H (2013) Função da Ciência do Direito Tributário: do Formalismo Epistemológico ao Estruturalismo Argumentativo. Rev Direito Tribut. Atual 29:181–204

Bachman G (2006) Private Ordnung. Mohr Siebeck, Tübingen

Bandeira LOVV (2022) Exceção de insegurança no direito brasileiro. Almedina, São Paulo

Barletta A (2012) Extra e ultra petição: studio sui limiti del dovere decisorio del giudice civile. Giuffrè, Milano

Bauer F (2023) Proportionality in private law: An analytical framework. In: Bauer F, Köhler B (eds) Proportionality in private law. Mohr Siebeck, Tübingen, pp. 15–25.

Belmonte E (2023) Compensazione e autotutela. Edizione Scientifiche Italiane, Napoli

Betti E (1959) Autotutela (dir. priv.). In, Enciclopedia del diritto, vol. IV. Milano, Giuffrè, pp. 529–537.

Beurskens M (2017) Privatrechtliche Selbsthilfe, Rechte, Pflichten und Verantwortlichkeit bei digitalen Zugangsbeschränkungs- und Selbstdurchsetzungsbefugnissen. Mohr Siebeck, Tübingen

Binenbojm G (2020) Poder de polícia, ordenação e regulação, transformações político-jurídicas, econômicas e institucionais do direito administrativo ordenador, 3rd edn. Fórum, Belo Horizonte

Bomfim NL and Fidalgo CB (2008) Releitura da autoexecutoriedade como prerrogativa da Administração Pública. In, Direito administrativo e seus novos paradigmas. Belo Horizonte, Fórum, pp. 269–303.

Bongiorno G (1984) L'autotutela esecutiva. Giuffrè, Milano

Braga PS (2008) Aplicação do devido processo legal nas relações privadas. Juspodivm, Salvador

Brandon D et al (1984) Self-help, extrajudicial rights, privileges and remedies in contemporary American society. Vanderbilt Law Rev. 37(4):849–1040

Brito TQD (1994) O direito de necessidade e a legítima defesa no código civil e no código penal. Lex, Lisboa

Cabral ADP (2024) Repensando a autotutela, conceito e limites no direito brasileiro. In: Eid EP (ed) Ensaios sobre autotutela. Thoth, Londrina, pp. 39–66.

Callies G (1999) Prozedurales Recht. Nomos, Baden-Baden

Candeias H M (2023) O abuso do direito de retenção. Exercício desproporcional do direito de retenção. Revista da Faculdade de Direito da, Universidade de Lisboa, LXIV, 1:2, pp. 885–930.

Canotilho JG (2003) Direito constitucional e teoria da constituição, 7th edn. Edições Almedina, Coimbra

Carimini F (2018) Sequestro convenzionale e autotutela. Edizione Scientifiche Italiane, Napoli

Carvalho Filho JDS (2011) A autoexecutoriedade e a garantia do contraditório no processo administrativo. Revista do Ministério Público. Rio Jan. 39:75–97
Castro CRDS (2010) O devido processo legal e os princípios da razoabilidade e da proporcionalidade, 5th edn. Forense, Rio de Janeiro
Cipriani N (2000) Patto commissorio e patto marciano. Proporzionalità e legittimità delle garanzie. Edizione Scientifiche Italiane, Napoli
Comoglio LP (2000) Mezzi alternativi di tutela e garanzie costituzionali. Rev Processo 99:262–265
Cretella Júnior J (1963) Executoriedade do ato administrativo unilateral. Rev Direito Adm 71:16–28
D'Acunto L (2018) Recesso e autotutela nei rapporti di consumo. Edizione Scientifiche Italiane, Napoli
Dagnino A (1983) Contributo allo studio dell'autotutela privata. Giuffrè, Milano
De Belvis E (2018) L'esecuzione privatizzata. Edizione Scientifiche Italiane, Napoli
Díaz Alabart S (2007) La autotutela. In, Liber Amicorum Guido Alpa, Private Law Beyond the National Systems. London, British Institute of International and Comparative Law, pp. 1–15.
Didier F Jr (2009) Subsídios para uma teoria das impenhorabilidades. Rev Processo 34(174):30–50
Didier Jr F & Fernandez L (2023) A autotutela administrativa no sistema brasileiro de justiça multiportas. In, Tesolin FR and Machado AA (coord) Direito Federal brasileiro. Londrina, Thoth, pp. 177–198.
Didier F Jr et al (2017) Curso de direito processual civil, execução, vol 5, 7th edn. Juspodivm, Salvador
Dinamarco CR (2020) Instituições de direito processual civil, vol I, 10th edn. Malheiros, São Paulo
Dinamarco CR (2022) O processo arbitral, 2nd edn. Editora Direito Contemporâneo, Curitiba
Dinamarco CR (2024) Instituições de direito processual civil, vol IV, 5th edn. Malheiros, São Paulo
Duque MS (2019) Eficácia horizontal dos direitos fundamentais e jurisdição constitucional, 2ª edn. Editora dos Editores, São Paulo
Fantini A (2024) Sul sistema delle risoluzioni per inadempimento, autotutela ed effettività rimediale. Edizione Scientifiche Italiane, Napoli
Fazzalari E (1975) Istituzione di diritto processuale. CEDAM, Padova
Follieri L (2016) Esecuzione forzata e autonomia privata. Giappichelli, Torino
Follieri L (2023) L'autotutela esecutiva. In: Albanese A et al (eds) La responsabilità patrimoniale "sostenibile". Giappichelli, Torino
Fonseca RG (2012) O fundamento da autotutela executiva da Administração Pública, contributo para a sua compreensão como problema jurídico-político. Almedina, Lisboa
Frazão A (2022) Julgamentos algorítmicos, a necessidade de assegurarmos as preocupações éticas e o devido processo legal. In: Colombo C et al (eds) Tutela jurídica do corpo eletrônico. Editora Foco, Indaiatuba, pp. 579–596.
Gabrielli E (2016) Appunti sulle autotutele contrattuali. Riv dirit priv XXI(4):491–530
Godinho RR (2022) A autocomposição no processo coletivo entre o discurso e a possibilidade. Rev Minist Público Estado Rio Jan 84:171–206
Gold A S (2020) The Meaning of Self-help. In, The Right of Redress. Oxford, Oxford University Press, pp. 160–181.
Greiner J, jiménez D, lupica LR (2017) Self-help, reimagined. Indiana Law J 92:3,
Grinover AP (2007) A inafastabilidade do controle jurisdicional e uma nova modalidade de autotutela (parágrafos únicos dos artigos 249 e 251 do Código Civil). Rev Bras Direito Const – RBDC 10:13–19
Grinover AP (2018) Ensaio sobre a processualidade, fundamentos para uma nova teoria geral do processo. Gazeta Jurídica, Brasília
Hanau H (2004) Der Grundsatz der Verhältnismäßigkeit als Schranke privater Gestaltungsmacht. Zu Herleitung und Struktur einer Angemessenheitskontrolle von Verfassungs wegen. Mohr Siebeck, Tübingen
Hess B (2010) Different Enforcement Structures. In: Van Rhee CH, Uzelac A (eds) Enforcement and Enforceability. Tradition and Reform, Intersentia, Antwerp

Jouannaud V (2023) The various manifestations of the constitutional principle of proportionality in private law. In: Bauer F, Köhler B (eds) Proportionality in private law. Mohr Siebeck, Tübingen
Justo AS (1993) A execução, pessoal e patrimonial. Sep Rev Direito III-IV:125
Kelsen H (1992) Reine Rechtslehre, 2 Auflage edn. Österreichische Staatsdruckerei, Wien
Kenett W (2021) Civil enforcement in a comparative perspective. A public management challenges. Cambridge, Intersentia
Klatt M, Meister M (2012) The constitutional structure of proportionality. Oxford Press, Oxford
Klingbeil S (2019) Selbsthilfe als private Zwangsvollstreckung. In: Tim H et al (eds) Strukturwandel und privatrecht. Nomos, Baden-Baden, pp. 185–214.
Korybut M (2014) The uncertain scope of revised article 9's statutory prohibition of exculpatory breach of peace clauses. Hastings Bus. Law J 10:2
Larenz K, Wolf M (2004) Allgemeiner Teil des bürgerlichen Rechts, 9 Auflage edn. C. H. Beck, München
Leite CFL (2024) Execução arbitral sob perspectiva da Análise Econômica dos Métodos de Solução de Conflitos. Rev Processo 49:349
Lepore A (2019) Autotutela e autonomia negoziale. Edizione Scientifiche Italiane, Napoli
Lichtman DG (2004) How the law responds to self-help. In: John M olin program in law and economics working paper, vol 232, Chicago, pp. 1–73.
Loterstein A (2013) Law-enforcement officers and self-help repossession. State Action Approach Mich Law Rev 111:7
Lucca RR (2024) Direitos potestativos, autotutela e resolução de compromissos de compra e venda. In: Eid EP (ed) Ensaios sobre autotutela. Thoth, Londrina, pp. 299–328.
Marino S (2024) La risoluzione dei conflitti per via di autotutela in prospettiva storica. In: Eid EP (ed) Ensaios sobre autotutela. Thoth, Londrina
Marques Neto FDA (2007) Ensaio sobre o processo como disciplina do exercício da atividade estatal. In: Didier F Jr, Jordão EF (eds) Teoria geral do processo, panorama doutrinário mundial. JusPodivm, Salvador, pp. 261–286.
Matri D (2017) Covenants and third-party creditors. Empirical and law & economics insights into a common pool problem. Springer, Switzerland
Mattos SLW (2009) Devido processo legal e proteção de direitos. Porto Alegre, Livraria do Advogado
Mcrobert R (2012) Defining "breach of the peace" in self-help repossessions. Wash Law Rev 87(2):569–594
Medauar O (2021) A processualidade no Direito Administrativo, 3rd edn. Fórum, Belo Horizonte
Minami MY (2020) Da vedação ao non factibile, uma introdução às medidas executivas atípicas, 2nd edn. Juspodivm, Salvador
Miragem B (2021) Causas de justificação do comportamento causador do dano na responsabilidade civil. In: Simão JF, Pavinatto T (eds) Liber Amicorum teresa ancona lopez – estudos sobre responsabilidade civil. Almedina, São Paulo, pp. 43–52.
Montecchiari T (2019) Ius singulare e autotutela privata, contributo allo studio di uma categoria. ESI, Napoli
Moraes JR (2009) Evolução histórica da execução civil no Direito lusitano. Editora da Universidade de São Paulo, São Paulo
Moraes MZD (2022) Processo criminal transformativo, modelo criminal e sistema processual não violentos. D'Plácido, Belo Horizonte
Morato García RM (2011) Derecho de resistencia y ejercicio irregular del poder de dirección. Editorial Comares, Granada
Möslein F (2018) Rechtliche Grenzen innovativer Finanztechnologien (FinTech), smart contracts als selbsthilfe? Z Bankr Bankwirtsch. 30(4):208–221
Mouzalas R (2024) Autotutela privada no direito brasileiro. Thoth, Londrina
Murino F (2010) L'autotutela nell'escussione della garanzia finanziaria pignoratizia. Giuffrè, Milano
Noronha CS (2016) Repensando a tutela dos direitos. Revista da Faculdade de Direito da UFRGS, 1:32, pp. 76–97.

Novais JR (2022) As restrições aos direitos fundamentais não expressamente autorizadas pela Constituição, 3rd edn. AAFDL Editora, Lisboa
Nurra MT (2022) La legittima difesa nel sistema del diritto privato. Roma, Inschibboleth
Patterson D (2019) Rechtsdurchsetzung ohne staat, paradigms of enforcement – justice vs. efficiency. In: Schmidt-Kessel M (ed) Rechtsdurchsetzung ohne Staat. Mohr Siebeck, Tübingen
Paulus CG (2000) Die Privatisierung der Zwangsvollstreckung – oder, Wie der Rechtsstaat an seinem fundament erodiert. Z Rechtspolit. 33(7):296–297
Peppe L (2009) Riflessioni intorno all'esecuzione personale in diritto romano. Ann semin giurid 53:117–162
Raimo RD (2018) Autotutela satisfattiva e giustizia "voluntaria". Riv Dirit Cost 3:67–85
Renner M (2021) Private ordering. In: Stefan G, Hans-W. M, Moritz R (eds) New private law theory, pp. 193–204. Cambridge University Press, Cambridge
Repgen T (2019) § 229 Selbsthilfe. In: Schilken E et al (eds) §§ 164–240, Stellvertretung, Zustimmung, Fristen, Verjährung, Selbsthilfe, Sicherheitsleistung. Otto Schmidt/De Gruyter, Berlin
Ricciardoni ADS (2011) L'autotutela civile. Jovene, Napoli
Rodrigues AB (2023a) Em defesa da legítima defesa. Um olhar sobre os limites da justificação na dogmática civil moderna. Rev Fac Direito Univ Lisb 1:1:183–239
Rodrigues MA (2021) Execução por quantia certa contra devedor solvente. Foco, Indaiatuba
Rodrigues MA (2023) Responsabilidade patrimonial pelo inadimplemento das obrigações. Indaiatuba, Editora Foco
Romano S (2021) Introduzione allo studio del procedimento giuridico nel diritto privato. ESI, Napoli
Rosenberg L et al (2018) Zivilprozessrecht, 18. Auflage edn. C.H. Beck, München
Roxin C, Greco L (2020) Strafrecht allgemeiner Teil. Band I – Grundlagen Der Aufbau der Verbrechenslehre, 5 Auflage edn. C. H. Beck, München
Salles RBDO (2019) Autotutela nas relações contratuais. Editora Processo, Rio de Janeiro
Saturno A (1995) L'autotutela privata. I modelli della ritenzione e dell'eccezione di inadempimento in comparazione col sistema tedesco. Edizione Scientifiche Italiane, Napoli
Schinemann CCB (2023) Arbitragem e execução, divisão de competências, poderes do árbitro e limites subjetivos. Editora Revista dos Tribunais, São Paulo
Schirato VR (2010) O processo administrativo como instrumento do Estado de Direito e da Democracia. In: Odete M, Rhein SV (eds) Atuais rumos do processo administrativo. Editora Revista dos Tribunais, São Paulo, pp. 9–51.
Silva GMD (1967) A tutela dos direitos da acção directa. Rev Ordem dos Advog 27:5–81
Silva VAD (2002) O proporcional e o razoável. Rev dos Trib 91(798):23–50
Silva VAD (2021) Direito constitucional brasileiro. Editora Universidade de São Paulo, São Paulo
Sinel Z (2009) Causes of action and self-help remedies. Restit Law Rev 17:122–132
Siqueira TF (2021) Limites objetivos da coisa julgada, objeto do processo e questões prejudiciais. Juspodivm, Salvador
Sundfeld CA (2000) Processo e procedimento administrativo no Brasil. In: Sundfeld CA, Muñoz GA (eds) As leis de processo administrativo, Lei Federal 9.784/99 e Lei Paulista 10.177/98. Malheiros, São Paulo, pp. 12–35.
Talamini E (2003) Tutela relativa aos deveres de fazer e de não fazer e sua extensão aos deveres de entrega de coisa (CPC, arts. 461 e 461-A; CDC, art. 84), 2nd edn. RT, São Paulo
Talamini E (2022) Poder geral de adoção de medidas coercitivas sub-rogatórias nas diferentes espécies de execução. In: Talamini E, Minami MY (eds) Medidas executivas atípicas, 3rd edn. Juspodivm, Salvador
Talamini E (2023a) Adjudicação compulsória extrajudicial, pressupostos, natureza e limites. Rev Processo 336(48):319–339
Talamini E (2023b) Fundamentação da sentença arbitral e devido processo. Rev Processo 48(334):433–459
Verkuil PR (2005) Privatizing due process. Adm Law Rev 57(4):963–994

Winship P (2019) An historical over view of UCC article 9. In: Secured transactions law reform. principles, policies and practice. Hard Publishing, pp. 21–39.
Yarshell FL (2009) Antecipação da prova sem o requisito da urgência e direito autônomo à prova. Malheiros, São Paulo
Yarshell FL (2024) O devido processo legal na excussão de bem alienado fiduciariamente. In: Eid EP (ed) Ensaios sobre autotutela. Thoth, pp. 139–155.
Yarshell FL, Rodrigues VS (2020) Desjudicialização da execução civil, uma solução útil e factível entre nós? In: Reflexões sobre a desjudicialização da execução civil. Juruá, pp. 361–372.
Yoshikawa EH (2010) Execução extrajudicial e devido processo legal. Atlas, São Paulo

Chapter 5
Systematic Profile of Self-Help

In this final chapter, a systematic overview of self-help will be presented. The criteria used for this purpose have already been discussed in earlier chapters. Now, they will be outlined as the focus, given the importance of classifying the forms of unilateral protection. Just as legal remedies are categorized based on the nature of the solution, the interests protected, the timing of their application, and so on, the same applies here. This analysis is conducted within the context of Brazilian law. Although this may seem obvious, it is common for specific categories from foreign legal systems to be imported without proper context or demonstrated usefulness, as has been demonstrated. For this reason, the framework of self-help is presented within the national legal environment, whether to align it with other forms of interest protection or to facilitate its identification according to specific requirements control.

5.1 Legal Framework of Self-Help

The legal framework of self-help can be either public or private. This division has led to a common separation in legal literature, which, for a long time, failed to link the powers of unilateral protection held by the State and private individuals. From the beginning, this study has aimed to show the error of this separation and the issues it causes, including challenges to individual autonomy in self-protection, the extent of the State's monopoly on the use of force, the application of strict legality to fundamental rights, and the supremacy of the State over the individual.[1] However, the unitary perspective highlights the existence of this power of unilateral protection under both public and private legal regimes. It does not solely focus on the competition between the State and private entities, since each has its scope defined by these frameworks.

[1] Blomeyer (1982), p. 1.

E. Pierre Eid, *Self-Help as Method of Conflict Resolution*,
https://doi.org/10.1007/978-3-032-13905-4_5

To define them, identifying the agents involved is not enough. Saying that State agents carry out public self-help, while private self-help, which individuals exercise, does not fully address the issue. These regimes may be applied in different contexts.

From the perspective of Public Administration, the application of the private legal regime will occur under certain circumstances, in which there is an equalization of power with private entities and individuals.[2] Article 173, § 1, item II of the Brazilian Federal Constitution of 1988 states that when the State directly engages in economic activity, it is subject to the "legal regime applicable to private companies," so that the resulting self-help will be governed by private law.[3] The instrumental power exercised here is subject to the principle of freedom, guided by both general and specific powers. This also applies, for example, to contracts entered into by the Public Administration where the private legal regime applies, giving the parties the freedom to include self-help provisions and remedies.[4]

Although it is most common to consider the relationship between the State and private individuals, as well as the self-executing nature of acts, as limitations on fundamental rights, the importance of this power to realize, protect, or satisfy interests also applies to relationships between State entities. In cases of public self-help, it is evident how the relationship between them is influenced by the ability to protect interests unilaterally. For example, Article 160, caput of the Brazilian Federal Constitution of 1988, prohibits withholding or restricting the transfer or use of resources allocated to States, the Federal District, and Municipalities. However, this rule has an exception in the first paragraph, which permits the withholding of transfers by the Union or the States for the payment of outstanding debts owed by the recipient entity (item I) and for compliance with the budgetary rules outlined in Article 198, §2, items II and III of the Constitution II).[5]

From the perspective of a private individual, whenever they are subject to the public legal regime, self-help will be governed by that legal system framework.[6] There are numerous examples of the exercise of instrumental power in such cases, such as expropriation carried out by a concessionaire granted specific powers for this purpose, as well as mechanisms of self-help in administrative contracts, including acts based on the exception of non-performance of a contract. Therefore, the methodological approach of many studies on private self-help, which is often treated as synonymous with self-help exercised by private individuals, is doubly incomplete: it assumes that only private individuals can exercise private self-help and presumes that they carry out no public self-help.

Therefore, the significance of classification based on the legal regime lies in defining the boundaries of actions permitted by the legal system, especially in relation to freedom and legality, the involved agents, and the expected outcomes. Public and private self-protection are simply a division based on the criterion currently being

[2] Mendonça and Bento (2024), pp. 211–212.

[3] Grau (2015), pp. 115–119.

[4] Justen Filho (2015), p. 495.

[5] STF, RE 509.984 AgR, Justice Ayres Britto, Second Chamber, judged on 28/02/2012.

[6] Klein (2022), pp. 342–343.

examined, which underscores the need for a joint analysis of the phenomenon linked to the unilateral protection of those who have been infringed upon or whose interests are threatened.

5.2 Sources of Self-Help

From the sources, one derives the rules concerning general and specific powers for unilateral protection. In Chapter 3, these powers were presented as developments of typicality and atypicality. The approach is conducted on two levels: to identify possible sources and the relevance of non-binding prescriptions, such as soft law and doctrine, in strengthening self-protection. The aim is to demonstrate the same importance of this study, which has already been recognized in other forms of interest protection.[7]

At the level of identification, the boundaries between private and public self-protection are relevant to this consideration. Given the application of the principles of legality and freedom, respectively, the impacts on the sources may differ.

In public self-protection, where authorization is required to act unilaterally, the main source is the text stemming from a legitimacy parameter based on the deliberation of a representative body. This is a result of a general binding of recipients, guidance on freedom and property, and the imposition of rights and duties. Laporta's observation highlights the significance of a democratic process in creating and incorporating normative texts into the legal system, serving both as a means of legitimization and ensuring compliance with the limits established by the Brazilian Constitution.[8] Therefore, the idea of legality as the basis for public self-protection must consider the enactment of laws under the following conditions: the Constitution, the laws of various federal entities, and international treaties. Suppose the material and formal limits of these laws are respected. In that case, the normative and conventional actions of the Public Administration can create, specify, clarify, and delegate this instrumental power, as is often seen in regulated economic sectors.

The freedom that guides private self-protection broadens the sources of instrumental power. In addition to the sources mentioned earlier, agreements between parties can lead to unusual forms of unilateral protection, either by extending beyond what the typical power already establishes or by creating forms not anticipated by the legislator. Moreover, the observation that custom serves as a source is valid. The lack of formally proclaimed rules or principles, which are spontaneously and commonly adopted and accepted by the parties in legal relations, it may result in the self-protection of their interests. An example is the usage and customs in the field of international trade, which Goldman referred to as the new *lex mercatoria*,[9]

[7] Pereira (2024), pp. 259–263.

[8] Laporta (2007), p. 152.

[9] Goldman (2009), pp. 211–230.

and which incorporate mechanisms such as the retention of goods, set-off, or credit restrictions in the event of default.[10]

In both systems, precedent is also a key source. Some examples in this study come from how courts interpret texts and apply rules related to unilateral protection. Much of precedent's importance lies in defining when unilateral conduct is allowed, its scope, and its legality. The link between precedent and legal certainty helps guide behavior, provides predictability, and reduces uncertainties about the extent of authorization for actions by the active party. An example of case law as a source of self-protection is the decision by the Brazilian Supreme Federal Court (STF) in RE 633.782 (general repercussion theme 522), which established the principle that "it is constitutional to delegate police powers, by law, to private legal entities that are part of the indirect Public Administration, with a majority public shareholding, which provide exclusively public services that are inherent to the State and on a non-competitive basis."

Among the main points addressed by the judgment, the possibility of delegating acts of coercion was also accepted: "there is no reason to exclude the attribute of coercibility inherent to the exercise of police power, under penalty of undermining the very purpose for which those entities were created."[11] In other words, the STF not only stated that the powers of order, consent, or police supervision could be delegated, but also emphasized the main element for establishing unilateral protection, which is the police sanction. This reinforces the premise that the alleged monopoly should no longer be recognized or upheld.[12]

Regarding non-binding sources, legal scholarship has played a crucial role in advancing the study of self-help internationally. Martins-Costa emphasizes the epistemological authority of doctrine, as it is through doctrine "that the law progresses without uncertain leaps or excessive upheavals, since its role is constructive and progressive."[13] By fulfilling prescriptive, interpretative, classificatory, and investigative functions, the literature focused on unilateral remedies has evolved over recent decades—while still acknowledging earlier studies that, since the eighteenth and nineteenth centuries, have challenged dogmas still maintained today regarding the use of force and the autonomy of protection—at least along four main lines: (i) the reaffirmation of private self-help, emphasizing contractual remedies and extrajudicial measures enforcement[14]; (ii) advances brought about by technology, expanding the scope for self-regulation and the use of self-help as governance mechanism[15];

[10] Callies (2002), p. 194, 2002.

[11] STF, RE 633.782, Justice Luiz Fux, Plenary, judged on 26/10/2020.

[12] Souza (2014), pp. 167–168.

[13] Martins-Costa (2014), p. 26.

[14] Murino (2010), pp. 54–57. Gabrielli (2016), pp. 515–516. Carimini (2018), p. 59. Lepore (2019), pp. 33–38. Salles (2019), pp. 70–86. Theodoro Jr. (2023), pp. 97–99.

[15] Poncibò and Dimatteo (2019), pp. 125–126. Paulus and Matzke (2017), p. 770. Möslein (2018), p. 220. Duden (2023), pp. 321–323. Santisteban Castro (2023), pp. 596–597. Yarshell and Rodrigues (2021), p. 422. Talamini and Cardoso (2022), pp. 196–199.

(iii) the reevaluation of the scope of state powers to regulate private parties[16]; and (iv) the effort to establish autonomous contours and identify unilateral remedies.[17]

Not by chance, during this same period, specific soft law guidelines have also gained importance in the study of self-help: the examples previously mentioned of the European Bank for Reconstruction and Development (EBRD), the United Nations Commission on International Trade Law (UNCITRAL), and the International Institute for the Unification of Private Law (UNIDROIT) regarding security rights,[18] as well as the Tallinn Manual, a non-binding document that offers interpretations of international law to guide *jus ad bellum* and *jus in bello* within the context of cyberattacks,[19] point in two directions. The first is the pursuit of interpretive and applicative uniformity of rules at the supranational level, aiming to facilitate the enforcement of unilateral remedies and ensure their benefits are recognized in commerce, consumer relations, and non-material areas, such as the digital world. The second is the dominance of these guidelines in guiding the development of self-help and countering the still standard view that it is merely residual and exceptional.

5.3 Individual and Collective Interests

The interests harmed or threatened, protected, satisfied, or realized by unilateral remedies may be either individual or collective. Just as there are individual and collective proceedings, as well as individual and collective arbitration, there are also individual and collective settlements. Self-help will be classified based on two factors: the number of active parties required for the effective exercise of the act, and the legal interest to be protected.[20] Thus, it is possible to have both the unilateral protection of collective interests and the collective unilateral protection of individual interests, reflecting the established distinction between the protection of collective rights and the collective protection of rights.[21]

The distinction between individual and collective self-help depends on the legal protection involved. The harm or threat may affect one or a few individuals, a specific group, or an unspecified collective. Therefore, self-help is considered individual when it focuses on protecting, satisfying, or directly and solely enacting the interests of those performing the acts, or collective when it targets the protection, satisfaction, or realization of interests related to a specific or unspecified group.[22] At this

[16] Schimpfhauser (2009), pp. 70–71. Pieroth (2011), p. 57. Gutmann (2011), p. 38. Hamburger (2014), p. 129. Klein (2022), pp. 325–326.

[17] D'Acunto (2018), p. 38. Montecchiari (2019), pp. 35–37. Klingbeil (2017), p. 40. Beurskens (2017), pp. 298–299.

[18] Stănescu and Gikay (2017), pp. 101–103.

[19] Schmitt (2017), pp. 9–10.

[20] Geri (1988), pp. 290–291. Scarpelli (1993), pp. 120–121. Carinci (2001), p. 961.

[21] Zavascki (2017), pp. 35–37.

[22] Grinover (2012), pp. 27–30.

point, the theoretical framework concerning the procedural nature of homogeneous individual rights also needs to be questioned. The protection provided by self-help, even when formalized as a procedure, operates at the substantive level; therefore, the independence of an interest is not necessarily compromised simply because the harm or threat originates from the same source (Article 81, III of the Brazilian Consumer Defense Code).[23] These interests, threatened by a common cause, can be self-protected by the group of active subjects if they choose to do so. For this reason, self-protection is allowed concerning diffuse interests, collective interests, and homogeneous individual interests.

As an example of self-protection of diffuse interests—understood as interests relating to an indeterminate group—one could cite the actions of the Public Administration in revoking an environmental license previously granted to a company that repeatedly fails to meet its obligations not to pollute. The administrative prohibition of the legal entity's activities is a partial but necessary measure to prevent further environmental harm.

As an example of self-protection of collective interests in the strict sense, one might refer to a strike by employees of a particular company. In this case, the demand itself does not constitute a form of unilateral protection but instead functions as an indirect enforcement measure to achieve those objectives. The work stoppage more closely resembles acts of suspension of contractual obligations due to breaches by the employer, which indeed constitutes a case of unilateral action protection.[24]

As an example of self-protection of homogeneous individual interests, one may cite the case of a group of individuals harmed by a construction company, who, by collective decision, resolve to remove it from its role in real estate development due to repeated delays, the use of substandard materials, and labor debts. By collective decision of this group of contracting parties—each suffering distinct losses arising from the common cause of non-performance—they assume responsibility for managing the execution, budget, and contracting related to the project.

These cases highlight an important point about the characteristics of the active subject. It is crucial for self-protection that the active subject is the party responsible for making decisions in favor of their interests that have been infringed or threatened. In this collective context, the active party also acts to protect the interests of others, whether through substitution or representation. This does not change what has already been said about the unilateral power of this agent. For example, in the self-protection of diffuse interests, the Public Administration safeguards the environment using police powers legally granted to it to regulate and oversee market activities that could harm this diffuse right. In the case of collective self-protection, a strike movement can only occur through the organization and action of a group of workers. Even if some choose not to participate and do not take direct action towards unilateral protection, the strike is still established, and any demands that are met tend to benefit all involved parties. Lastly, in the case of homogeneous individual rights, there is no role for representation or substitution as forms of collectivization, since the goal

---

[23] Talamini (2016), pp. 118–119.

[24] Mallet (2015), pp. 25–27.

of unilateral protection is only achieved through the convergence or aggregation of those involved. Even if the majority, rather than all, of those harmed are interested, dissenters are bound by the collective decision's outcome—not because they are subject to the effects of representation or substitution.

5.4 Object of the Exercise of Power

Another classification considers the purpose of exercising power. This involves identifying the target of the active subject's actions in trying to influence the passive subject.[25] This criterion is crucial in defining the limits of action for protecting, satisfying, or realizing the infringed or threatened interest, in line with the criteria outlined in the previous chapter. There are three possible objectives: personal, proprietary, and formative, which lead to self-protection aimed at the individual, property, or with the goal of changing a legal position.[26]

These objects illustrate the evolution in the recognition and use of unilateral protection. Traditionally viewed as the exercise of physical force, aggression, and the dominance of the stronger over the weaker, it has become common to associate self-protection with physical subjugation.[27] The development and inclusion of specific powers into legislation have emphasized two main aspects. Acts aimed at the physical, moral, and psychological integrity of individuals have become limited, restricted to urgent situations and immediate responses to unjust aggression, such as self-defense, legitimate defense, necessity, or strict compliance with legal duties to disperse violent protesters. Most specific and general powers, when exercised properly within the boundaries set by the legal system, do not follow this pattern. When classified as personal, self-protection can have broader applications in cases involving non-proprietary rights, such as freedom of association, business activities, and so on forth.[28] Another aspect is the confirmation of these premises through the proliferation of specific self-help powers related to conduct against property, such as various forms of unilateral enforcement, or formative powers, such as the provisions that give the active party the authority to change a legal position within a certain context conflict.[29]

The development described above reverses the logic of this traditional view on self-help. On one hand, legal and theoretical advances have not only shown a growing acceptance of both specific and general self-help powers but have also limited a residual and conditional role for unilateral protection of personal integrity. This concern can be summarized as the effort to balance unilateral protection with the preservation of fundamental rights, primarily restricting it to acts involving property

[25] Landmann (1975), pp. 45–47.

[26] Noronha (2016), p. 93.

[27] Santamaria (1937), pp. 55–56.

[28] Patterson (2019), pp. 68–69.

[29] Hanau (2004), pp. 100–101.

or personal development.[30] On the other hand, due to the dynamics of legal relationships, the most characteristic incentives for unilateral protection have proven more effective from this evolved perspective, which is detached from an exclusively or predominantly corporeal focus model.[31]

Therefore, the classification presented here should be clarified as follows: personal self-help includes actions against human integrity as well as those against non-proprietary freedoms, extending this criterion to legal persons; proprietary self-help involves actions directed at a set of assets to satisfy or protect the interests of the active party; formative self-help refers to unilateral conduct that alters legal positions, which is enough to fully or partially meet the claim of the agent.[32]

5.5 Types of Unilateral Protection

One of the main classification criteria considers the type of protection, enforcement, or satisfaction provided by unilateral protection. The classification given to judicial protection for this purpose reflects the way it is carried out and the purpose of legal remedies general.[33] This result is the correspondence achieved, in whole or in part, with the material exercise of the claim by the active party.[34] From this perspective, self-help can be executive, constitutive, or declaratory, depending on the specifics of the dispute and how it impacts the legal realm of the active party.[35]

An observation should come before this division. Judicial protection can be analyzed based on its purpose concerning the claim, that is, whether it aims to satisfy or to protect it.[36] Accordingly, judicial remedies are categorized as either satisfactory or precautionary. Similarly, one can also refer to satisfactory or precautionary self-help. However, it is not the element of finality or temporality that defines them. As previously discussed, using the degree of stability as a parameter for unilateral protection is imprecise, since this is an incidental rather than an essential characteristic. It would also be inappropriate to consider the summary or exhaustive nature of the protection, as both are cognitive parameters whose assessment is equally affected by the unilateral nature of the protection act.[37] Nevertheless, the actions of the active party may serve two purposes, without undermining the goal of protecting the infringed or threatened interest: to satisfy it or to safeguard it.

The difference between satisfaction and precaution relates to self-help by considering two criteria. The first is to reference the claim of the active party regarding

---

30 Díaz Alabart (2007), pp. 24–25.

31 Popineau-Dehaullon (2008), pp. 382–386.

32 Helmreich (1967), p. 39.

33 Bedaque (2010), pp. 523–524.

34 Riehm (2017), pp. 355–356.

35 Schünemann (1985), pp. 40–41.

36 Bedaque (2021), pp. 120–121.

37 Saturno (1995), p. 244.

the harm or threat faced. The second is to identify the purpose of their actions using this reference. Ultimately, given the many different forms of conduct, unilateral protection may be appropriate either to satisfy, to safeguard, or only for one of these reasons scenarios.[38] Therefore, the relationship between executive, constitutive, and declaratory self-help is directly connected to the satisfactory or precautionary purpose.

Establishing a clear distinction between satisfactory and precautionary self-help will not be easy. The criteria provided serve as guidelines to help define the scope of the active party's powers,[39] as some examples demonstrate. Many actions taken by the Public Administration in exercising police powers serve a precautionary purpose: for example, when items are removed from circulation, smuggled medicines are seized, or expired foodstuffs are confiscated, public health is protected. However, the primary and most effective measure is the imposition of a sanction on the offending party. In such cases, the seized goods may not fulfill the purpose of sanctioning the individual, but the State's action is crucial to safeguard the public legal interest and to put an end to the unlawful conduct.

5.5.1 *Enforceability*

The recent focus on self-help is also due to the enforceability modality.[40] Whether because it took time to recognize the existence of a power to enforce claims to performance held by the Administration and private parties, or because the exercise of this power has become encouraged both by convention and law, it is important to highlight the characteristics of this type from three perspectives: how unilateral executive protection is structured; which enforcement acts qualify as self-help; and how the relationship is established between the coercive enforcement of an obligation and the division between judicial and extrajudicial processes enforcement.

A material to an unfulfilled obligation must fulfil the right to an unfulfilled obligation. Such non-performance may involve an obligation to pay a sum or deliver an item, to do something, or to refrain from doing something. Enforcement procedures exist to make this happen, either by forcibly replacing the will of the debtor or by encouraging the debtor to comply. Judicial enforcement is, therefore, the means by which a claim for an unfulfilled obligation is enforced. The connection between substantive and procedural law becomes clear because these procedural steps serve to achieve what could not be done within the scope of substantive legal relations. For this purpose, enforcement actions are categorized into direct and indirect acts.

---

[38] Bongiorno (1984), pp. 52–53.

[39] Follieri (2021), pp. 39–40.

[40] Bongiorno (1984), pp. 52–53. Lepore (2019), pp. 131–132. Purpura (2020), pp. 193–194 Follieri (2023), p. 97. Fonseca (2012), pp. 47–48. Loterstein (2013), pp. 1372-1373. Hattenhauer (2011), p. 271. Duchstein (2015), p. 105. Klingbeil (2019), p. 185.

Direct acts include subrogation actions, such as a "substitution of activities",[41] which should have been voluntarily carried out by the debtor. Indirect acts are those meant to instill fear in the debtor of staying in default, aiming to encourage compliance.[42]

Firstly, when acting as the adjudicator of the claim, the conduct of the active party within the legal sphere of the passive party is no longer performed by an impartial third party with the authority to infringe upon the patrimonial and personal realms. The boundaries in each context are very different. As discussed in Chapter 3, the initiative of the active party is subject to objective restrictions imposed by the legal system, both in contractual and non-contractual contexts, through the barriers of civil and criminal law liability.[43] Therefore, the combination of general and specific powers directly connects enforcement, legal authorization, and conventional authorization to act unilaterally in the satisfaction of obligations.

Secondly, the enforced claim to performance can also be carried out through acts of subrogation or by indirect actions.[44] In this case, subrogation by force exercised by the active party may lead to (i) expropriation, such as retaining deposits to satisfy damages caused by the debtor.[45]; (ii) transformation, as provided for in the only paragraphs of Articles 249 and 251 of the Civil Code, which authorize the creditor, in urgent cases, to carry out or undo, either personally or through a third party, the acts that the debtor committed to do or not to do[46]; and (iii) dispossession, as in the extrajudicial search and seizure of movables property.

Indirect enforcement, however, requires more careful analysis. As it does not represent conduct aimed at satisfaction on the creditor's initiative, it cannot always be described as self-help.[47] Many extrajudicial measures taken by the creditor aim to pressure the debtor into voluntary compliance. These include spreading negative information about the contracting party in the market to harm their relationships with other creditors and using default to block new contracts with companies affiliated with or controlled by the creditor, among other actions. Such actions should not be confused with the narrowly defined concept of unilateral protection discussed in the first chapter. The establishment of a direct causal link between conduct and legal protection[48] shows that indirect enforcement can only be linked to self-help when the conduct in question is part of the factual basis for the protection, satisfaction, or realization of the injured or threatened interest.

For example, in the event of default in ongoing contracts, the harmed party may be compensated for the losses incurred and may demand the performance of outstanding obligations. The exception of contract non-compliance will justify taking measures to suspend obligations by the harmed contracting party and, consequently, make the

---

[41] Dinamarco (2024), p. 44.

[42] Minami (2020), pp. 242–244.

[43] Stamm (2007), pp. 44–45.

[44] Purpura (2020), p. 197.

[45] Belmonte (2023), pp. 231–233.

[46] Grinover (2007), p. 19.

[47] Tesheiner (2007), p. 380.

[48] Sinel (2017), p. 33.

production and continuity of the debtor's activities unfeasible. The interruption of services or supplies to the harmed party would already be enough to put significant pressure on the debtor to resume contractual performance and, consequently, achieve the primary objective, which is compensation.

Finally, the doctrine of administrative law has already compared self-executing powers to the authority exercised by a judge in favor of the holder of an enforceable title.[49] The comparison is only partly accurate. The unilateral instrumental power to resolve disputes should not be confused with the effectiveness granted by law to enforce decisions proceedings,[50] The primary purpose of which is to satisfy the claim. The former has a material origin, while the latter does not grant the holder coercive enforcement power but instead the right to initiate enforcement proceedings or the compliance phase, in which the State will act coercively. The enforceable title is the legal mechanism that allows such acts of interference with the personal or proprietary sphere. The power of executive self-protection grants the same permission but with different requirements, such as the absence of a need for documentation to evidence this authorization, relying instead on a legal or contractual basis source,[51] as well as representing authorization for the creditor to act against the debtor without the need for intermediaries, sometimes and restrictively without procedural formalities.

5.5.2 Formative

Unilateral relief is constitutive when it creates, modifies, or extinguishes a legal position.[52] This foundational ability to resolve disputes served as the starting point for the doctrinal re-examination of the subject under study here.[53] It involves observing the implementation of such changes to legal positions without needing judicial intervention or cooperation from the other party. It is, therefore, a matter of exercising this power specifically, based on the requirements of self-protection, especially when the holder's interest is harmed or threatened.

The various examples already discussed, such as express termination clauses, revocation of powers of attorney, removal of fake profiles from social networks, and invalidation of administrative acts granting authorizations that private individuals have disregarded, demonstrate the frequent overlap between the power of self-protection and formative power. According to some authors, self-protection would constitute a formative right.[54] This study takes a different approach, defining it as an instrumental power existing within other categories, such as subjective rights,

---

[49] Cretella Júnior (1972), p. 241.

[50] Sica (2017), pp. 229–230.

[51] Tavormina (2003), p. 75.

[52] Motto (2012), pp. 79–82.

[53] Helmreich (1967), p. 39.

[54] Betti (1959), p. 529. Geri (1971), p. 60.

duties, and exceptions. Indeed, it is essential to acknowledge that not every exercise of a formative right constitutes an assertion of self-protection. The reliance on the requirements for the formation of this power excludes, for example, the right of option from its scope. The fact that exercising these active legal positions involves submission, without any direct link to harm or threat to the interests of the active subject, results in the regular exercise of a right or strict adherence to a legal duty, without involving the power of self-protection.[55]

At the heart of exercising these powers inherent in formative rights is, once again, the division of responsibilities between the State and private parties. Some of these powers rely on an authoritative act by a third party capable of executing them, due to the holder's own inability or insufficient action.[56] In some instances, however, the law may modify these provisions, expanding or limiting the scope for direct action or changing the authority of that third party. The recent example of Law No. 14,382/2022, which introduced extrajudicial compulsory conveyance, is one such case. As a common example of substitute judicial relief for a declaration of intent,[57] the promissory buyer or seller was required to initiate a legal action to obtain a decision substituting the volitional act, which would serve as the instrument for formal registration of the transfer.

In addressing the new law, Talamini emphasizes that this is not a case of self-protection, since extrajudicial compulsory conveyance "cannot operate against the express opposition of the other party".[58] However, compulsory conveyance only occurs due to the refusal or inaction of the promissory seller to transfer, or the refusal or inaction of the promissory buyer to accept. This is already enough to cause harm to the interest in receiving or transferring ownership respectively.

Article 216-B, §1, item I of Brazilian Law 6015/73 (Public Records Law) establishes the requirement for a document evidencing the refusal of any of the parties to the transaction, which, in this case, is also presumed by failure to comply with the fifteen days set out in the extrajudicial notice provided for in the provision. The procedure conducted at the registry office is primarily intended to ensure the transfer based on consensus or to demonstrate the absence of the right, should there be voluntary action and expression. The compulsory transfer of ownership will occur precisely because, in addition to the initial refusal, a second refusal occurred due to non-compliance with the notice. Thus, as with other procedures for consolidating ownership due to default (such as in fiduciary guarantees),[59] extrajudicial compulsory adjudication constitutes a form of constitutive self-help, as the element of conflict exists and the active party initiates the process, if the transfer does not result from consensus or if the absence of the applicant's right is not demonstrated.

Examples like this once again show the legislator's concern to expand certain powers to private individuals. By allowing them to exercise unilateral protective

---

[55] Bötticher (1964), p. 4.

[56] Fornaciari (1999), pp. 113–115.

[57] Yarshell (1993), pp. 37–40.

[58] Talamini (2023), p. 329.

[59] Conti (2022), pp. 55–58.

powers directly through a formative right, especially when the realization of such power previously depended on a third party, it demonstrates the state's encouragement of self-help.

5.5.3 *Declaratory*

The purpose of declaratory relief is to eliminate a state of legal uncertainty.[60] Such uncertainty stems from an objective context that questions the existence, non-existence, or nature of legal relationships, as well as the authenticity or falsity of documents, within the limits established by the Brazilian Code of Civil Procedure. Considering these factors—usually discussed in the context of judicial protection—it is important to determine whether they are compatible with unilateral protection.

The first consideration is whether self-help is declaratory in nature. Although not as common as other types, it is admissible when the active party can eliminate uncertainty, and it is enforceable against the passive party. This differs from the view that denies this possibility,[61] for declaratory self-help to exist, the passive party must be subject to the declaration issued by the active party. These conditions show that it is not simple to classify such unilateral measures, as the imposition of a declaratory result requires some level of binding force, whether conventional or authoritative.[62]

The second consideration is to contextualize unilateral declaratory protection in light of the various aspects of declaratory acts.[63] Recognizing the constitutive elements of self-help enables an understanding of the purpose of a declaration by the active party to bind the passive party. The goal of this bond is to eliminate doubt for those affected and to reach those who caused it. Even though such acts may produce effects to mitigate or resolve a conflict, the elimination of uncertainty by the party who caused it does not constitute self-help, just as the legal recognition of a declaratory claim means that the defendant has accepted the active party's demand. Moreover, the content of the declaratory act is crucial: there must be a match with the removal of legal uncertainty resulting from conduct or positions that make it difficult to perform, interpret, or determine a fact or the applicable rules.[64] Therefore, a simple unilateral declaration by the debtor about their own default does not qualify as self-help; nor does a declaration by the Public Administration certifying the absence of tax debts on the part of the taxpayer.

The purpose of unilateral declaratory protection is to have the active party make a declaration to remove the uncertainty caused by the passive party. To keep its unilateral nature, making this declaration does not require the passive party's agreement, although it still binds them. The effects of the declaration occur without their consent

60 Cunha (2009), p. 177.

61 Yoshikawa (2008), pp. 24–25.

62 Sassani (1999), pp. 34–35.

63 Carnelutti (1940), p. 17, 1940.

64 Cabral (2021), pp. 106–107.

or acknowledgment. Therefore, the doctrinal approach that recognizes these features in bilateral declaratory legal transactions should be excluded from the concept self-help.[65] Although there may be legal transactions aimed at this purpose, the hallmark of the unilateral nature of the declaration must be maintained. This highlights the limitations on the use of declaratory self-help. Three requirements must be satisfied: the declaration by the active party to defend their infringed or threatened interests, the binding effect on the passive party's conduct, and the reduction or elimination of the uncertainty caused by the latter.

The third consideration is to recognize declaratory self-help beyond the limits of judicial protection of this type. The debates about the inability to declare facts, legal positions, or the proper way of interpreting and applying the law, based on the traditional restriction presented by early twentieth-century doctrine,[66] become irrelevant within the scope of unilateral protection due to the existence of an interest in effectively resolving the uncertainty that harms the active party's interests, which may appear at various levels. The characterization of the declaratory interest in self-protection is not subject to the same restrictions discussed regarding the interest to act in judicial declarations.

As an example of this narrow view of unilateral declaratory protection, consider the actions of the Administration when interpreting and applying a tax rule. Consider a situation where this rule has been subject to significant interpretive differences, both among tax inspectors—who have varied in how they understand and apply it, sometimes issuing assessments and other times not—and among taxpayers, due to differing perspectives on whether a taxable event has occurred, especially as formalized in administrative challenges. The stance taken by the Tax Authority, in addition to binding and requiring inspectors to follow it, also constrains the individual within the administrative system and removes uncertainty about whether the event will be considered within the scope of the rule hypothesis.

5.6 Timing of the Exercise of Self-Protection

The classification based on exercise timing considers unilateral protection as either reactive or preventive. Under this criterion, the reference point is the occurrence or threat of an unlawful act or damage, as established for judicial purposes protection.[67] This point, however, may involve some complexities. When discussing the temporal criterion for self-protection, reference was made to the difficulties in clearly determining whether the active party is genuinely acting preventively or if this is simply a mistaken assessment of the facts. It should be noted that this discussion is not hypothetical. In Chapter 3, the doctrinal proposal to treat smart contracts as a case of preventive self-protection concerning all obligations was questioned, based on

[65] Pucci (1926), pp. 158–160. Grande (2010), pp. 251–253. Lepore (2019), pp. 77–83.

[66] Kisch (1903), pp. 24–25.

[67] Marinoni (2022), pp. 20–23.

automation and the prevention of default by one of the parties.[68] Taken to its logical conclusion, this line of thought would suggest that any situation where one party fulfills an obligation could be seen as self-protection, even if there is no sign of harm or threat to the active party's interest.[69]

If, in reactive self-protection, there are already cognitive obstacles and limitations inherent in a unilateral assessment to determine when and how the harm or threat occurred, in preventive self-help, these difficulties are even greater, as it falls to the active party to assess whether there is an imminent risk of harm or damage, or whether the facts do not support such a conclusion. If, for reactive self-help, heteronomous protection with a certifying function is relevant, then for preventive self-protection, this combination is even more important. Before exercising unilateral protection, the active party must gather information and evidence of the imminent threat of harm or damage to avoid engaging in unlawful behavior.[70]

Two examples clearly illustrate the uncertainty in this identification. Article 477 of the Brazilian Civil Code authorizes a party to refuse performance of their obligation if the other contracting party suffers a "diminution in their assets capable of compromising or casting doubt on the performance of the obligation they have undertaken." In other words, to refuse performance, the party must be sure that these objective conditions in the provision have occurred. The party needs reliable and concrete evidence to justify suspending the performance of the contract, such as clear signs of the other party's financial insufficiency, made public or formally announced in the market.[71] Another example is the preventive response in legitimate self-defense: the same burdens of awareness and confirmation of the danger apply to the active party to ensure their actions are genuinely measures to prevent a risk or if there has been a mistaken assessment of the facts, under penalty of criminal liability (Article 20, §1 of the Brazilian Penal Code).

This does not mean that preventive self-protection loses its usefulness. In many cases, it occurs as a response to an objectively verifiable fact, especially as a contractual remedy. In the context of linked contracts, it is common for parties to agree on clauses that allow for the accelerated maturity of all debts in the event of a default in any one of them. While in one agreement the unlawful act is completed, in others it signals that further defaults may happen. This example demonstrates that the usefulness of preventive self-protection increases when the burden of verifying facts is reduced, which can be achieved through objective data, whether provided by an authority exercising independent oversight or through specific contractual rules.

[68] Santisteban Castro (2023), pp. 596–597.

[69] Ricciardoni (2011), pp. 10–12.

[70] Morato García (2011), pp. 390–391.

[71] Trimarchi (2010), p. 54.

References

Bedaque JRS (2010) Efetividade do processo e técnica processual, 3rd edn. Malheiros, São Paulo
Bedaque JRS (2021) Tutela provisória: analisada à luz das garantias constitucionais da ação e do processo, 6th edn. Malheiros, São Paulo
Belmonte E (2023) Compensazione e autotutela. Edizione Scientifiche Italiane, Napoli
Betti E (1959) Autotutela (dir. priv.). In: Enciclopedia del diritto, vol IV. Giuffrè, Milano
Beurskens M (2017) Privatrechtliche Selbsthilfe, Rechte, Pflichten und Verantwortlichkeit bei digitalen Zugangsbeschränkungs- und Selbstdurchsetzungsbefugnissen. Mohr Siebeck, Tübingen
Blomeyer A (1982) Substantive law and judicial remedies. In: Cappelletti M (ed) International encyclopedia of comparative law, vol XVI (civil procedure), Ch. 4. Tübingen, Mohr Siebeck. The Hague, Nijhoff
Bongiorno G (1984) L'autotutela esecutiva. Giuffrè, Milano
Bötticher E (1964) Gestaltungsrecht und Unterwerfung im Privatrecht. Walter De Gruyter & Co., Berlin
Cabral ADP (2021) Negócio de certificação, introdução, objeto e limites. Revista de Direito Civil Contemporâneo 29(8):89–145
Callies G (2002) Reflexive transnational law, the privatization of civil law and the civilization of private law. Zeitschrift für Rechtssoziologie 23(2):185–216
Carimini F (2018) Sequestro convenzionale e autotutela. Edizione Scientifiche Italiane, Napoli
Carinci MT (2001) L'improbabile rilievo constituzionale dell'autotutela collettiva di lavoratori autonomi, professionisti e piccoli imprenditori. Argomenti di diritto del lavoro 3:931–980
Carnelutti F (1940) Note sull'accertamento negoziale. Rivista di Diritto Processuale Civile 17(1):3–24
Conti BCTD (2022) Garantias fiduciárias. Almedina, São Paulo
Cretella Júnior J (1972) Da autotutela administrativa. Revista de Direito Administrativo 108:47–63
Cunha LJCD (2009) Interesse de agir na ação declaratória. Juruá, Curitiba
D'Acunto L (2018) Recesso e autotutela nei rapporti di consumo. Edizione Scientifiche Italiane, Napoli
Díaz Alabart S (2007) La Autotutela. In: Liber Amicorum Guido Alpa, private law beyond the national systems. British Institute of International and Comparative Law, London
Dinamarco CR (2024) Instituições de direito processual civil, 5th edn. Malheiros, São Paulo
Duchstein M (2015) Die Selbsthilfe. Juristische Schulung (JuS) 2:105–109
Duden K (2023) Digitale Sachherrschaft. Mohr Siebeck, Tübingen
Follieri L (2021) Dall'esecuzione forzata all'autotutela esecutiva nel terzo millennio. Nuovo Diritto Civile, anno VI, n 4:35–66
Follieri L (2023) L'autotutela esecutiva. In: Albanese A et al (eds) La responsabilità patrimoniale "sostenibile". Giappichelli, Torino
Fonseca RG (2012) O fundamento da autotutela executiva da Administração Pública, contributo para a sua compreensão como problema jurídico-político. Almedina, Lisboa
Fornaciari M (1999) Situazione potestative, tutela costitutiva, giudicato. Giappichelli, Torino
Gabrielli E (2016) Appunti sulle autotutele contrattuali. Rivista di diritto privato, XXI 4:491–530
Geri LB (1971) Profili sistematici dell'autotutela privata. Giuffrè, Milano
Geri LB (1988) L'occupazione d'azienda come possibile forma di autotutela. In: Rapporti giuridici e dinamiche sociali, principi, norme interessi emergenti. Giuffrè, Milano, 292–299.
Goldman B (2009) Frontières du droit et Lex Mercatoria. Revista de Arbitragem e Mediação 22:211–230
Grande G (2010) L'autotutela consensuale. In: Gianniti P (ed) La disciplina dell'autotutela nel diritto costituzionale, civile, penale, del lavoro, amministrativo, tributario, comunitario ed internazionale. CEDAM, Padova
Grau ER (2015) A ordem econômica na Constituição de 1988 (interpretação e crítica), 17th edn. Malheiros, São Paulo

Grinover AP (2007) A inafastabilidade do controle jurisdicional e uma nova modalidade de autotutela (parágrafos únicos dos artigos 249 e 251 do Código Civil). Revista Brasileira de Direito Constitucional–RBDC 10:13–19

Grinover AP (2012) A tutela coletiva dos investidores no mercado de valores mobiliários, questões processuais. In: Yarshell FL, Pereira GS (eds) Processo Societário. Quartier Latin, São Paulo

Gutmann T (2011) Die Grenzen staatlicher Gewalt. In: Gutmann T, Pieroth B (eds) Die Zukunft des staatlichen Gewaltmonopols. Nomos, Baden-Baden, 33–52.

Hamburger P (2014) Is administrative law unlawful? The University of Chicago Press, Chicago

Hanau H (2004) Der Grundsatz der Verhältnismäßigkeit als Schranke privater Gestaltungsmacht. Zu Herleitung und Struktur einer Angemessenheitskontrolle von Verfassungs wegen. Mohr Siebeck, Tübingen

Hattenhauer C (2011) Einseitige private Rechtsgestaltung. Mohr Siebeck, Tübingen

Helmreich H (1967) Das Selbsthilfeverbot des französischen Rechts und sein Einfluß auf Gestaltungs- und Gestaltungsklagerecht. Duncker und Humblot, Berlin

Justen Filho M (2015) Curso de direito administrativo, 13th edn. Editora Revista dos Tribunais, São Paulo

Kisch W (1903) Beiträge zur Urteilslehre. Verlag von C. L. Hirschfeld, Leipzig

Klein AL (2022) Poder de polícia e poderes privados. In: Klein AL, Marques Neto FPA (eds) Funções administrativas do Estado. Editora Revista dos Tribunais, São Paulo

Klingbeil S (2017) Die Not- und Selbsthilfe, eine dogmatische Rekonstruktion. Mohr Siebeck, Tübingen

Klingbeil S (2019) Selbsthilfe als private Zwangsvollstreckung. In: Hussman T et al (eds) Strukturwandel und Privatrecht. Nomos, Baden-Baden

Landmann V (1975) Notwehr, Notstand und Selbsthilfe im Privatrecht. Schulthess Polygraphischer Verlag, Zürich

Laporta FJ (2007) El imperio de la ley, una visión actual. Trotta, Madrid

Lepore A (2019) Autotutela e autonomia negoziale. Edizione Scientifiche Italiane, Napoli

Loterstein A (2013) Law-enforcement officers and self-help repossession. State-Action Approach Mich Law Rev 111:7

Mallet E (2015) Dogmática elementar do direito de greve, 2nd edn. LTR, São Paulo

Marinoni LG (2022) Tutela inibitória e tutela de remoção do ilícito, 8th edn. Editora Revista dos Tribunais, São Paulo

Martins-Costa J (2014) Autoridade e utilidade da doutrina: a construção dos modelos doutrinários. In, Martins- Costa J (org) Modelos de Direito Privado. São Paulo, Marcial Pons, 9–40.

Mendonça JVS, Bento D (2024) Autoexecutoriedade pública e autotutela privada? Caminhos que se cruzam. In: Eid EP (ed) Ensaios sobre autotutela. Thoth, Londrina

Minami MY (2020) Da vedação ao non factibile, uma introdução às medidas executivas atípicas, 2nd edn. Juspodivm, Salvador

Montecchiari T (2019) Ius singulare e autotutela privata, contributo allo studio di uma categoria. ESI, Napoli

Morato García RM (2011) Derecho de resistencia y ejercicio irregular del poder de dirección. Editorial Comares, Granada

Möslein F (2018) Rechtliche Grenzen innovativer Finanztechnologien (FinTech), Smart Contracts als Selbsthilfe? Zeitschrift für Bankrecht und Bankwirtschaft 30(4):208–221

Motto A (2012) Poteri sostanziali e tutela giurisdizionale. Giappichelli, Torino

Murino F (2010) L'autotutela nell'escussione della garanzia finanziaria pignoratizia. Milano, Giuffrè

Noronha CS (2016) Repensando a tutela dos direitos. Revista da Faculdade de Direito da UFRGS 1(32):76–97

Patterson D (2019) Rechtsdurchsetzung ohne Staat, Paradigms of Enforcement – justice vs. efficiency. In: Schmidt-Kessel M (ed) Rechtsdurchsetzung ohne Staat. Mohr Siebeck, Tübingen

Paulus CG, Matzke R (2017) Digitalisierung und private Rechtsdurchsetzung. Relativierung der Zwangsvollstreckung durch smarte IT-Lösungen? Computer und Recht. 13(12):769–778

Pereira CFB (2024) Revisitando a fonte de normas processuais. In: Yarshell FL et al (eds) 50 anos da Teoria Geral do Processo no Brasil. Thoth, Londrina
Pieroth B (2011) Das staatliche Gewaltmonopol – ein Verfassungsrechtssatz? In: Gutmann T, Pieroth B (eds) Die Zukunft des staatlichen Gewaltmonopols. Nomos, Baden-Baden
Poncibò C, Dimatteo L (2019) Smart contracts. Contractual and Noncontractual Remedies. In: The Cambridge Handbook of Smart Contracts, Blockchain and Digital Platforms. Cambridge University Press, Cambridge
Popineau-Dehaullon C (2008) Les remèdes de justice privée à l'inexécution du contrat. Étude comparative. LGDJ, Paris
Pucci L (1926) Contributo allo studio dell'accertamento privato. Giuffrè, Milano
Purpura A (2020) Autonomia privata, responsabilità e attuazione coattiva del credito. Giappichelli, Torino
Ricciardoni ADS (2011) L'autotutela civile. Jovene, Napoli
Riehm T (2017) Rechtsgrund–Pflicht–Anspruch. Zur Dogmatik des Schuldverhältnisses. In: Auer M et al (eds) Privatrechtsdogmatik im 21. Jahrhundert. Festschrift für Claus-Wilhelm Canaris zum 80. Geburtstag. De Gruyter, Berlin
Salles RBDO (2019) Autotutela nas relações contratuais. Editora Processo, Rio de Janeiro
Santamaria MF (1937) La giustizia privata. Jovene, Napoli
Santisteban Castro M (2023) La incidencia de la autotutela en los smart contracts. In: J P i J (ed) Aspectos críticos del derecho procesal. Diálogos hispano-italianos en homenaje a Angelo Dondi. JM Bosch, Barcelona
Sassani B (1999) Impugnativa dell'atto e disciplina del rapporto. Contributo allo studio della tutela dichiarativa nel processo civile e amministrativo. CEDAM, Padova
Saturno A (1995) L'autotutela privata. I modelli della ritenzione e dell'eccezione di inadempimento in comparazione col sistema tedesco. Edizione Scientifiche Italiane, Napoli
Scarpelli F (1993) Lavoratore subordinato e autotutela collettiva. Milano, Giuffrè
Schimpfhauser EM (2009) Das Gewaltmonopol des Staates als Grenze der Privatisierung von Staatsaufgaben. Peter Lang, Frankfurt am Main
Schmitt MN (2017) Tallinn manual 2.0 on the international law applicable to cyber operations. Cambridge University Press, Cambridge
Schünemann W (1985) Selbsthilfe im Rechtssystem, eine dogmatische Studie am Beispiel der. J.C.B. Mohr (Paul) Siebeck, Tübingen, pp §§ 227–229 ff
Sica HVM (2017) Cognição o juiz na execução civil. Editora Revista dos Tribunais, São Paulo
Sinel Z (2017) De-ciphering self-help. Univ Tor Law J 67:1
Souza RP (2014) Empresas estatais constituídas para o exercício de poder de polícia. In: Medauar O, Schirato VR (eds) Poder de polícia na atualidade. Belo Horizonte, Fórum
Stamm J (2007) Die Prinzipien und Grundstrukturen des Zwangsvollstreckungsrechts. Mohr Siebeck, Tübingen
Stănescu CG, Gikay A (2017) The reluctance of civil law systems in adopting the UCC article 9 'without breach of peace' standard—Evidence from national and international legal instruments governing secured transactions. J Civ Law Stud 10:1
Talamini E (**2016**) A dimensão coletiva dos direitos individuais homogêneos, ações coletivas e os mecanismos previstos no Código de Processo Civil de. 2015. In: Didier F Jr, Zaneti H Jr (eds) Repercussões do novo CPC–Processo coletivo. Juspodivm, Salvador
Talamini E (2023) Adjudicação compulsória extrajudicial, pressupostos, natureza e limites. Revista de Processo 336(48):319–339
Talamini E, Cardoso AG (2022) Smart contracts, "autotutela" e tutela jurisdicional. In: Bellizze MA et al (eds) Execução civil, novas tendências. Editora Foco, Indaiatuba
Tavormina V (2003) Il processo come esecuzione forzata. Jovene, Napoli
Tesheiner JMR (2007) Jurisdição, execução e autotutela. In, Instrumentos de coerção e outros temas de direito processual civil – estudos em homenagem aos 25 anos de docência do Professor Dr. Araken de Assis. Forense, Rio de Janeiro

Theodoro H Jr (2023) Autotutela executiva, execução extrajudicial positivada. Forense, Rio de Janeiro

Trimarchi P (2010) Il contratto, inadempimento e rimedi. Giuffrè, Milano

Yarshell FL (1993) Tutela específica nas obrigações de prestar declaração de vontade. Saraiva, São Paulo

Yarshell FL, Rodrigues VS (2021) Contratos inteligentes e execução civil, diálogo possível e útil? In: Cabral TNX et al (eds) Tecnologia e justiça multiportas. Editora Foco, Indaiatuba

Yoshikawa EH (2008) Da autotutela. RDDP 66:19–32

Zavascki T (2017) Processo coletivo: tutela de direitos coletivos e tutela coletiva de direitos, 7th edn. RT, São Paulo

Chapter 6
Conclusions

This study aimed to contribute to the dogmatic characterization of self-help, both in its fundamental elements and in its limits within the national legal system. The arrangement of ideas presented in the previous chapters allows for conclusions that confirm the thesis advanced, as summarized below:

1. It would be difficult to support the idea that the State has replaced or overshadowed self-help with jurisdiction. By deductive reasoning, it is hard to believe that, during times of more disorganized and decentralized societies, the power of unilateral protection would have vanished. However, it was observed that this rivalry between self-help and jurisdiction peaked right when the State needed to assert its sovereignty and dominance over individuals.
2. This discourse, besides being imprecise, was partisan. The self-help that challenged State authority was private, meaning the self-defense of interests carried out by private individuals. None of this was compared to the broad powers of the State to enforce administrative acts, which in many cases amounted to exercising public self-help. From this perspective as well, it is confirmed that behind the repressive discourse against unilateral protection was the need to uphold the values of an authoritarian era of public authority functions.
3. The right of action follows the same line of reasoning. For many, this is a right to extend judicial protection universally, based on the idea that self-help is prohibited. This prohibition, it's important to repeat, was created from a private perspective, not a public one. However, the principles of the right of action were developed in isolation as a fundamental right. It was overlooked that many other fundamental rights also support self-protection and self-defense, some of which date back even before the public and unconditional view of the right of action.
4. The right of action is not an exclusionary principle. It does not exist to prevent the development and constitutional foundation of other means of dispute resolution. Instead, it is a fundamental security principle that guarantees the State's obligation to provide solutions to disputes through the judicial process in an effective and just manner.

E. Pierre Eid, *Self-Help as Method of Conflict Resolution*,
https://doi.org/10.1007/978-3-032-13905-4_6

5. The idea that self-help is banned, residual, or relies on explicit legal provisions, still found in current Procedural Law studies, should be examined critically. This notion stems from private self-help. However, the broadness of this concept is challenged by two aspects: the assumption that strict legality would govern private self-help relations and the neglect of the extensive powers of the State self-satisfaction.
6. The division between public and private self-help is outdated. Both are simply categories based on the legal regime of authorization, scope, and limits for the conduct of the active subject. The redefinition of this division should be understood through the principles of legality and freedom. Public self-help is governed by the principle of legality, representing the normative force that regulates State power and the limits set by individuals' fundamental rights. Private self-help is guided by the principle of freedom, which acts as an interpretive guide regarding the extent of unilateral powers self-protection.
7. The traditional view advocating limiting private self-help should be reconsidered. The principle of freedom permits the sharing of specific and general powers of unilateral protection, with a broad conventional scope. There is no constitutional basis to justify applying strict legality to private relations solely in the context of self-help.
8. Article 345 of the Brazilian Penal Code does not protect an objectively and clearly defined legal interest. Its conception dates to a time when criminalizing private self-help was common and mistaken, as it was linked to illegality. Much of the case law shows that unilateral unlawful acts are absorbed by other offenses, which confirms the theoretical and practical difficulty of establishing the autonomy of the criminal type in this provision.
9. Article 345 of the Brazilian Penal Code was created for acts of substitution by authorities. However, such conduct, without legal or conventional approval, often amounts to more serious crimes like robbery, theft, homicide, etc. The requirement for approval aims to prevent criminal liability in these situations, not to broadly ban self-help, especially when the acts don't involve property or personal harm aggression.
10. There is no criminal liability in private self-help when it is supported by specific powers, including those of conventional and general origin. In the latter case, the legal system assigns the grounds for excluding unlawfulness to the limits of an active person's extra-contractual conduct subject.
11. The emphasis on private self-help ignores the fact that, in public self-help, the agent may also face criminal, administrative, and civil liability if they exceed their authority. Therefore, using criminal laws to universally prohibit unilateral protection, whether public or private, does not make sense, as it is necessary to establish the objective and subjective elements of the offense in each case.
12. Self-help is a form of dispute resolution. Unlike what traditional doctrine suggests, it is a means capable of providing the claimant with legal protection of their interests. This is where self-help differs from other legal concepts: it is a specific exercise of power aimed at protecting, satisfying, and realizing

infringed or threatened interests. As a form of power, it must be capable of subjecting the respondent to its influence outcome.

13. The central element of this characterization is conflict. Self-help is not just the routine exercise of a subjective right, a formative right, or the fulfillment of a duty, but a power linked to all these concepts, specifically aimed at preventing or fixing an infringement or threat to the claimant's rights interests.
14. As a means of dispute resolution, self-help should be considered within the broader context of other mechanisms that serve this purpose. Currently, there is increasing concern in Brazilian legal scholarship about the integration, organization, classification, and systematization of theories to address these various means. As discussed, the theories proposed so far, such as the Theory of Procedure or the Multi-Door Justice Theory, are inadequate for addressing the specificities of non-institutionalized, non-procedural, and atypical methods. The proposal in this study is to view self-help within a broader context, provided by a Theory of Dispute Resolution, based on the framework outlined in Chapter 1.
15. As a unilateral power of dispute resolution, this authority is essential. It is materially essential because it defines the scope for substantive rules to offer solutions and act as sources of this power to resolve disputes (advocated as the instrumentality of substantive law). It is also essential in terms of its functionality, as it extends across various private and public legal relationships, giving the claimant the ability to realize, satisfy, or protect infringed or threatened rights interests.
16. The traditional view of the division between public and private self-help is unbalanced. It was created under the principles of State dominance over individuals, so that people's ability for self-protection is taken away in favor of public protection, which controls the use of force and coercion of rights. This perspective is now outdated. Both private individuals and State agents share responsibilities and powers of independent protection, just as there are both public and private spheres for dispute resolution.
17. As a fundamental force, the influence of traditional doctrine, which promotes the residual role of self-help, has prevented many forms of unilateral protection from being recognized as such. The daily lives of individuals and public entities are shaped by this power, both in exercising it and in being affected by it. From the most common to the most complex forms, the presence of this power underscores its pervasive nature and the importance of studying it subject.
18. This power exists in legal relationships even before the development of other dispute resolution methods, such as State proceedings. However, there was a discourse that separated theory from reality, given the increasing claim that this power was residual, despite it being routinely exercised by its holder. Recently, the instrumental function of this power has been reaffirmed with the rising interest in self-help because of its speed and efficiency, which are characteristic of unilateral actions action.

19. This recent concern reaffirms its essential role with examples of self-regulation, where self-help serves as an important tool for governance, control, and management. This is widely seen with the growth of unilateral protection resulting from technological advances developments.
20. Self-help should be understood considering the existence of both public and private dispute resolution spaces, as well as the division of responsibilities between the State and private individuals for this purpose. In addition to the presence of this authority in the hands of both, the arrangement established by the principles of legality and freedom grants general and specific powers of action. Some of these powers involve the dispersion of imperium merum through executive self-help.
21. The relationship between self-help and imperium contradicts another premise often found in the literature, namely the State monopoly on force. Although this assertion could have been challenged long ago, it is increasingly clear that individuals and State agents share powers to enforce their interests, albeit to varying degrees. Subject to the limits of civil and criminal liability, these agents, by explicit legal provision, through powers of unilateral protection, act in a cooperative, shared, or complementary way to achieve such coercive satisfaction.
22. Contrary to the traditional view, the State encourages self-help practiced by private individuals in at least two ways: through the legal granting of specific powers, especially those enabling enforceable self-help along with expropriation; and through the delegation of State authority, as seen in the debate over delegating police powers, including the authority of coercion.
23. With the overcoming of many dogmas surrounding self-help, the unresolved question even in specialized scholarship remains the definition of its limits. There is an effort to generalize proportionality and reasonableness as measures to control unilateral action. However, these two elements are incidental. They will not always be sufficient, nor will they always be necessary, and they do not distinguish between public self-protection and private self-protection concerning the precedence of rules over principles. For this reason, the study aimed to identify five criteria of control, especially because the national legal system, unlike some foreign systems, does not provide such guidelines.
24. From this perspective, two important points of balance emerge. As a means of dispute resolution, self-protection must adhere to the requirements of due process of law. This principle sets specific and adaptable conditions for protecting rights. Therefore, there is a relationship of adjustment and alignment of unilateral protection to ensure compliance with due process. Another key point of balance involves pursuing procedural safeguards in the unilateral actions of the active party. In many cases, it becomes clear that the protection provided by infra-constitutional rules is insufficient to meet the requirements of due process and to facilitate the proper exercise of rights of self-protection.
25. Unilateral protection is a type of safeguard for interests that are either infringed upon or threatened. Additionally, there is self-composition, which can lead to bilateral or multilateral protection, and heteroprotection, provided by a third

party to the dispute. As a form of legal protection, it must be classified to systematize it within Brazilian law. The classification considers the legal regime, the source, the nature of the interest, the type of unilateral protection, and the timing of its use. Therefore, various forms can be identified, such as public, formative, collective, constitutive, and repressive self-protection, as well as private, conventional, individual, personal, executive, and preventive protection self-protection.

26. These classifications serve a dual purpose beyond just systematization, which is lacking in both national and foreign literature. The first is to provide guidance, supporting both the recipient and the interpreter of the rules on self-protection in understanding the scope of action and the respective boundaries of lawfulness. The second is to utilize these same factors for oversight, which a third party often conducts.

MIX
Papier aus verantwortungsvollen Quellen
Paper from responsible sources
FSC® C105338

If you have any concerns about our products,
you can contact us on
ProductSafety@springernature.com

In case Publisher is established outside the EU,
the EU authorized representative is:
Springer Nature Customer Service Center GmbH
Europaplatz 3, 69115 Heidelberg, Germany

Printed by Libri Plureos GmbH
in Hamburg, Germany